Stephen Wangh

An Acrobat of the Heart

Stephen Wangh studied with Jerzy Grotowski in 1967. Since 1973 he has taught acting in Europe, Boston, and New York, where he is currently Master Teacher at the Experimental Theatre Wing at New York University. He is a playwright, lyricist, and director, and has been Artistic Director of The New York Free Theater, Reality Theater, and Present Stage. He was dramaturg for Moisés Kaufman's *Gross Indecency: The Three Trials of Oscar Wilde,* and was Associate Writer of the Tectonic Theater Company's *The Laramie Project.* His own plays include *Class, Calamity!* and *Goin' Downtown,* as well as numerous collaborative theater pieces.

An
Acrobat
of the
Heart

An
Acrobat
of the
Heart

A Physical Approach to Acting

Inspired by the Work of Jerzy Grotowski

Stephen Wangh

Vintage Books

A Division of Random House, Inc.

New York

Library of Congress Cataloging-in-Publication Data
Wangh, Stephen.
An acrobat of the heart : a physical approach to acting inspired by the work of Jerzy Grotowski / Stephen Wangh. — 1st. ed.
p.   cm.
ISBN 0-375-70672-0
1. Movement (Acting)   2. Acting.   3. Grotowski, Jerzy, 1933–   I. Title.
PN2071.M6 W36 2000
792'.028—dc21
00-036470

www.vintagebooks.com

For Suzanne

*It would be disastrous for an acrobat to go off wool
gathering just before he performs a* salto mortale *or other
neck-risking stunt! . . . He must jump, come what may.
This is exactly what an actor must do when he comes to
the culminating point of his part.*
—CONSTANTIN STANISLAVSKI

*When you perform a somersault in space which you are
usually not able to do because it seems impossible, you
regain some trust in yourself. . . . It is not knowing how
to do things that is necessary, but not hesitating when
faced with a challenge.*
—JERZY GROTOWSKI

The actor is an athlete of the heart.
—ANTONIN ARTAUD

Acknowledgments

This book owes the greatest debt to Jerzy Grotowski, whose teaching inspired so much of my work. But it also owes much to many other teachers—including Helen Houston, Martha Stodt, Alan Levitan, Omar Shapli, Kristin Linklater, Alan Miller, and Linda Putnam—who taught me what a bountiful act teaching can be. And it owes special thanks to Tom Crawley, whose journal, *The Stone in the Soup,* provides a unique record of Grotowski's teaching work.

The writing was made possible by Una Chaudhuri, Chair of the Undergraduate Department of Drama at the Tisch School of the Arts at N.Y.U., and Kevin Kuhlke, Head of the Experimental Theatre Wing. Their encouragement and support provided the time and supplied me with the fortitude to finish this work. Thanks are also due to New York University and the Tisch School of the Arts, whose Research Challenge Fund and Senior Faculty Grants provided financial support.

For assistance with the research, I am indebted to Raïna Fernandez von Waldenburg, who provided the main logistical, editorial, and moral support for this project. Thanks also to those who read the manuscript and whose insightful suggestions clarified the writing: Chris Rohmann, Pamela Ricard, Jan Cohen-Cruz, Walton Wilson, Kristin Dombek, and Amanda Gronich. To Nanc Allen for her administrative assistance, and to the students of the Experimental Theatre Wing for their courage and dedication. To Moisés Kaufman for his encouragement, and to Michael Earley of Methuen for his editorial suggestions. Before and after all, I am grateful to my first reader and loving accomplice, Suzanne Baxtresser, and to Noah Nuriel Alim Baxtresser Wangh.

Contents

Preface

FOUR WEEKS WITH JERZY GROTOWSKI

One afternoon in October 1967, Ted Hoffman, chairman of the Theatre Program at the New York University School of the Arts, called together twenty acting and directing students. He told us that he had invited a young Polish theater director named Jerzy Grotowski to lead a four-week workshop at N.Y.U., and that we were to be his first American students. None of us had ever heard of Grotowski, and Hoffman didn't give us much to go on. He simply told us to show up on the first Monday in November—the men in shorts, the women wearing leotards—prepared to work hard.

In 1967 it was just three years since Grotowski had moved his Polish Laboratory Theatre from the small town of Opole to the city of Wrocław in southern Poland. Grotowski had given a few workshops in Europe, and in 1966 the company had made its first international tour. But to the theatergoing public in the United States—and to most of us—he was utterly unknown.

Some of us quickly read the two short articles on the Polish Laboratory Theater that had recently been published in *TDR*, but our main source of information was a rumor. The rumor had it that when Grotowski had conducted a workshop at the Royal Shakespeare Company in 1965, several of Peter Brook's actors had dropped out because the work was too strenuous.

———

Room 2H was the largest studio in the 40 East Seventh Street building, a long, blue-carpeted room with two small windows at the far end. During our year at N.Y.U., most of us had attended voice or acting classes there. But when the studio door was opened on that Monday, the space looked unfamiliar. Folding chairs had been arranged in three rows in front of the windows, and to the side of the chairs, along the left wall, stood a long table with three more chairs behind it. The center of the studio was completely empty. It was, we were told, a sacrosanct space where we should trespass only in order to work.

We entered silently, walking carefully along the perimeter of the room, and sat down on the cold metal chairs in our shorts and leotards, feeling naked and apprehensive. When we were all seated, Ted Hoffman, Richard Schechner, editor of *TDR*, and several other N.Y.U. dignitaries ushered in two men who sat down behind the table along the wall to our right. One of the two was pale and rotund. He wore a blue suit and dark glasses; his face was expressionless, but there was something imposing and enigmatic about his presence. The second man looked younger, more physical, his eyes were alert and intense.

The dignitaries made introductory speeches. The enigmatic man in the blue suit, they said, was Jerzy Grotowski, the famous Polish director. The younger man was Ryszard Cieślak, the leading actor of Grotowski's Polish Laboratory Theatre. And we students should feel honored that we were to be in Grotowski's first American workshop.

After the introductions, the dignitaries left (though Schechner remained to observe the workshop), and Grotowski began to speak to us. He spoke in French with quiet intensity, his words translated by a woman who sat by his side. "I can give you no positive techniques," he said, "no tricks or systems to use, only a negative training to remove personal blocks you might have in expressing creative acts" [Crawley, I, 3].[1] For us,

1. Citations from Grotowski's 1967 N.Y.U. workshop are from Tom Crawley's unpublished journal of that event, *The Stone in the Soup, A Journal of Jerzy Grotowski's First American Workshop.*

used as we were to teachers who offered "methods" and "techniques," this seemed an ominous beginning. Grotowski then described three principles of his work: The first was that the actor must use himself—his own feelings, thoughts, and opinions—in the work. The second was that all acting was to be thought of as a series of "units of exchange," moments of listening and reaction that could be "scored" as one might score music. The third principle was that "the actor, if he is to reveal something significant, personal and profound . . . must reach into the depths of himself, through whatever psychic or physical blocks might impede such expression." He concluded by declaring, "The actor will do, in public, what is considered impossible" [Crawley, I, 6, 7].

While we sat bewildered by this astonishing speech, Cieślak silently stripped to his shorts, went out to the middle of the empty studio and proceeded to demonstrate the "impossible" for us. With incredible ease and precise physical control, he performed a series of headstands, rolls, and backbends, each flowing into the next, each completely centered and yet somehow off-balance and dynamic. His body seemed to be made of liquid muscle, enormously powerful, yet utterly soft and supple. He moved with the strength and precision of an accomplished gymnast, yet there was something in his face, in his searching eyes, that removed his work entirely from the world of gymnastics. It was as if the enormous muscular energy we witnessed was merely the exterior emanation of an even more intense inner life.

Then Grotowski indicated it was our turn. *"Alors, vous tous, faîtes le même."* (Now, all of you, do the same.)

And so it went. Four days a week for the next four weeks, we met for six hours a day. Some days Grotowski spoke philosophically about things like the importance of precision, or the value of silence. At other times he coached our monologues and scenes or commented pointedly on our work. Cieślak, for his part, demonstrated impossible exercises. And we Americans tried to emulate his work . . . until we began to understand that "emulation" was not what this class was about.

At first, many of us were so overwhelmed by the pure physical challenge of Cieślak's exercises that we could not see beyond the technical difficulties we encountered. Our headstands were wobbly, and our leaps were hesitant. When Cieślak demonstrated his "rivers" of "*plastique*" body isolations, kinetic and dramatic impulses seemed to flow through his entire body as if it were made of molten metal. When we tried, our rivers alternately surged and froze, creaking through our torsos by rusty jerks. The infinite agility, the intense concentration, and the wonderful precision with which Cieślak glided effortlessly from headstands to backbends to leaps and rolls seemed entirely beyond our abilities. But even harder to grasp was Grotowski's assertion that the physical problems we were encountering were not really problems at all. On the contrary, he maintained, they were advantages! "The real value [of the exercises]," Grotowski insisted, "lies in [your] *not* being able to do them" [Crawley, II, 13]. For us young Americans, schooled for years in the supreme importance of "success," the idea that the value of this work lay in the struggle, rather than in the victory, was baffling, frustrating . . . and at the same time wonderfully liberating.

Grotowski's vocal work was even more mysterious. The man urged us to speak as if we had mouths all over our bodies. "*La bouche ici!*" he would say, clapping an actor between the shoulder blades—"Your mouth here!" Then he would instruct us to listen for a response at an "external point of contact." A response from whom? From the wall? From an invisible person? From the empty space? Again and again Grotowski turned our attention to the space around us, until finally we began to perceive that the world we inhabit is not actually empty at all. It is filled with the imagery that we project into it, and therefore **everything an actor does is not so much an act of *doing* as it is a *response* to a real or an imaginary partner.**

Starting the second week of our workshop, Grotowski began to coach us in monologues and scenes from Shakespeare. And here again his approach was baffling, for he seemed to work differently with every actor in the group. Tom Crawley and Rae Allen had chosen a scene from *Antony and Cleopatra*, and Grotowski began their work process by questioning them thoroughly about their personal connections to the characters. Then he led Tom through a long exploration of two sides of himself, *le petit* Tom and *le grand* Tom, an exploration that depended upon Tom's control of his facial muscles! The requisite emotions, Grotowski explained, would arrive on their own if Tom would just pay attention to the physical details. "Emotions come; they happen to us; they are not voluntary," he told Tom [Crawley, VI, 6]. Making a technical, physical choice, Grotowski insisted, could produce emotional truth.

When he coached Trazana Beverly and me in the murder scene from *Othello*, Grotowski began instead by directing the scene. He told me to dispense with the candle I was using and to avoid looking at my hands: "Shakespeare's murderers all over the world look at their hands, and that's reason enough not to do it. Even if you have an honest, sincere impulse to look at your hands, you mustn't do that" [Crawley, VIII, 2]. He urged me to treat the scene not as a murder but as a sexual seduction, and then, at the climax of the scene, when I was choking Desdemona to death, Grotowski ordered me to freeze with my hands around her throat. The remarkable thing was that this external, directorial instruction, rather than taking me out of the reality of the scene, seemed instead to intensify my internal frenzy and anguish. As I held my thumbs frozen around Trazana's throat, my need to finish the act only grew stronger. I was told later that this moment had also been quite powerful for our audience, but all I was aware of at the time was that this seemingly arbitrary physical choice had transformed my experience of acting itself.

Until that moment, although I had often enjoyed performing, being on stage had always made me self-conscious. My mind would always race ahead of me, anticipating my cues while I pretended to listen to the actor speaking opposite me. And never had I felt entirely at home in my body. That was one of the reasons I had chosen to stop acting and to direct instead. But here in Grotowski's workshop, there was suddenly no time for me to anticipate the cues, and no space in which to feel self-conscious. I was working so hard with my body and with my imagination that my thoughts and emotions seemed to take care of themselves. Moreover, the exhilaration of the bodily exertion itself seemed to spur my emotional courage. For the first time in my experience on stage, I felt fully "present" in my body and in the work.

And I was not the only one whose life and whose work were deeply affected by those four weeks in November 1967. It was after observing that workshop that Richard Schechner founded the Performance Group, where he employed Grotowski's techniques to create *Dionysus in '69*. Meanwhile several other members of our class became the nucleus of André Gregory's Manhattan Project, whose remarkable production of *Alice in Wonderland* grew directly out of Grotowski's work.

During the next three years, Grotowski's fame grew throughout the world. As a teacher of acting, he was acclaimed as the greatest investigator since Stanislavski. And as a director, he was credited with having revivified the experiments of Vsevolod Meyerhold, for like the famous Russian director, he dared to deconstruct and recompose dramatic texts and to alter the actor-audience relationship radically. In 1969, when the Polish Laboratory Theatre brought its productions of *Apocalypis cum Figuris* and *The Constant Prince* to New York, tickets were scalped at $200 a seat.[2]

But by the time the world had started treating him as a "star," Grotowski himself was moving on. In 1970, at the height of his international fame, he stunned the theater world

---

2. A complete account of the productions of The Polish Laboratory Theatre can be found in Jennifer Kumiega's *The Theatre of Grotowski* (London: Methuen, Inc., 1985).

by declaring, "We live in a *post-theatre* age. What is coming is not a new wave of theatre, but something that will take the place occupied by it" [Burzynski, p. 101]. So saying, Grotowski turned to the creation of "holidays," para-theatrical rural retreats in which he invited nonactors to experience the "active culture" of the artist. Then in the late 1970s, he changed directions again, abandoning these participatory experiments to initiate "The Theatre of Sources." For this experiential research, Grotowski invited shamans and teachers of ritual from all over the world to lead his students in a quest for "those elements of the ancient rituals of various world cultures which have a precise and therefore objective impact on participants" [Wolford, p. 9]. This "Objective Drama" work, in turn, led Grotowski onward to what Peter Brook has called "Art as Vehicle," the investigation of how gesture, sound and personal images can transform not the audience, but the actor himself. It is this extremely personal and demanding version of his work that Grotowski pursued from 1986 until his death in 1999 at the Centro per la Sperimentazione e la Ricerca Teatrale in Pontedera, Italy.[3]

BRIDGING THE GAP

Today, in the year 2000, Grotowski's directorial legacy is still very much alive. His innovations have spawned thousands of experiments in textual deconstruction and environmental theater. Yet his remarkable actor-training work has made only minor inroads upon more traditional acting techniques. A few teachers, including Zygmunt Molik of the original Polish Laboratory Theatre, continue to give workshops in physical acting,

3. For a description of Grotowski's work at the Workcenter of Jerzy Grotowski in Ponte-derra, Italy, see Thomas Richards, *At Work with Grotowski on Physical Actions*.

but in spite of its transformative power, Grotowski's approach
to actor training has not proliferated. Why is that?

Why, thirty years after Grotowski introduced his vision of a
body-centered actor training, are there still so many actors
whose voices and bodies seem quite disconnected from their
emotional instruments? So many whose "internal" acting technique leaves them wanting in the very kind of precision that
Grotowski's training inspired? And why, in all this time, have
so few teachers integrated Grotowski's important insights into
their curricula? I think there are several reasons.

One is that Grotowski, himself, was always wary of undermining the learning experience or the creative event by reduc-
ing it to words. As his collaborator Ludwig Flaszen wrote of the
early rehearsals with the Polish Lab:

> Grotowski . . . didn't want [actors] to be intellects at
> work. . . . We "discussed" through our actions. . . . For
> example, when language must be used in the work, either
> by Grotowski or among the actors themselves, it is a lan-
> guage of images, not the language of things by their
> names. [Flaszen, pp. 305, 316]

Grotowski was also worried that others might misinterpret
his work. He perceived that those who studied with him frequently became enthralled by the physicality of the work and
lost sight of the deeper acting values. During a workshop in
Denmark in 1968 Grotowski was heard to complain:

> [The] American work was too mechanical, the creative
> work depended too much on techniques foreign to Amer-
> ican sensibility. [Grotowski] criticised all the groups
> present for using his exercises without the images to sup-
> port them, reducing them to acrobatics, to zero. [Croy-
> den, p. 182]

Grotowski was also disturbed by the tendency of some of those who worked with him to become acolytes to a received teaching. When he saw that former students and other artists were looking to him for guidance or trying to reproduce his work, Grotowski cautioned them to avoid following in his footsteps. His lessons, he insisted, were never meant to be a universal map for all travelers to follow but simply a starting point from which an actor might begin to explore his or her personal unknown territory. "If a pupil senses his own technique," Grotowski encouraged in 1969, "then he departs from me. . . . Every other technique or method is sterile" [Grotowski, 1980, p.119].

In addition to all these factors, there is, I believe, one more important circumstance that has militated against the spread of Grotowski's physical acting training:

The physical acting process as Grotowski taught it during the 1960s included a discontinuity, a *gap* between the training exercises on the one hand and their application to text and scene work on the other. It was a gap that the actors in the Polish Laboratory Theatre never had to face because they did both their *training* and their *rehearsing* under Grotowski's personal guidance. Similarly, when Grotowski worked with us at N.Y.U., we never had to figure out for ourselves how to apply the physical and vocal training to our scene rehearsal process. Grotowski himself slid effortlessly back and forth between his teacherly insights and his directorial intuitions, so he was able to guide us directly from the *corporel* and *plastique* exercises into specific tasks that served the texts we had chosen.

But in the "real" world, actors rarely work with directors who are also consummate acting teachers, so they require work methods that can help them bridge the gap between personal investigation on the one hand, and rehearsal and performance skills on the other. Since Grotowski did not supply such bridges, it was difficult for those who studied with him to connect the physical acting training they had received to the various "real world" acting circumstances they faced. And it was even more difficult for Grotowski's students to communicate to others how the training should be applied.

During the past twenty-five years, my teaching work has been devoted to finding work methods that can bridge this gap.

At the close of our workshop in 1967, however, I was not ready to take up that task. The training had been a wonderful experience for me, but I believed I had more important theater work to do. The war in Vietnam was expanding every month, and I was the director of an antidraft street musical, *Brother You're Next*, which I and several other N.Y.U. students performed each week on street corners all over the city. This political action seemed to me the most valuable thing I could do with my theater skills. Grotowski, however, disdained such pragmatic uses of theater. He had grown up in Poland during World War II, and during the "Polish October" of 1956, he had flirted with political activism, becoming a Secretary of the Central Committee of the Socialist Youth Movement and publishing several political articles. But by 1967, he was thoroughly disenchanted with politics, and one day during our workshop, he declared that art and politics should have nothing whatsoever to do with one another. At the end of class that day, I approached the enigmatic *éminence grise*. He had seemed quite absolute in his opinion, but since my street theater was the most important thing in my life, I felt I must justify myself to him. In the best French I could muster, I struggled to explain that my government was killing people every day, and that therefore I could not, as a human being and an artist, simply stand by. I don't remember exactly what I said, but I must have spoken with considerable passion, because, after remonstrating for a few minutes, M. Grotowski said, "Well, if it is that important to you, then you must do it."[4]

---

4. Many years later, Grotowski declared that his work was, in fact, "social activity through culture." See the section called "Is Acting a Political Activity?" in the last chapter of this book.

It was not until five years later, after stints with two political theaters and a short career as a newspaper reporter, that I revisited the lessons I had learned from Grotowski. By the spring of 1973 I had quit my fifty-dollar-a-week freelance job at *The Boston Phoenix* to devote myself to writing a play. Linda Putnam, another participant in Grotowski's N.Y.U. workshop, was also a refugee from a political theater company and had also moved to Boston. And she, like me, was broke. When we joined forces to found the Reality Theater Acting Growth Program, we had two clear aims: One was to build a theater that would explore the connections between personal transformation and social consciousness. The other was to try to support ourselves by teaching acting.

In the fall of 1973 we opened the Acting Growth Program. I taught theater games and Linda taught physical acting. It was as I watched Linda teach that I really began to understand how Grotowski's exercises functioned. I could see that even without his guidance, the physical training itself could transform actors. And, watching Linda, I began to understand how a teacher could sense what was going on within a student and serve as a catalyst to the learning process.

In 1976 Emerson College offered me a teaching position, but they wanted me to teach a scene-study class. Suddenly I was face-to-face with the *gap* between the physical training and its application to scene work. I knew that Grotowski's physical acting training could help an actor make connections between his body and his emotional life, but I didn't know how to help students make the transition into text and character work. At first I tried coaching the actors across the gap as I had seen Grotowski do, directing their physical choices as they worked on scenes. But I wanted to find exercises that would permit actors to bridge the gap for themselves, forms that would serve them while they rehearsed on their own. And I wanted to create a workspace that would encourage actors to explore, to take risks and to discover new forms on their own when they needed them.

The work in this book is the result of those efforts. Though it is grounded in Grotowski's physical training, it includes a great deal of work drawn from other sources, from Linda Putnam's work, from the techniques that Kristin Linklater and Tina Packer created with Shakespeare and Company, and from the theater games exercises of Viola Spolin and Omar Shapli. It also includes exercises I have developed with the assistance of hundreds of students at Emerson College, Reality Theater, The Actor's Space, and the Experimental Theatre Wing at N.Y.U.

Of course I am aware that in writing this book, I run the very risks that Grotowski foresaw years ago: the risk of being misunderstood, the risk of being taken too literally, and the risk of transforming a living process into a fixed system. I am also aware that my style of teaching is very different from Grotowski's, and that, even in those exercises that I derive directly from his work, I may be altering or even contradicting his aims. If I do "remain true" to Grotowski's intentions in some of what I teach, however, it is not because I think there is any particular value in "remaining true" to a teacher or to a teaching. It is simply because I have found that these exercises and these approaches to acting technique have proved effective for hundreds of actors over the past twenty years.

But in the end, it depends on you, the reader, to keep this work from being misunderstood or misused or reified. Remember as you read this book: **The very essence of the learning process this book describes is that it depends on the individual actor to transform it from a mere collection of interesting exercises into a living practice.** As Yoshi Oida has written:

Don't try to exactly copy another person's path; use their knowledge, but remain aware that the particular "landscape" of your own path is unique. However, the paradox remains: you must discover your own path, but you can't perceive it while you are on it, only after you have traveled it. [Oida, 1997, p. 125]

Introduction

A LITTLE HISTORY

*The soul desires to dwell with the body because without
the members of the body it can neither act nor feel.*
> —Leonardo da Vinci, quoted by Michael Chekhov,
> *To the Actor, on the Technique of Acting*

Four hundred years ago, Hamlet expressed his consternation at
the art of acting:

> *Is it not monstrous that this player here,*
> *But in a fiction, in a dream of passion,*
> *Could force his soul so to his own conceit*
> *That from her working all his visage wanned,*
> *Tears in his eyes, distraction in his aspect,*
> *A broken voice, and his whole function suiting*
> *With forms to his conceit; and all for nothing!*
> [2.2. 507–13]

And ever since, performers and audiences have argued about
how it is that actors manage this feat. At the core of the argument lie two related questions. The first is, Must actors really
feel the emotions they *portray*? And the second is, Do they
achieve their portrayal by controlling the *external expression* of
emotion or by inducing the *internal experience*? In 1773 the
French critic Denis Diderot put the problem this way:

xxxii   INTRODUCTION

The actor who has nothing but reason and calculation is frigid. The one who has nothing but excitement and emotionalism is silly. What makes the human being of supreme excellence is a kind of balance between calculation and warmth. [quoted in Strasberg, p. 34]

Fifty years later, the acting teacher François Delsarte concluded that the reason French actors had lost touch with real human feelings was because they had become entirely dependent upon declamation and rhetoric unconnected with physical gesture. "Gesture," he proclaimed, "is the direct agent of the heart. . . . In a word, it is the spirit of which speech is merely the letter" [Delsarte, pp. 446–47]. So saying, he set out to create an acting system that depended not on mental action but on physical gesture, declaring, "A perfect reproduction of the outer manifestation of some passion, the giving of the outer sign, will cause a reflex within" [quoted in Stebbins, p. 63].

The problem with Delsarte's method was that it tried to prescribe a fixed vocabulary of movements for each human emotion, as if emotional expression could be codified in a gestural dictionary. And although Delsarte's system worked for some (notably the American actor Steele MacKay), it led others into stereotyped and melodramatic gesticulation, devoid of the very "heart" that Delsarte had sought to restore.

It was just such empty, "external" acting that Konstantin Stanislavski witnessed as a young man on the Russian stage, and that he himself adopted when he began acting. But after seeing performances by the great Italian actors Tommaso Salvini and Eleanora Duse, Stanislavski realized that these great performers did not just "portray" their roles externally; they seemed to actually "live" on stage. Inspired by these performances, Stanislavski set out to discover a method by which he could make his own acting "logical, coherent, and real," not just on occasion, by accident or inspiration, but in a dependable, repeatable fashion [Stanislavski, 1936, p. 43].

The problem, Stanislavski felt, was that "mechanical" actors depended entirely on *external* means, "showing your teeth and rolling the whites of your eyes when you are jealous, or covering up the eyes and face with the hands instead of weeping; [and] tearing your hair when in despair" [Stanislavski, 1936, p. 24]. In reaction against this error, he searched for a method that would depend on *inner*, psychological practices. The French psychologist Théodule-Armand Ribot (1839–1916) "provided Stanislavski with a key to unlock the actor's unconscious. According to his theories, the nervous system bears the traces of all previous experiences. They are recorded in the mind, although not always available. An immediate stimulus—a touch, a sound, a smell—can trigger off the memory" [Benedetti, 1982, p. 31].

Armed with this key, Stanislavski developed the sense-memory and "affective memory" exercises that became the mainstay of his early work. It was these "internal" techniques that Stanislavski's students Richard Boleslavsky and Maria Ouspenskaya brought from Russia to New York in 1923. And it was this work that they taught at their American Laboratory Theater where Harold Clurman, Stella Adler, and Lee Strasberg came to study. "The aim of affective memory," Strasberg recalled later, "is not really to feel or see or touch something—that is hallucination—but to remember the mood when doing that" [Strasberg, p. 69].

From this work Strasberg developed what he called the "emotional-memory" exercise:

In the emotional-memory exercise, the actor is asked to recreate an experience from the past that affected him strongly. The experience should have happened at least seven years prior to the time that the exercise is attempted. I ask the student to pick the strongest thing that ever happened to him, whether it aroused anger, fear, or excitement. [Strasberg, p. 149]

Thus over the years, what Stanislavski began as a method of stimulating memory by means of sensory recall was transformed into a method of stimulating emotion by means of personal memory.

But while Strasberg was creating this "American Method" technique based on Stanislavski's early work, Stanislavski himself had begun to reconsider his emphasis on these internal "psycho-techniques." He realized that by concentrating so completely on the actor's mind, he had ignored the actor's body. In his later years Stanislavski developed a system of what he called "physical actions." In his book *Creating a Role*, which was not published in English until 1961, Stanislavski writes: "In every *physical action*, unless it is purely mechanical, there is concealed some *inner action*, some feelings" [Stanislavski, 1961, p. 228][1]

The actor Vasily Toporkov, who worked with Stanislavski during the 1930s, describes his late work this way:

> Konstantin Stanislavski directed our attention to what is the most tangible, the most concrete in each human action; its physical aspect. Especially in his last years, he gave the greatest importance to this aspect of the life of the role, beginning his work on a character with it. Diverting the attention of the actor from "feelings," from psychology, he directed it toward the carrying out of purely physical actions. In this way the actor could penetrate in a natural way into the sphere of feelings. [Toporkov, p. 216]

During the 1930s, Michael Chekhov, who had been a member of Stanislavski's First Studio, brought his own version of

---

1. In the same book Stanislavski also writes: "With faith in your physical actions you will feel emotions, akin to the external life of your part, which possess a logical bond with your soul. . . . Your body is biddable; feelings are capricious. Therefore if you cannot create a human spirit in your part of its own accord, create the physical being of your role" [p. 154].

Stanislavski's physically based techniques to New York. Chekhov (nephew of the author Anton) had worked closely with Stanislavski's protégé Eugene Vakhtangov and developed an approach to acting based on what he called the "psychological gesture." Also at that time, Sonia Moore, who had studied with Stanislavski during his last years, reported that Stanislavski was teaching actors to access their emotions by means of muscular choices. But in spite of these developments the influence of Strasberg and the "American Method" remained pervasive in drama schools through the 1980s, and the reputation of Stanislavski as a teacher of inward, mental techniques continued to be promulgated.

During the past twenty years, however, even some of Strasberg's own students have rediscovered the physical counterpart of emotional life. In 1988 acting teacher Warren Robertson said:

I often have an actor do an Affective Memory Exercise on his feet instead of sitting in a chair. And at moments I'll have him try to integrate feelings into his body. I'll have him lift his hand and wave goodbye, and he will remember, without even trying, who he is waving goodbye to. The body is a means of finding a specific feeling. [Mekler, p. 113]

Thus, although Stanislavski had rejected "external" approaches to acting early in his life, he (and many of his followers) later rediscovered the basic insight that François Delsarte had made one hundred years before—that the body can indeed provide a direct route to the emotions.[2]

Grotowski picked up the investigation where Stanislavski had left off. Jennifer Kumiega, who chronicles Grotowski's the-

2. This controversy between the "internal" and "external" theories of acting parallels a similar dispute between "mental" and "physiological" theories of psychology, with Ribot and Freud as exponents of the mental school and William James and Wilhelm Reich the physiological one.

ater work in her book *The Theatre of Grotowski* [Methuen, 1985], puts his conception this way:

> We do not *possess* memory, our entire body *is* memory, and it is by means of the "body-memory" that the impulses are released. [Kumiega, p. 120]

A corollary of this axiom is that an actor who has learned to "listen" to his body will find that character "actions," "intentions," and "objectives" arise organically within the work itself, without the actor needing to sit down and do "table work" to figure them out.

In fact, the physical approach to acting is not an abandonment of "internal" technique but an extension of it. Therefore, as you progress through this book, you may find that many of the physical acting exercises it contains connect directly with methods of training you have studied elsewhere. The "image" work we study may seem similar to the "sense memory" techniques of Lee Strasberg. The "listening" work may remind you of Sanford Meisner's exercises. And the "physical character" work may resemble the teachings of Uta Hagen.

There are many connections between Stanislavski's and Grotowski's approaches to acting, but ultimately the correspondences between the two lie not in the details of the techniques but in their outlook on art, and work and life:

• Both approaches have the same aim: To free the actor from those blocks that prevent him or her from embodying emotional truth and creativity.

• Both are based on the conviction that great acting is not simply a "career," or a "profession" or a "craft." It is also a way of being in the world, an art that requires openness and generosity to the work and to one's coworkers.

• And both demand that actors ask themselves the most basic questions about their art: Why am I an actor? What is "true" in theater? What is theater for?

EXPERIMENTAL THEATER

Actor training is a heuristic activity, which means that although you know the methods by which to proceed, you do not know what the outcome will be until you achieve it. It is like climbing a mountain in a fog; you know you must try to keep moving upward, but you do not know what the peak looks like until you get there.

—Richard Hornby, *The End of Acting*

There is nothing like trial and error. There is no better method in the world.

—John Strasberg, in Mekler,
The New Generation of Acting Teachers

The work this book describes has been called *experimental theater*. But when people say "experimental theater," they often seem to think the word *experimental* means "new" or "nonrealistic" or "weird." But in fact, what makes experimental theater experimental is exactly the same thing that makes experimental physics experimental—that it proceeds by means of *experiments*, by people trying things out to see what works, rather than by holding to a belief in a system, or by dedicating themselves to one or another theory or aesthetic.

In Peter Shaffer's play *Amadeus*, Mozart's nemesis, Salieri, perceives that Mozart has a direct connection with the heavenly source of music. "What was evident," he says, "was that Mozart was simply transcribing music completely finished in his head." But most of us are not Mozart. We are rarely blessed with such divine inspiration. To find our way in the wilderness of artistic creativity, we must stumble around, "experimenting" with different solutions before we are satisfied with the answers we find. The central idea of experimental theater is that this process of "stumbling around" is, in fact, an excellent way to proceed. It can lead us to discoveries we might never have made if we had confined our explorations to those pathways for which we had maps, and it instills in us a willingness to enter each new project with an open mind and with the (supremely important) courage to make mistakes.

The processes described in this book are not well-marked, limited-access highways for you to follow; they are simply pathways into the vast playgrounds of your own creativity. Because each artist is unique, each will find some of these pathways more useful than others. To find out which ones serve *you* best you must experiment, trying each exercise not with any expectation of results but with an expectancy of discovery. If you do so, you will find

• Encouragement for the basic activity of searching for those pathways that inspire you.

• Methods of engaging whatever difficulties you may encounter along the way: bridge-building skills you can use when you run across chasms, and swimming skills you can use when the water gets too deep for wading.

• Moral companionship. The knowledge that although you must find your own path, you are not alone in your solitude. The solitude you feel is one that others also experience, and the path you walk runs parallel to tracks that others have walked before.

The external forms this book teaches include the *plastique* and the *corporel* exercises of Jerzy Grotowski. But as you study these forms it is important to remember that the exercises themselves are not a "method"; they are merely provocations, hints, ways of posing questions that can serve as trailheads into the wilderness of your personal process. **The essential "technique" of experimental theater does not lie in the exercise forms or even in the particular answers you may find while using those forms. It lies in the centrality of the act of questioning itself.**

THE *VIA NEGATIVA*

The actor must discover those resistances and obstacles
which hinder him in his creative task. . . . By a personal
adaptation of the exercises, a solution must be found for
the elimination of these obstacles which vary for each
individual actor. . . . This is what I mean by **via negativa***:*
a process of elimination.

—Jerzy Grotowski, *Towards a Poor Theatre*

What we usually call "developing one's talent" is often
nothing more than freeing *it from the influences that*
hamper, occlude and frequently destroy it entirely.

—Michael Chekhov, *To the Actor*

When we were very young, our emotions were as sudden and
as dramatic as summer thunderstorms . . . and they passed as
quickly. We could run laughing and shouting with joy, fall
down, cry wildly for a few moments, and then get up and laugh
again. If we were denied something we wanted, we could
scream with rage, and then a moment later, we could drop our
rage when something else distracted us. And each emotion we
encountered would course through our whole body and our full
voice with no holding back. As acting teacher Richard Hornby
writes, "We should recall that in the infant, the emotions
always involve strong physical manifestation. We are not born
repressed, but howl or shudder or laugh lustily" [Hornby,
p. 127].

But as we grew older, most of us learned how to suppress our
emotions. We learned that some emotions were to be expressed
only under certain circumstances, that many were to be hidden
from the outside world at all costs, and a few were to be hidden
even from ourselves. Some of us learned never to cry, "like a
baby." Some of us learned never to show our anger. And some

to hide our fear, or our need for love. Exactly which emotional displays we learned to hide depended on the particular family and environment in which we grew up. Some of us were punished for noise and violence, others for being sissies. Some may not have been punished; we just noticed that our parents and our friends never cried in public or showed their deepest feelings, and we slowly accommodated ourselves to their repressed style. But almost all of us learned to hide at least a few of our emotions—just as surely as we learned to cover our bodies with clothes. To clothe our emotional lives, we constricted our voices and armored our bodies with muscular tensions. At first, perhaps, we simply held back our screams by clenching our jaws, and our tears by closing our eyes. But when these primary defenses became too obvious, we moved the disguises one layer deeper, stifling our screams with a tightened larynx and covering our tears with false smiles.[3]

For most people in our society, it is a strictly personal matter whether or not they are satisfied to live with these emotional restrictions. But for actors, emotional expression is essential to our craft, so learning to become an actor necessitates overcoming whatever emotional blocks we may have accumulated along the way.

The amazing thing is that even after years of hiding our emotions from the world (and from ourselves), our abilities to experience and to express our passions are not dead; they are merely hibernating within us. The process of freeing these imprisoned abilities is what Grotowski terms the *via negativa*, the "road backward." By this he means that acting training is not so much a process of learning new skills as it is a process of uncovering old abilities that we still carry deep within.

Of course, not all of acting training is a "road backward." There are also "positive" skills to be learned, skills like char-

---

3. In his book, *The Function of the Orgasm*, Wilhelm Reich suggests that the process of emotional suppression begins as a conscious act and only later becomes unconscious and automatic. See also *The Drama of the Gifted Child* by Alice Miller and *The Betrayal of the Body* by Alexander Lowen.

acter work, for instance. These skills are like putting on new clothing, on purpose. But before we can put this new clothing on, we must first remove the old clothes we've been carrying around for years. Therefore the work in this book begins with the *via negativa*—the task of *un*doing—and only later does it move on to the tasks of *doing*, those that necessitate *precision* and *choice*. Thus

• **In the body work**, we learn to activate all the parts of our bodies and to move fully and freely . . . before we study precision gesture or working with props.

• **In the voice work**, we learn to free our breathing and to open every resonator before we try to employ text.

• **In our emotional training**, we learn how to let strong emotion pour through us and how to receive an impulse from another actor before we study how to choose acting beats, or to play a character.

Note: Some actors find it easier to enter strong emotional work after creating character. In his book, The End of Acting, *Richard Hornby writes: "For such actors, mask work, dialects, animal studies, experiments with makeup, and working with period costumes and properties, are essential right from the beginning" [Hornby, p. 251]. If you suspect this may be true for you, you may want to experiment with character (see the chapter entitled "Character Work") even while you explore the physical and emotional exercises that appear in the early chapters of this book.*

To the Reader

This book is written for all actors who wish to connect their bodies more fully with their acting work. It is a workbook, so its lessons include detailed directions for the exercises they describe. But since many of the most important questions about this work arise in practice, the book also follows the experiences of a group of acting students as they study for a semester in my acting class. These students are fictional. The questions and problems they encounter in my class are drawn from the experiences of hundreds of students I have taught during the past twenty years. Their questions may or may not be yours. You have your own body, your own mind, and your own history, so your experience of the very same exercises may be different.

Each exercise in this book is here because I have found it to be effective for *some* students of acting, but that does not mean that each one will work for you. If you try an exercise and you find, after making a real effort, that the exercise does not "click" for you, move on to something else. Perhaps it will serve you at another time.

Ultimately, no one can learn acting from a book. So to make the best use of this curriculum, you must find or create a space in which you can transform these inanimate pages into action—with a partner, with a group, or in a class.

An
Acrobat
of the
Heart

An Actor's Warm-Up

ASKING QUESTIONS

On the first day of class, the students who have just joined the Experimental Theatre Wing at N.Y.U. enter a long, narrow studio and put down their bags below the north-facing windows. It is September in New York City. The air is still a little hot and heavy with summer, and the tall building across Waverly Place blots out most of the sky. Some of the students move out onto the floor to stretch, but most of them sit finishing their coffee or staring out the windows at the street below. In the corner one young man plays a guitar. Some people who have worked together in the past chat with their old friends, but most of the students in this class are strangers to each other and sit silently, waiting for the class to start.

When I enter the classroom, the guitarist finishes his phrase with a flourish and puts his instrument away. I sit down on the floor and call the group together in a circle. This is a "transfer track" class, for students who have spent the past two years studying at other acting studios and have chosen to transfer into the Experimental Theatre Wing. Since none of them have worked with me before, I tell them a little about myself. Then I ask them to introduce themselves and to say a few words about why they have chosen to come to E.T.W.[1]

The first to speak is a dark-haired, heavyset woman named

1. There are usually at least sixteen actors in my class, but in this book we will follow just eight of them.

Veronica. She feels she has learned a great deal from the acting techniques she has been studying, but that they have left her feeling out of touch with her body. "Of course, we had dance classes," she says, "but the body work never seemed to connect with the acting. I've come here because I want to connect my body with my mind."

Brian is a tall, gangling young man with a small goatee and a touch of sadness in his eye. He brushes his long hair out of his face as he says, "Being on stage for me is a little like being at one of those parties where you don't know what to do with your hands. I feel like all the acting I've studied has only made me more mental, more self-conscious."

Maria is a small woman who speaks softly with a light Spanish accent. She says she has always felt as though her body was not strong enough. "In my other acting classes they never talked about it. They just told us to relax and to sense things. But I think I was never really *there*. I know I have to work on my body. I just hope the work here isn't too hard for me."

Aisha is the only African-American in the group. She has short-cropped hair, a muscular body, and she wears a guarded smile. "I want to be a director and to make my own shows, not just to act. I want to make shows full of movement, so I came to E.T.W. for the self-scripting and because I want to understand how to use space and movement on stage."

Peter has a broad face and straight blond hair. As he speaks, he looks around the circle as if he were quite comfortable with these strangers. "I'm just excited," he says. "I feel like I've learned a lot about acting, but most of it seems like rules and ideas in my head. When I've seen productions at E.T.W., though, I always come out feeling like I do after a ball game, you know, alive. That's what I want."

Carlos is the guitarist, a muscular young man with dark eyebrows and an ironic smile. "I am here," he says, "because I want to work harder. I was studying musical theater, and I enjoyed it, but it didn't go deep enough. I want to put my music and my acting and dancing all together. I like to believe that I could do impossible things. Do you know what I mean? I want to learn to fly."

Sandra is next. She is a tall woman with long, blond hair and quiet blue eyes. But there is something distant in her gaze. "I don't know," she begins. "I liked the studio I was in, but I felt like I'd learned all I could there. It's just the vague feeling that there must be something more, something different. I think acting is such a hard profession, you know, and if it doesn't become more exciting for me, I may not have the energy to stick it out."

The last to speak is a pale young woman with intense green eyes. Her name is Joan. She wears her long red hair pulled back tightly in a bun at the nape of her neck. As the others spoke, she rarely reacted to their stories and almost never smiled. "I've been in dance classes since I was about seven years old," she begins. "But now I feel like I have lost something I used to have. When I was a kid, performing was pure fun, but somewhere along the line it turned into work. My acting teachers would tell me only what I was doing wrong, and now I don't trust myself anymore. I mean, if it doesn't make me happy, what's the point?"

"I agree," I say. "There are many jobs in this world that you can do well even if they are no fun. But you cannot act without joy. On the other hand, learning to act can also be hard work. So maybe the first question we must ask is, How can you work hard at something that is, basically, pure fun? Or, to put it another way, How can you remember to have fun, even in the depths of the hardest, most serious acting work?"

"So," says Carlos when I finish, "what's the answer?"

"The answer? I don't know. Our work here is fundamentally the process of asking questions. In fact, in this process, the asking of questions is often more important than the particular answers you find."

So this is how my first class begins with a group of students. Now, in this same spirit, I turn to you, the reader, and ask you to pose a few questions to yourself:

- Why are you reading this book?
- What do you hope to find here?
- At this point in your life, how do you approach acting?
- What has the study of acting been like for you up until now? What ways of working have served you best, and what difficulties have been left unresolved?

Your answers to these questions may help determine how you want to approach this book. For instance, if you have come to physical acting because you are frustrated by techniques that require you to discover your emotions while sitting in a chair, you may want to read a little and then plunge into one of the physical exercises, just to see how it feels to act and to move at the same time. If, on the other hand, you come to this work after having had an unpleasant training experience, you may want to read the whole book before trying out the exercises, to be sure that you are not getting yourself into another approach you can't trust.

And there is another reason to take a moment for self-reflection before you plunge into this work: entering a new discipline can be very exciting, but it can also inspire the thought, "Oh no, I feel like I don't know *anything*." And that is usually not the case. So it can be worthwhile to take note of the skills (techniques, methods, ways of working) you already possess.

What is written here is not meant to undermine or to invalidate techniques that already work for you. The work in this book should be about opening new doors, not about closing old ones.

TUNING YOUR INNER STRINGS

Nearly seventy years ago, Konstantin Stanislavski wrote:

You know that a sculptor kneads his clay before he begins to use it, and a singer warms up his voice before his concert. We need to do something similar to tune our inner strings, to test the keys, the pedals, and the stops. [Stanislavski, 1936, p. 250]

But how do you knead the "clay" of acting? How do you test "the keys, the pedals, and the stops" when the instrument you are playing is your body, your voice, and your entire emotional life? Ballet dancers have their "barre," and soldiers do calisthenics, but what can actors do to prepare, not just for speaking and moving, but for falling in love and raging and crying? Is there some kind of warm-up that can prepare all these different parts of the actor's instrument and at the same time connect the body, voice, and emotional life with each other?

I first confronted this question a few years after studying with Grotowski. I had joined a theater group that was touring New England performing a play about the National Guard shootings at Kent State, and before rehearsals the members of our troupe would warm up by practicing yoga *asanas*. After I had been doing this for several weeks, I began to notice that while I was twisting my body this way and that trying to achieve the correct yogic posture, I was also thinking a great deal. I was thinking about the pain. I was worrying that I was not doing the *asana* correctly. I was ruing the fact that I had not started yoga when I was younger. And I was comparing my position with that of one of the other actors—and realizing my body would never be able to do what *her* body did. And then, the more I thought about her body, the further and further my mind drifted from the yoga. It became clear to me that while my body was practicing yoga, my mind was engaged in a very different sort of warm-up, a kind of express-train monologue that whizzed right past the lumbering local on which my yoga body was traveling. Of course, with a little concentration, I could bring my mind back to what my body was doing, but that mental gymnastic often came with an extra little kick, a judgment like "Wake up, you're supposed to be concentrating on *your* body, not *her* body, you idiot!" So by the end of my yoga session my mind was as full of distress as my body was. There had to be a better way to prepare myself to perform.

As I struggled with this question, I realized that the work I had studied with Grotowski a few years before had provided just such a method of warming up my body and my mind together, as if they were one entity, not two. When I began to teach this work I came to understand that the essence of what I had learned with Grotowski lay not in the particular exercises, but in an awareness of the connections between the body, the mind, and the emotions, an awareness that can be reawakened and strengthened every day as part of the warm-up process.

So to start creating an actor's warm-up for yourself you don't need to learn any new exercises. You can begin by using forms you already know, and then as you acquire more acting tools you can add them to your warm-up little by little. This warm-up is not a fixed regimen; it is a practice that will grow and change as your acting skills and your circumstances change. It begins with asking questions, and the first question we ask is simply, *Where* do you choose to do your warm-up?

FINDING SAFE SPACE

The essential problem is to give the actor the possibility of working "in safety." The work of the actor is in danger, continuously supervised and observed. One must create an atmosphere, a working system, in which the actor feels that he can do anything, and that nothing he does will be mocked, that all will be understood.... Often, the moment the actor understands this, he reveals himself.

—Jerzy Grotowski, *Les Lettres français*

At the beginning of Carlos Castaneda's book *The Teachings of Don Juan: a Yaqui Way of Knowledge*, Don Juan and Castaneda sit together on the porch of Don Juan's house. The sorcerer tells Castaneda that before a student can receive his teachings, he must first find the one place on the porch where he can "feel naturally happy and strong." So Castaneda spends all night walking and rolling around the porch in search of the "spot where I could be at my very best." In *The Teachings of Don Juan* this process of finding the right place seems profound and mysterious. But actually it is a skill we all exercise every day.

Right now, for instance, you have probably chosen a "comfortable" place in which to read this book, a place in the room to sit (or stand or lie down) that allows you to concentrate on the task of reading. Similarly, when you enter a dance studio, you choose a place on the floor that "feels right" for dancing. If one day you were to notice that a section of the dance floor was wet, you would look for a dry area in which to work because it would be foolhardy to practice leaps and pirouettes on a wet floor.

In the same way, when you walk into an acting studio, you automatically seek out a place in which you feel comfortable doing your acting work. Acting requires emotional leaps, and you need as much safety as you can get before engaging in pirouettes of the heart. Perhaps the first thing you do when you enter the studio is to find someplace to put down your bags. Then, before you sit, maybe you go to the window to look out, or perhaps you stare at a picture or read a newspaper. When you sit down, maybe you choose to sit alone or maybe you sit near your friends. And when the class is about to begin, perhaps you move again to sit nearer or farther from the teacher. So without thinking about it you constantly adjust your relationship to the space to make yourself feel safe and comfortable. All these adjustments are actually the beginning of your warm-up. They are the ways in which you "warm up" your relationship to the workspace.

But what is it that actually makes one place on the floor seem more "comfortable" to you than another place? How does your body "know" that one place is better than another? What signal is it responding to?

The only way to answer these questions is to notice how you feel as your body explores the space. So before I start my first warm-up class with my new students, I ask them to spend a few minutes **Finding Safe Space** (1.1).

In this exercise, the body's sense of actual, physical space acts as a barometer of inner, emotional space. Thus this seem-

---

Finding Safe Space (1.1)

This is an exercise you can explore at the beginning of an acting class or a rehearsal, or even now, while you read this book.

At the beginning of acting class or rehearsal, a group of actors can try the exercise this way:

1. First, spend a few minutes just wandering around the work-space, "looking for" the best place to work.

2. Try out places that seem appealing to you, but also try out places that you suspect you won't like. Sense what the difference between them is.

3. Try sitting, standing, jumping, kneeling, lying down, and rolling to see how different activities feel in each space.

4. Do you feel safer and more comfortable in the middle of the floor or near a wall? In the light or in the dark? Facing others or facing away?

5. After three minutes of exploration, choose a place in the room where you can make yourself as comfortable as possible to start your warm-up. (Of course, if someone else is already in the space where you want to be, that changes the whole space for you.)

6. Let yourself be aware of how you "knew" which place to choose.

To try while reading:

1. Take a moment right now to notice where you are: this is the place you have chosen (consciously or unconsciously) in which to do this reading.

2. Now get up, move someplace else with the book and try reading there.

3. Repeat this process in several other places in the room.

4. Is there a difference? Can you sense how or why you chose that first place in which to read?

ingly "external" exercise is at the same time an "internal" practice in self-awareness. Often we are unconscious of the connection between our outer actions and our inner state. But in this exercise, the inner state is directly linked to clear actions we take in the real world: In order to satisfy our sense of safety and comfort, we move our bodies to another place in the room. Thus the process of searching for a Safe Space is a first step toward connecting our conscious and our unconscious processes: it utilizes a conscious outward behavior to stimulate our inner awareness, and it uses that inner awareness to initiate clear, physical actions. And that is exactly what the physical approach to acting is about: **not physicality for its own sake, but physicality because the body serves as a *pathway* into our emotional life and as a *means* of knowing and expressing what we feel.**

This simple space exploration of ours provides two benefits:

• First, it offers you some control over your feeling of safety in the work.

• At the same time, it helps you develop an awareness of the connection between your external choices and your internal feelings—the perception that something as simple as moving your body from place to place can have an immediate effect on your mental and emotional state.[2]

THE STREAM-OF-CONSCIOUSNESS WARM-UP

In Grotowski's training, the asanas *are fluid and transformative, never freezing into fixed positions, facilitating the practitioner's active attention to flow and requiring constant movement of the spinal column. In yoga, by con-*

2. "Viewpoint technique," to which we return when we deal with scene work and blocking on page 190, carries this kind of sensitivity to space many steps further.

> *trast, positions are fixed and held, with the goal of bring-*
> *ing the practitioner to a passive state and halting various*
> *physical processes. Grotowski found that the goals of the*
> *hatha yoga exercises were counterproductive to the Labo-*
> *ratory Theatre's work, as the state they produced was*
> *antithetical to the receptivity and dynamic attention nec-*
> *essary for the actor.*
>   —Lisa Wolford, *Grotowski's Objective Drama Research*

After all the members of my acting class have found safe
space, I say, "Now, just begin *any* warm-up you would like to
do. It doesn't matter what training it comes from; it might be
something you learned in a dance class, or it might be from
your soccer team calisthenics, but it must be something in
which you work actively with your body."

Then, after the actors have been moving their bodies for a
few minutes, I suggest that they start to notice what is happening in their minds while their bodies move, "Just notice when
something changes in your mind and mark that moment by
changing what your body is doing." A few minutes later, I make
the task more specific, asking them to search for a physical
form that reflects the new event that is happening in their
minds. "If your mind is racing, you might literally run around
the room. If you feel depressed, you could try huddling in a
corner. But each time your mind changes course, you must let
your body change with it."

Since this is just the first day of class, the students are still
strangers to each other. When they begin the exercise, they are
working in isolation, performing stretches or calisthenics they
have learned in the past. But as the warm-up progresses, and
as they attempt to find physical expressions for their inner
states, more and more of them begin to move around the space,
to make sound, and sometimes even to make contact with each
other. I encourage them to trust their impulses and to allow
their bodies to exteriorize the contents of their minds (the
Stream-of-Consciousness Warm-up, 1.2). At the end of another

five minutes, I ask them to take a quiet moment to sense how they feel and to remember what they did. Then I call them together. "But," I say, "take a couple of minutes returning to the circle, and as you do, notice how the simple act of joining the circle changes your relationship to the space. Take the time you need coming together, just as you did when we explored the room at the beginning."

When the whole group has gathered, I ask people to comment on what this new warm-up was like for them. Several comment that it was entirely different from warm-ups they have done in the past. Joan, who had spoken so bitterly about her recent acting classes, seems quite surprised at her experience: "This was the first warm-up I ever really enjoyed. I've gotten so used to accepting the forms that teachers give me. It was nice not to feel confined. It had never occurred to me before that just warming up could actually be fun."

Brian reports that when he began today's class he was feeling depressed and angry, but he says that he feels different now and more present.

"And do you know exactly when your mood changed or what you were doing when it did?" I ask.

"Yes," he says, smiling for a moment, "it changed when I started throwing punches and yelling, 'Go to hell.'"

"And do you know at whom you were throwing punches and yelling?"

"Yeah," he says. "You see I live in a small apartment with—"

"No," I say, "don't tell us. It's your image. I was just wondering if it was clear to you."

"Real clear. He drives me nuts."

"So you discovered that one thing a warm-up can do for you is to put you in touch with energy you have been holding inside: Your stream of consciousness can inspire your body to throw punches or to cry tears that have been waiting inside you for a chance to show themselves. Perhaps it is a little like sweeping your mental attic to make some space in which to do your work."

"But it's not gone," Brian protests. "I mean, right now I'm still angry with him."

"That's right. One sweep does not eliminate all the dust. But you said that after you threw those punches you felt better. You had swept one corner of your mental attic clear enough to notice that, *in addition to the dust*, there is also some sunlight shining in the attic window. The anger is not gone. It is at the side, where you have swept it, and if you wanted to use it for a scene now, you'll know right where to find it. Meanwhile, you feel less depressed, not because you have *eliminated* that emotion, but because you have *separated* yourself from it a little by letting it course through your muscles. We are not talking about primal therapy or self-realization here, just about clearing enough mental space to be able to do our acting."

Most of the students seem quite pleased with what they discovered, but Carlos is not. He seems troubled, and as he speaks he presses his dark eyebrows together. "My mind kept changing so quickly that there was no way I could keep up with my body. I don't think I could ever put all those thoughts into my work."

"You're absolutely right," I say. "If you watch a movie that is being projected slower than sixteen frames per second, you will see flicker because your brain is so fast that it can process sixteen visual images every second. When you add to that all the other senses, plus memory and fantasy and thought, you realize that the number of perceptions that can pass through your mind each second is enormous. There is no way your body could possibly keep up with them all. And there is no need. Let yourself pick and choose. Bring your body to one thought or feeling or image, follow it for a while, and then choose another. In a little while it will become clear to you that many of these thought-moments are trivial, while some of them contain a great deal of energy, and that energy is something you can capture with your body and put into your work."

While I have been speaking, Sandra has been staring out the window, her wide blue eyes constantly escaping the room and searching out the little patch of blue the city reserves for the sky. Now she turns to me and says, "Does that mean that *any*thing can become part of the work?"

"That's exactly the question."

"And the answer?"

"It may be different for different people. For instance, just now before you spoke, you were staring out the window."

"Yes."

"Were you aware that you also looked out there often while you were doing your warm-up stretches?"

"A little." Sandra looks embarrassed. Her eyes look down and long blond hair falls across her face.

"And when you found yourself looking out, what did you do?"

"I don't know. When I became aware of it, I just concentrated back on my work."

"Right, and concentration is a very important tool. But the purpose of this work is to suggest that there is another choice available to you: instead of bringing your mind to your body, you could bring your body to your mind."

"You mean just keep staring out the window while I work?"

"No, I mean literally letting your body *join* your eyes. I don't know what it is that your eyes were craving out there. But once you *notice* that your eyes are drawn to the window, you could move over to the window like this, and then you might lean against it and crane your neck up toward the sky, like this. As you allow your body to follow your eyes, you might find that you are actually doing the stretch your body was working on before, but at the same time you are also exploring your inner yearning for blue sky."

"But I need to concentrate," Carlos chimes in. "If I don't do my yoga, my mind is always scattered."

"Then by all means, do it. I'm not saying you shouldn't do things that center you. Centering is definitely one of the things a warm-up can do for you. If you feel scattered, I would definitely recommend that you do something that centers you: yoga or a breath meditation, or even just standing still or sitting quietly with your eyes closed while you sense how you feel."

"I don't understand," Sandra protests. "I thought you said I shouldn't try to bring my thoughts back from the window."

"No, I think concentration is important, too. But sometimes the effort of trying to concentrate can exacerbate our fear that things like a strong desire to look at the blue sky are somehow mistakes or distractions from the work. What I am suggesting is that there is also another way to achieve center: by treating those distractions themselves as sources of energy.

"Over the years, many of us have been taught that certain things are clearly *not* part of our work: things like our opinion of other students or of the teacher, and things like what we would like to eat for lunch, or how we feel about whatever happened last night. In fact, an enormous amount of our energy is locked up in the thoughts we have labeled 'not part of the work.' What I am proposing here is a process by which you can liberate some of that energy. It is not that you should never do yoga or concentration exercises that bring your mind to your body. It is just that there is also an opposite way to build the connection between your body and your mind—by bringing your body to your mind, noticing what is actually happening in your mind and finding a physical form that can *embody* that energy.

"Using this process you may find three things changing:

• One is what we have just been talking about: that those things that were formerly distractions from your work are no longer so distracting because the distractions are being reprocessed into work energy.

• The second change you may notice is what Brian discovered: that your general mood and energy problems like feeling depressed or tired may start to crack open and reveal the variety that exists within them, that even something like general gloom contains the seeds of sadness and anger and laughter.

• And the third thing that you may find is that after bringing the body to the mind for a while, you have a much easier time concentrating when you go back to it."

"I don't get that," says Carlos, clearly hoping that this process will not deprive him of his yoga.

"Think of it this way: At first perhaps your body is doing slow, methodical stretches while your mind is running all over the place. But then if you allow your body to join your mind in its frenetic marathon, you compel the two parts of yourself to run alongside each other long enough for them to begin to link up. Then, if you return to your slow stretches, your body can more easily pull the mind along with it into its concentration. Ultimately, you will find that these two ways of working— bringing the body to the mind and bringing the mind to the body—slip back and forth quite effortlessly. And both of them serve the purpose of centering you."

The Stream-of-Consciousness Warm-Up (1.2)

This is an exercise you can do alone or with a group.

1. To begin, make sure you are in a place in which you feel comfortable. If during the work you realize that you want to be somewhere else, move.

2. Now, begin any warm-up you would like to do for your body: Stretches, yoga, jogging, push-ups. It doesn't matter what you start with as long as your body is doing something active.

3. When you have done that for a few minutes, the next step is to notice what is going on in your mind as you work. (To help you notice, you can try mumbling your stream of consciousness out loud.) Sometimes you will find that you are thinking about what your body is doing, but at other moments you may notice that you are thinking about other things: Perhaps you are noticing the space or the people around you, or perhaps you are daydreaming, or staring out the window, or judging your work. In any case, **don't try to stop your mind from wandering**. Just continue doing your warm-up while allowing yourself to notice your mind's activity.

4. After this double task is clear to you, do this: Every time your mind enters a new thought or feeling, purposefully change what you are doing with your body. Change it fully, to something very different from what you were just doing. The important thing is to <u>notice</u> the changes in the inner world, and to <u>mark</u> those changes by changing your outer activity.

5. The next step is to make your outward choices reflect your inner states. For instance, if your mind is racing around nervously, you might literally race around the room. If you feel angry and frustrated, you might kick or punch the air. If you are feeling lost, you might crawl into a corner. You don't have to find exactly the right thing to do; just let your body somehow reflect the mind's activity. But be sure that <u>each time</u> a new thought enters your mind, you stop what you are doing and do something entirely new, something that allows your whole body to reflect the new emotion or mental activity.

6. Continue to work this way until the process of noticing and changing is clear to you, at least six or seven minutes.

7. Now stop and take a minute with your eyes closed to let yourself reflect on what you have gone through, and on how you feel now. Remember what happened. How do the condition of your body and of your mind now compare with their condition before you started this warm-up? How do they compare with how they feel after your usual warm-up?

A BALANCING ACT

An actor is never unconcentrated. He's just concentrating on something that he doesn't think he should be concentrating on.

—Michael Kahn, in Mekler,
The New Generation of Acting Teachers

There are two ways to keep a broomstick upright and stationary as you balance it in your hand. The first is to grip the broomstick tightly and keep it from tilting with the strength of your muscles. The second is to place it on your open palm and to move your hand underneath it as the broomstick begins to fall one way or another. These two methods are physical examples of the opposite approaches to mental centeredness.

Many schools of acting teach techniques of concentration, ways of maintaining a kind of "one-pointedness" that can keep the mind calm and intent on one task even in the midst of external (or internal) chaos. Stanislavski begins *An Actor Prepares* by describing what he calls a "circle of concentration," which excludes disturbing influences (like the presence of the audience) from the actor's consciousness. Such concentration is a powerful tool, but it has two drawbacks:

1. While excluding *unwanted* stimuli (like the man coughing in the back of the audience), it can also shut out *wanted* signals (like the subtle changes in how your scene partner is smiling at you tonight).
2. Like holding the vertical broomstick stationary in your grip, this concentration requires energy.

But there is another method of centering, the one used in Zen meditation, in aikido, and by the circus juggler. In these disciplines, center is maintained not by *expending* energy to fight against distractions but by *absorbing* the energy of those distractions, and *including* that energy into the new center. In this way, each distraction is treated not as a *problem* that needs to be overcome but as a *source* of creative energy.

This is the way a circus juggler keeps a broomstick balanced on his hand: by constantly *redefining* center and moving the hand below the ever-falling stick. Of course, the expert juggler senses the tilting of the stick so quickly that he seems not to be moving at all. But his stasis is an illusion. It is a calm created out of constant motion, a seeming perpendicular created out of an endless series of falls, a concentration built out of the energies of distraction.

This is the technique the aikido practitioner uses, blending the energy of his opponent into his own. And this is the method underlying the Stream-of-Consciousness Warm-up: accepting all of our "irrelevant" thoughts and impulses as creative inspirations for our work.

SLOW MOTION

After our serious discussion about the Stream-of-Conscious-ness Warm-up, I get my class on its feet and announce that we are going to play tag, *slow motion tag*. Everyone knows the basic rules for playing tag; the only thing I need to explain is that in this version of the game whenever I call out "slow motion," everyone must move as if we were being filmed by a slow-motion camera. "But even in the slow motion sections," I say, "remember to play to win." Then I yell, "Not it!" and the game begins.

Tag is a wonderful container for the fear and excitement people bring to a first class; it is a game that immediately con-nects people's bodies and emotions; and above all, it is pure fun. We play hard for five or six minutes, long enough for people to notice that the "slow motion" is not quite as easy as it looks.

When I gather the group together again, I ask if anyone had any difficulties.

"Yes," Veronica reports. "It felt like there were certain parts of my body I couldn't quite control."

Brian adds, "I noticed that just a moment before the tag, my body would speed up or the person I was going to tag would suddenly change direction much faster than they really could have in fast motion."

"Right," adds Peter, "but how can you 'play to win' and hold yourself back at the same time?"

"That," I respond, "is a very important question, and it points to one of the reasons we are playing this game. But rather than trying to answer it intellectually, let's just spend a few minutes examining slow motion as a 'serious' question. And then we'll see if it is possible to add our serious work to the tag game without ruining the fun." With that, I lead the **Slow Motion Study** (1.3).

After everyone is deep in this studied slow motion, I simply

Slow Motion Study (1.3)

1. Begin by walking around the room normally. Walk easily, allowing your arms to swing freely.

2. The room is like a sea of air, and as your arms swing through it, feel how it pushes against them. Perhaps you can also feel the air sweeping past your face.

3. Try to feel the air as your feet swing through it, as your shoulders and pelvis cut through it, and as it eddies behind you. Sense it even through your clothes; feel how it presses against your knees as you lift them on each step and how it pushes against your chest as you move forward.

4. Now imagine that the air is filled with fog, a thick fog. You keep walking, but the fog is so thick that you can see it clearly, can see its color and texture. Picture how the fog curls around your body. Feel how it touches your hair, your arms, your hands, your fingers.

5. Allow the fog to become even thicker, so that it is almost a liquid. You just keep walking, but let the liquid work on you. Remember what it is like to walk in water, how your knee must lift through the liquid, how the calf must push to swing the foot forward, and how the foot must press downward through the water to reach the ground. Feel how if you lift your arm and then let it go the liquid supports it as it falls. Feel how if you lean to the side the water supports you.

6. And now let the liquid become even thicker, as if it were pea soup, or custard, or setting concrete. Feel its thickness against your whole body. Feel it around each finger. Feel it against your face. See its color and texture.

7. Try swinging your arm through this thick liquid, try turning your face and sensing how your nose, your chin, your whole profile cut their shape through the stuff.

8. Imagine that there is a beam of light shining from your eyes like the light from a lighthouse. If you sweep your eyes to the right or left, that whole beam must cut a swath through the liquid too.

9. Check through your body. If any body part tends to wobble, simply let the liquid be thicker around that part.

call "Not it!" again, loudly, but very slowly, "Noooooot iiiiit!" This time when we play tag there is almost no wobbling, and the moments leading up to each tag are no longer hurried past, but instead are extended microcosms of attack and retreat, little "scenes" of aggression and fear mutually created by the taggee and the tagger.

"So," I ask the group when we stop, "what happened to the wobbling?"

"Well," says Aisha, "having that thick custard out there meant I didn't have to hold myself back. It was holding me."

"But how is that possible?" I insist. "After all, there *was* no custard. There was nothing in this room but the same old air."

"Nothing but your words," adds Carlos, "and our imaginations."

At this point Veronica chimes in, "Are you saying that just believing in something makes it real?"

"No, what I'm suggesting is something much more specific: that surrounding your body with imagery seems to have an effect on the body itself. **If you fill the world around you with imagery, that imagery will work on you** *as if from the outside* **even though you know perfectly well it isn't there!** And that is the very core of the physical training we are going to be studying. It is not about our bodies alone, but about how our bodies and our imaginations work on each other.

"So this little game of tag is really an introduction to our whole study of acting. It demonstrates the connections between imagery, emotion, and the body. But it also starts to confront the paradox Joan brought up earlier, the paradox of how it is possible to have serious fun, no?"

"Yes," says Joan. "I must admit this was serious fun."

"Good. We'll stop here for today, but from now on, if you catch yourself having fun, remember, it's legal."

THE BODY PART WARM-UP

On the first day of work we examined warm-up as an external reflection of an internal stream of consciousness. Now we will try linking body and mind in another way: by thinking of your warm-up as a series of questions you ask your body—or as a series of gifts you give yourself. Questions like, "What do my feet need right now?" Or gifts like, "What is the best thing I can do for my legs in two minutes?" This is the approach of the **Body Part Warm-up** (1.4).

At the start of the next class, I take half an hour to lead the group through this questioning process, body part by body part, from their feet up to their heads. As they progress, I encourage the students to "listen" to their bodies, to see if they can actually satisfy their needs. Along the way, I make suggestions such as, "If you don't know what to do, just try something. If it isn't right, you'll know that right away, and you can try something else."

Then, when they have worked through all the parts of their physical bodies, I have them move on to the *body politic*: "When you were working on warming up your feet, many of you discovered that the best way to give a gift to your feet was to use your hands to give them a massage. Well, the same thing is true of this body politic, the group of people in this room. There are certain needs each of you has that can best be satisfied *in relation* to other people. So now let yourselves ask, 'What do I want *from others* in this group?' 'What gifts can we best give and receive from each other?'"

This question is a bit of a shock. Until this point, everyone has been very concentrated on his or her own body. Suddenly the actors are aware of each other. They hesitate, not knowing what to do. "Remember," I say, "when you were working with your own body, the only way to find out what you needed was to try something. Then if you didn't like what you were doing, you could try something else. The same is true now."

When they start to explore the question of their relationship to others, some of the actors begin by giving and receiving backrubs; others play games or dance together. But there are also a few who hang back from group involvement entirely. They seem to be circling around the outside of the group, as if they were waiting for someone else to initiate the contact. I don't interfere except to say, "Keep noticing what is going on for you now, and risk trying something new."

After about five minutes of this work I say, "When we had worked through all the body parts, then I had you warm up your body as a whole. So now let's try the same thing with this body politic. What is it that the *group* needs as a whole?" Again there is a moment of hesitancy. How is it possible for a group to *want* something? How can individual actors know what the group wants? How can the group figure it out? Again I remind them, "There is no way to find out except by trying." At first several different subgroups develop, each engaged in different activities. One group is dancing and clapping in rhythm, another is sharing shoulder massages in a circle. Suddenly the dancers surround the massagers, circling them with their rhythm. For a while the massage group sticks with its activity, but then one of the massagers begins to jump up and down in time to the rhythm while continuing to do his massage. Within a few minutes everyone is dancing—everyone, that is, except Sandra, who is moving slowly by herself in one corner of the room.

"Be aware of everyone," I call from the side. But when the group nears Sandra, she yells at them and runs to another corner.

"So how do you deal with that?" I yell over the rhythmic clapping. "What if not everyone needs the same thing at the same time?" The large group leaves Sandra alone and dances without her in the center of the room. Then, as the dance dies down, Aisha leaves the group dance and places herself beside Sandra as if she were mirroring Sandra's body position, but without looking at her at all. After a few seconds, she and Sandra begin to lean against each other a little. I cannot tell who initiated the lean, but they slowly tip further and further toward each other until they fall over. Suddenly they are both laughing and pushing against each other with their feet. Another person from the large group joins them. In the end, everyone joins Aisha and Sandra on the floor, all of them waving their feet in the air.

"One minute to the end of the warm-up," I say. The group moves less and less. Eventually they are all just breathing together.

"Good," I say. "Now, spend a few minutes alone. Let yourself sense how you are feeling at this moment. Sense what has changed since the beginning of the warm-up. What did you discover along the way? Are there any things you noticed that you would want to do more of, or less of, the next time?"

Now when we gather there is silence for a while. The exercise ended with a sense of group harmony, and perhaps no one wants to spoil that. "Maybe," I venture, "there are no questions that need asking."

Then Peter raises his hand. "Well," he says, "that was basically fine. But sometimes I needed more time." He smiles a little. "I mean, on certain body parts, I felt like I could have spent much longer."

"You are absolutely right. There is rarely enough time. It would be wonderful if you always had a year or more to rehearse a play, as Stanislavski did. And it would be nice if we had more than thirteen weeks together to study this physical acting curriculum. But we don't. If we spend a whole class on warm-up, we will never get to the rest of the work we need to do. And if your warm-up comes before a rehearsal, the time you take for your warm-up is time you no longer have for the rehearsal."[1]

"So what should we do?"

"Two things. One is to budget your time. Perhaps today your

---

1. See André Gregory's comments in his "Afterthoughts" at the end of this book.

feet or your pelvis or your voice need extra time, so perhaps you will have to spend less time on your hands or your arms. But it is necessary that each day you at least check in with each body part, because important material may be hiding out in one or another body part."

"And what is the second thing?"

"You're not going to like it."

"Oh, I know," Peter says, smiling again because he came to class late, "come on time."

"Worse. Come early. From now on we will be doing a warm-up at the beginning of every class, and once you start understanding how to listen to your body's needs, you will no longer need me here to get you started. Eventually you may be working with a director who does not provide any time for warm-up, so you will have to make that time entirely for yourself. Remember, one of the central lessons of today's work was that your warm-up is not a chore; it is a series of gifts you give yourself."

"And what," asks Joan, "if what your body needs is just to rest?"

"You mean like to go to sleep?"

"No, I mean relaxing your muscles, or just resting."

"Relaxation is fine," I say. "Some acting teachers consider it a necessary first step before all other work. A good relaxation can help get you in touch with both breath and body. But you have to be careful with relaxation because it can also be a way to avoid getting in touch with energy. Remember, one of the purposes of a warm-up is to get your energy up so that you are physically and mentally alive. And getting physically warm is also safer for your muscles. Sports coaches these days usually recommend doing something aerobic to warm up your muscles before you do your stretches. Ultimately there is a delicate balance between relaxation and energy. Both are necessary for the work."

No one seems to have any more to say, so I turn to Sandra and ask, "And how was that for you?"

"Well . . . by the end it was okay."

"And before that?"

"I don't know. I just didn't want to dance. I just wanted to be alone. You said we should see what the group needs, but what if you don't need what everyone else needs?"

"Well, are you a member of the group?"

"I don't know. I'm one person. Maybe I was avoiding something."

I turn to the others. "Well, what happened to the others of you when you saw that Sandra didn't want to join the dance?"

"It was okay with me," says Peter, "except that you said we should be aware of the whole group. Then I thought that maybe we should find a way to get Sandra to join."

"Right. Many theater classes nowadays teach ensemble work, exercises designed to build a strong bond between the members of a group. But there is a common misconception that to be a group you all have to be doing exactly the same thing. Of course, it is true that moments of group unison are very powerful. That is what you all discovered at the very end of your warm-up today. But to be aware of the group is not the same as insisting on unison. In this case to be aware may only have meant to keep Sandra and her needs in your view. In the end Aisha found a way to make a connection with her, and everyone else joined in. And it is always true that the unison discovered through that kind of negotiation is more powerful than the unison imposed as an ideal."

"But if everyone just stayed with their own needs," Carlos protests, "we would never get together."

"That's true. It is always a negotiation. And it was very important that Sandra, although she did not join the rest of you, kept in touch with you."

"In touch? By going off into the corner?"

"Yes. There are all kinds of ways of going off into the corner. If Sandra had simply ignored the group, or closed her eyes, or exited from the room, she would have cut off the connection. But as she moved away from you she yelled and made it very clear that she was saying, 'No, I don't want to play your game.' That was a gift also. Saying no clearly and openly is actually a very good way of staying in touch."

At this point I stop the discussion and we spend the rest of the class in physical training. But at the end of the day, I return to the question of warm-ups. "Tomorrow we will try to combine the different warm-up tools we have studied so far. But the conversation Peter and I had earlier about not having enough time reminded me of another thing we ought to try. I suggested to Peter that he could begin his warm-up on his own. But that practice is actually something useful for everyone. So when we meet next time, I will come to class late, on purpose. I want you all to start discovering what you must do to make your own transition into the work without a teacher to tell you when and how to begin."

The two approaches we have taken to warm-up so far—the Stream-of-Consciousness warm-up and the Body Part warm-up—are complementary, not mutually exclusive. Now it is up to you to start building a warm-up for yourself by "mixing and matching," combining different elements, experimenting with different orders to find out what works for you. You may begin by exercising one or another part of your body, and then, realizing that your thoughts are elsewhere, follow those thoughts as they lead you to another physical concentration. Or perhaps you start by simply moving around the space, sensing how your body feels as it moves through different spaces, and letting yourself ask, "What do I need now?"

ACTING ON IMPULSE

On the third day with my acting class, I enter the class late, as promised. Most of the group is already working, so I say, "Fine.

The Body Part Warm-Up (1.4)

You can do the first nine steps of this exercise on your own, but steps ten and eleven require that you work in a group:

1. Choose a place in which to begin your work, someplace you feel comfortable standing, sitting, and lying down. (If during the course of the work you realize you want to be someplace else, move.)

2. Begin by asking a question of your feet: What do your feet <u>need,</u> right now? If you had just two minutes to make your feet happy, what could you do for them? Take time to try things out. Note: you are trying to do the best you can <u>under these conditions</u>. If what your feet would really like is to run on wet sand but the nearest beach is five hundred miles away, you will have to make do with something else: perhaps you can run around the room and imagine the beach, or perhaps you can tickle your feet, pretending you have sand in between your toes. But it will not serve to simply lament reality.

3. Then move on to your legs: What do your legs want or need right now? What is the best thing you can do for your legs in a couple of minutes? As you work, let yourself ask the question several times. Sometimes you will find that after you have done one thing for a while, the body part craves something very different. If you don't know what to do, begin by trying anything. The process of questioning is an active one. If what you try doesn't seem right, try something else.

4. Now move on to the pelvis, the hips, and the groin. Of course there are probably lots of things that your pelvis would like, but again, you've got to make do with the best you can get under these conditions. Use your muscles and use your imagination.

5. Continue to work other body parts, spending about two minutes on each section of the body. After the pelvis we go to

the lower back, waist, and abdomen
the upper back and chest
the shoulders
the arms and hands
the neck, the head, and the face.

With each body part, let yourself really ask the question and search for the answer. This is a dialogue between you and your shoulder. Let the shoulder tell you how it feels. You may not find the perfect "gift" for your shoulder, but at least you will discover that some choices are better than others.

6. Now spend some time on just the eyes. Begin with the eyes as

muscles: do they want to be open or closed? How does it feel to let the lids be heavy? How does it feel to move the eyes rapidly or slowly?

7. Now try asking the question of the eyes in their other capacity, as sense organs. What do your eyes want to look at? The floor? Out the window? At another person? At something actually in the space or something in your imagination? Give your eyes the best visual "gifts" you can under these circumstances.

8. Now, what about the <u>whole</u> body? What does the body need as a whole, rather than as a collection of parts? Try some things that involve the entire body at once. If you want to, you can move in space. Are there things your body craves in relationship to the space? Does moving through the space then change what it is your body craves?

9. And now we move on to the breath and the voice: What does your breath need right now? What would make your voice feel best?

10. Okay, we've been through all the parts of the body, but there is more. When you were working on giving gifts to your feet, you may have found that the best way to make your feet happy was to give them a massage with your hands. In other words, the best way to satisfy one body part was with the help of another. Just so: there are some things that are achieved much more easily "with a little help from your friends." And just as all the body parts are parts of the whole body, so too, all the people in the room are parts of the "body politic." So, thinking of your <u>relationship</u> to others as if it were a muscle, what can you do for your relationship with other people in the room? This is another question that must be answered in the doing. Try something. If it isn't what you wanted, try something else. What can you do for your relationship to others . . . under these conditions? Work with one person for a while, and then move on to another.

11. Now, in the same way that you moved from working with all the individual body parts to working with the body as a whole, we move from working with relationships between individuals to working with the relationship of the group as a whole: What does the group as a <u>whole</u> need? Take time to experiment. As you try things out, keep letting your awareness spread out to everyone. If different parts of the whole seem to need different things at the same time, how can you accommodate that need?

12. When you finish, take some private time to digest what you have been through. How was this warm-up for you? Are there things you would want to do more or less of next time?

Just keep working while I talk a little. Today you have forty-five minutes for your warm-ups, but how you divide your time is up to you. I will say only that by the end of the time, you are responsible for having warmed up not only all the parts of yourself, but also your connection to others and to the group. And by the end of the warm-up you need to be ready to work with your full body."

As I watch the class today, I note that everyone seems very energized and engaged in what he or she is doing, but the energy is rather chaotic. Some people have begun by running around the space, while others are doing yoga. One couple spends a long time playing nonverbal games with one another. At one point in the middle of the warm-up, Aisha stops working entirely for a few minutes. I am about to ask her what is happening when she begins to work again, so I leave her alone. At the end of the time allotted the group again discovers a unified activity, but the mood is clearly less positive than it was the day before. After I allow some time for each person to think about what has happened, we gather in the center of the floor. As soon as we are together Carlos bursts out, "So what went wrong?"

"I'll tell you what went wrong," says Aisha. "You came up and invaded my space while I was trying to work alone."

"I was just trying to make some contact."

"Well, maybe I didn't want any contact right then."

"But didn't you say," Carlos says, turning to me, "didn't you say yesterday that the only way to find out what was right was to take the risk of expressing our needs?"

"But *my* need," Aisha responds, "was to keep working alone right then. It so happens that I had just gotten into something important."

"And are you still angry?" I ask her.

"Yes I am. He interrupted my work."

"And what did you do when he did that?"

"I turned away."

"And what were you thinking as you turned away?"

"I was thinking, 'Get the hell out of my face. I'm busy.'"

"Did you say that?"

"No."

"Well, let's try an experiment. Just turn to Carlos now and say the words."

"Really?"

"This is experimental theater, so we try experiments."

Aisha leans across Sandra who is sitting between them and says in Carlos's face, "Get the hell out of my face." Everyone laughs. And Aisha laughs.

"Now you're laughing," I point out. "Are you somewhat less angry than you were?"

"A little," she smiles.

"Why?"

"I don't know. Maybe 'cause I got it off my chest . . . somewhat. But are you saying that there, right in the middle of the warm-up, I should turn to Carlos and yell out, 'Get out of my face!'?"

"Well, Carlos, if Aisha said, 'Get out of my face' to you in the middle of the warm-up, what do you think you would do?"

"I'd probably just go get in someone else's face."

General laughter. "Okay, let's take a minute on that," I say. "Acting requires having emotions—not manufacturing emotions, but not blocking them either. So one of the things that a warm-up is about is allowing emotion to happen."

"That's just it," Aisha breaks in. "I was just getting in touch with *my* emotions when—"

"When Carlos came along and gave you the gift of another emotion: anger."

"Gift?! I wasn't working on anger. What if you get a gift you don't want?"

"Well, maybe you need to return it. Let's say, you were actually feeling sad—"

"How did you know?"

"Well, you're a good actress, so it shows." Aisha smiles in spite of herself. "But if you are given a gift of anger, you may need to unload that gift on Carlos so that you can get back to what you were doing before. I promise you, the sadness will still be there waiting for you. As a matter of fact, after unloading some anger, the sadness is likely to be even stronger than it was before. On the other hand, if you choose to turn away at that moment, as you did, you may end up holding on to your anger so that, as you see, it is still with you now."

Aisha sits thinking about what I have said, but now Peter is shaking his head.

"What's the matter?" I ask.

"But if each of us experiments with all of our impulses, there is no way we won't run into problems."

"If you call them problems." It is Brian who speaks now. For the past couple of days he has said very little, but now he takes the words out of my mouth. "It's not a problem if you can use it."

"Right. I understand that," says Peter. "But I can't believe that it will work for me to just follow every impulse I have." He turns to me. "I mean, I guess it's okay for Aisha to tell Carlos to get the hell out of her face. He can take it. But what if in response to that, his impulse was just to hit her in the face? Do you mean he should just hit her?"

I answer Peter by describing an event that happened in an acting class of mine a few years earlier.

A young actor named Leonardo was just discovering how enormously angry he felt much of the time. For years he had carried powerful impulses around inside him, and now, in acting class, he was discovering this fact about himself. It was a wonderful discovery for him, but, unfortunately, he sometimes experimented with this discovery by "acting out" his newfound impulses on other people. And he was pretty strong. One day he picked up a chair and was about to heave it at another student when I yelled, "Stop!" just in time, and I asked him, "What the hell are you doing?"

"I'm just following an impulse," he answered, still waving

the chair over his head. He glowered at the actor he had been about to clobber. "He yelled at me, so I just felt like picking up this chair and . . ."

"And what? Are you going to throw that chair at his head or at his feet?"

Leonardo stood frozen, with the chair wavering over his head and thought for a moment. "At his feet," he said. "I don't want to hurt him."

"Why not?" I asked. "Why not just bust him right over the head? After all, it's just 'an impulse.'"

"But . . ." As he thought, the chair slowly descended to the floor.

"Right, and if you can choose to direct the chair exactly *where* you want to hit him, isn't it also possible to choose to miss him entirely? And if it is possible to miss him entirely, might it not be possible to hit him with an imaginary chair? And, if it is possible to do that, would it possible to scream at him instead of heaving a chair at him?"

"No, no," he said, "the impulse is in my arms."

"Good," I said. "Pick up the chair again. And now get ready to throw it, but start to do the throw in slow motion. Good. Now, as you start the throw, let the chair become very heavy. Very, very heavy. Until finally it is so heavy that you cannot lift it."

He groaned as the chair sagged toward the floor.

"Now the chair is screwed into the floor. Try to lift it."

Leonardo struggled with the chair and started to yell at it.

"What did you say?" I asked.

"I said, 'Fuck you!'" he yelled.

"Okay," I said, "let's stop there." He stopped, exhausted. "Just now you were yelling, 'Fuck you' instead of moving your arms," I pointed out. "How did that angry impulse in your arms come to inhabit your voice instead?"

"I don't know," replied Leonardo, and he sat down to think about it.

———

When I finish telling this story to my class, I add, "The fact is, most of what we call impulses are actually mediated by rational choices anyway. For instance, during our warm-up, Peter, you had an impulse to run, am I right?"

"Yes."

"To run in a circle, or just to run?"

"Just to run."

"But, in fact, every time you reached the wall at the end of the room, you turned. If you were actually just moving on impulse, why didn't you just crash right into the wall? Because having an impulse doesn't mean being out of control. It just means allowing energy to flow through your body. How you *use* that energy is something else. At the same time, it is true that if you *stifle* an impulse, you may undermine the very freedom that you are learning to achieve in your warm-up. But an impulse can be redirected, turned, transformed and still be an impulse."

Now Aisha is confused. "So how do I know if it's okay for me to say, 'Get the hell out of my face,' or if I need to redirect that impulse and just grit my teeth or something?"

"Yes. That is a problem. Whenever you do anything that involves another human being, there needs to be a negotiation. In fact, there needs to be constant negotiation. Is it okay if I touch you like this? And like this? Can I push you this hard? Is it okay if I shove you against the wall? Was that fun? Are we still safe now? And now? And now?"

"But Aisha's impulse came in a split second," Carlos points out.

"The question and the answer may be just a sound, a breath, a smile, or a look. Remember what you yourself noticed about how many signals the mind can process in one second. A split second is actually plenty of time to ask a question and receive an answer.

"So, on the one hand, you *must* have safety in order to do your work. But, on the other hand, safety cannot mean avoiding risks. If you take safety to mean 'don't even try,' you will never

discover the excitement that arises from daring to risk something new. There is such a thing as playing it *too* safe.

"So, in the end, what is the solution? The answer will be different for each of you. Some people who have been very impulsive or very loud may need to experiment with redirecting their
energy, to ask themselves if it is possible to express their rage,
for instance, in slow motion. And others who find themselves
holding back from expressing certain impulses, as Aisha did
today, may need to stop being quite so careful and see what
happens if they just risk it. But, in either case, it is absolutely
necessary that you give clear signals to others.

"Remember, the warm-up is a *gift* you're giving to yourself
and to your coworkers. It is a gift you choose to help you grow
as actors. It can provide both safety and excitement. But **safety
without risk can be boring, and risk without safety is self-
defeating.**"

WHAT IS AN ACTOR'S WARM-UP?

A warm-up is a bridge between the conditions of mind, body,
and voice you have been using in everyday life and the conditions of mind, body, and voice you need in order to act. The
nature of that bridge depends on who you are and what your
particular voice, body, and psyche needs today, so no two
actors are likely to need exactly the same warm-up. Moreover,
the kind of bridge you need on a particular day also depends on
where you are "coming from" and what you are warming up for
that day. So even for the same actor there is no such thing as *the*
right warm-up to do every day. For instance, on a day when you
are coming to the studio after two hours at the gym, your physical needs will be different from what they are on a day when
you're coming from typing for eight hours. And the year that
you're breaking up with your boyfriend, your emotional needs
may be different from what they were the year when you were
falling in love. And the week that you are rehearsing a play by

Pinter, your warm-up will probably need to be different from the one you require before commedia dell'arte rehearsals.

A warm-up is not a regimen or a particular set of exercises. A warm-up is a process, one that can keep growing and changing, and one that you must constantly reinvent. As you progress through this book, you will find that many of the body, voice, and image exercises you learn can be integrated into your warm-up. But you must keep experimenting and noticing what works for you. How do you feel entering the work after yoga? After aerobics? Or after receiving a massage? How much contact with other actors do you need in your warm-up? What do you need to change when you are tired? And so on. **If you try different things, your body will give you clear answers.** You may discover that there are certain things you need to do every day, and that there are other practices you need to employ only every once in a while.

One way to look at this warm-up process is to put it in a larger context. The Body Part Warm-up gives you a certain structure to work in, a simple, external form within which to improvise. The Stream-of-Consciousness Warm-up, on the other hand, is a method of playing with structure or of *breaking* structure. So these two approaches to warm-up also represent the two poles of all creative work: form and formlessness, structure and freedom. All of our work, in fact, all artistic activity, involves learning how to play between these two extremes. And each artist must find his or her own balance between the two. Structure, rules, and technique provide the safety and concentration we need. Impulse, risk, and freedom provide the energy. Both are necessary.

Above all remember, the warm-up is not an assignment, not calisthenics, and not a chore. **It is a questioning process and a gift you are giving to yourself.** In the end, you will find that your warm-up can serve you in many ways: it can clear your mind, energize your body, and, later on, it can help you to prepare for your stage entrances and to develop your characters.

Although there is not one particular warm-up that will serve

every actor under all conditions, there are certain basic questions every warm-up can address. The **Outline for an Actor's
Warm-up** (1.5) is a list of questions to which a warm-up can
respond. The first seven are items we have already touched on;
the others are suggestions you can add as you progress through
this book.

Outline for an Actor's Warm-Up (1.5)

1. What is my relationship to the space? Do I have safe space in
which to work?
2. Do I need centering? Can I bring my mind to my body? Can I
bring my body to my mind?
3. How do I feel today? Am I carrying around emotions or images
I need to spend some time dealing with?
4. What does my body need? Do I have tensions I need to relax?
Do I have muscles I need to awaken?
5. How is my overall energy level today?
6. What does my voice need today? Are my voice and body connected?
7. What is my relationship to the other actors, and what needs do
I have in relationship to them?
8. What is my relationship to the group?
9. Are all emotions and image worlds available to me?
10. Are all rhythms and tempos available?
11. Are there particular tasks or problems I need to spend time on
today? Do I need to concentrate on scene preparation or character
work?

In addition to these particular questions, there are some overall con-
cepts to keep in mind as you build your warm-up:

• **Trajectory**. A warm-up is a voyage from a condition you find
yourself in at this moment of your day to a condition you want to be in
when you enter your acting work. So you need to be aware of where
you're coming from and what you're getting ready to do. The question,
"What am I warming-up for?" is always important. If you are entering
physical acting work, you should probably do something aerobic and
some stretches before the work. If you will be working on a scene,
there may be images or character traits that you need to practice

before entering the work. You also need to take account of how much time you have so that you can be sure to cover each thing you need to.

• **Checking in.** To get what you want, you have to let yourself <u>know</u> what it is that you need. And, since your needs may change <u>during</u> the warm-up, you have to keep checking in with yourself to notice the changes.

• **Additive process.** Once you've got one part of you warm and connected, be careful not to lose touch with it as you move on to another part of the body. (This applies especially to the lower body, which tends to go back to sleep while we work with our upper body or on our voices.)

• **Putting everything in.** Warming up is about making connections. As you become aware of parts of yourself (thoughts, emotions, judgments, and so forth) that seem to sit outside the work, you can use your warm-up to capture and recycle that energy.

• **Looking for variation.** If you find yourself "stuck" in one rhythm or mood or kind of imagery, spend some time in another mode.

WORK CLOTHES

When an actor puts on shoes, the movements of his feet are limited. Stamping, sliding, walking pigeon-toed, walking bowlegged—all of these are virtually denied him.
—Tadashi Suzuki, *The Way of Acting*

Before we leave the question of warm-ups, there is one more technical problem for you to think about: work clothes. On the face of it, the issue seems a simple one: **Since this work is physical, you need to wear clothes that don't get in your way. Because some of the work is strenuous, you should have layers of clothing that you can remove or put back on if you get too hot or too cold. Since you must communicate with your body, your clothing should not hide it. Since you need to express things with your face, your hair should stay out of the way, and since you will be in contact with others' bodies, you must free yourself of any jewelry that might be dangerous.** That's it, basically.

When I worked with Grotowski, he insisted that all the men

wear nothing but shorts and all the women, leotards. But I find things are not so simple. For many people, clothing, jewelry, and hair have become extensions of the self. To take off a ring that you have worn for years, to pull your hair out of your eyes or give up your makeup, may make you feel somehow "not yourself." Of course, when you need to portray a character unlike yourself, the external things that make you uniquely "you," like your jewelry, your hairdo, and even your tattoos can be impediments. Character work requires putting on a costume, so you don't want to be wearing one already. But on a more subtle level these outward manifestations can interfere with the basic task of self-revelation.

When you dress to go to a party or a job interview, you put on different clothes and jewelry—and attitudes—in order to present a certain "self" to the world. These are the character layers you can easily put on or take off. But many of us have gotten in the habit of putting on certain character traits that we almost never take off. And sometimes, to secure these traits, we attach them to our self-image with the help of external things such as clothing, jewelry, and makeup—superficial signifiers that help us confirm who we are, or who we are trying to be.

But as Grotowski suggests, acting training is first of all a process of stripping away, of giving up those things that hide the feelings, the images, and the "selves" we carry within us. And one of the ways in which we hold on to these "selves" is with our external decorations. For some people, it can be as hard to remove a favorite necklace as it is to dispense with a "cool" attitude. For others, removing a baggy sweatshirt can make them feel as vulnerable as crying in public. But, after all, that is what acting is about—being vulnerable, sometimes even crying in public. So the baggy sweatshirt can be a real impediment—and taking it off can be very liberating.

A number of years ago, I taught a woman who always wore little cloth bracelets, one on each wrist. They did not get "in the way" of her movement work or endanger her or her work partners, so I did not make an issue of them. But one day when she was working on a monologue that required her to express some rage, she seemed stuck in her work. Each time as her voice seemed about to scream, she would pull back, avert her eyes, and lose her concentration. When I suggested that she was not allowing the energy of the scene to enter her hands and fingers, she shut down even further. Finally, I suggested that she might try removing the bracelets. She explained to me that they were a gift from a friend who had died and that she had not taken them off for five years. "Maybe," I said, "your friend would understand. Besides, if it doesn't work, you can simply put them back on."

She spent a few minutes taking off the bracelets, clearly going through some emotion as she did so, and then she returned to the work. It took her some time to rediscover the images she had been working with and to allow the energy to refill her body. But this time, when I said, "And now the hands," her fingers curled into claws and slashed at her imagery, her voice grew louder, and her eyes flashed as she spoke. After the work, she spent some time alone. She cried a little and then smiled. She picked up the cloth bracelets, folded them, and put them in her purse.

In this year's class, I have noticed that several people continue to wear their jewelry while working. And although I have reminded her several times, Aisha keeps "forgetting" to take off her shoes before starting her warm-up. So at the end of class, I tell the group the story of the cloth bracelets. Then I add, "No one but you knows how your everyday 'costume' serves you, what energies or images it projects or hides. Perhaps even you do not know. But your job as an actor is to be able to employ *all* of yourself on stage, so I suggest that you just experiment with your costume. See what happens to you and to your work if you remove some of the externals to which you are attached. Don't rush yourself. Don't rip off all your jewelry tomorrow without allowing yourself to sense what happens to you as you do so. If taking off your shoes makes you feel uncomfortable, how can you put that uncomfortable feeling *into the work*? Does going barefoot hold memories for you? If so, what imagery and emotions do those memories inspire? When you feel the hardwood floor on your skin, how does your connection with the floor change?

"Unfortunately, you cannot make gestures with your earrings or scream with your hair. And it is not your clothing that receives the pleasure of a kiss or the pain of a slap. You act with your body and your voice. Everything else is extra."

Les Exercises Corporels

A sense of danger is essential to all theatre.
            —Yoshi Oida, *An Actor Adrift*

On November 7, the second day of our workshop in 1967, Ryszard Cieślak demonstrated the *exercises corporels*[1] for our workshop. With lightness and ease, his lithe body moved from headstand to backbend to leap . . . and then, with no apparent effort, he walked around the studio on his hands. As Cieślak finished, Grotowski turned to us and said, as if it were a simple axiom, "You see, it must be as easy for you to enter the stage walking on your hands as on your feet."

Our dismay at this pronouncement turned to curiosity when he explained the corollary to this axiom: **This means, it should be as difficult for the actor to enter the stage on his feet as on his hands.** In other words, every step we take with our feet and legs should be as meaningful, as justified, as *conscious* as if we were walking on our hands. The point was that we have become so out of touch with our lower bodies that we often treat them as if they were no more than trucks that carry our expressive upper bodies from place to place. By walking on his hands, Cieślak was forcing us to take our legs seriously.

---

1. Ever since the seventeenth century, when the Polish throne was allied with that of France, French has been the second language for many Poles. When Jerzy Grotowski came West to teach during the 1960s, it was a matter of course that he spoke in French, referring to exercises he taught as the *exercises plastiques* (movement isolations) and the *exercises corporels* (full-body exercises).

The *exercises corporels* are a method of reconnecting with the enormous energies that lie locked in the lower half of our bodies. The **Cat,** the **Headstands, Backbends,** and **Rolls** force us out of the perpendicular and put us back in touch with our pelvis, with our legs, and with the ground itself. At first blush, these exercises seem "gymnastic" or "acrobatic," and they do require real effort and practice to accomplish. But in the final analysis, "accomplishing" them is not what is important. What is important is what you discover about yourself in the process.

Note: *If you have a back that is prone to pain or injury, begin this work with caution, doing only what is safe and comfortable for you. If you are not sure, talk to a teacher or a physical trainer before you start.*

THE SPINE

The vertebral column is the centre of expression. The driving impulse, however, stems from the loins. Every live impulse begins in this region, even if invisible from the outside.

—Grotowski, *Towards a Poor Theatre*

Normally we don't think of our backs as being particularly expressive body parts, but, in fact, our spines serve as the central energy transportation and communication lines for our body. If our spines are inflexible, they can block impulses and feelings from being felt or expressed. And conversely, if our backs are supple, they connect our mind with our whole body and permit impulses to flow from one part of our being to another.

Our backs are also vulnerable to tension and injury, so before entering energetic physical work with the lower half of the body, it is vital that we activate our backs and that we know their limits. Before I start this first lesson of the *exercises corporels*, I ask students to bend their backs gently in each direction, carefully stretching their muscles and sensing the range of movement that is safe for them. Then I have them work back-to-back with partners, to explore how they can communicate with their backs and to discover the simple joys of physical expression. After these preparations we are ready to study the **Undulations** (2.1–2.4).

UNDULATIONS

In a way, spinal movements act as a kind of massage for the entire nervous system.

—Yoshi Oida, *The Invisible Actor*

An *undulation* is a wave. It is a movement that begins at one end of the spine and flows along the vertebrae all the way to the other end, allowing energy and emotions to travel from the lower half of our bodies to the upper, and vice versa.

There are two undulations to try: The **Undulation from the Pelvis Up** (2.1) and the **Undulation from the Head Down** (2.2). Note: If your back has given you problems in the past, be careful. If you encounter pain, ease off! (You don't get extra points for injuring yourself.)

A second way to begin exploring the Undulation from the Pelvis Up is just to stand relaxed in the middle of the floor and imagine that you have been kicked in the rear end. As the kick

The Undulation from the Pelvis Up (2.1)

1. Stand facing away from a wall with your heels about six inches from the wall.

2. Begin the undulation by tilting your pelvis backward so that your rear end touches the wall.

3. Now start to tilt the pelvis forward, bending the knees slightly as you do. As the pelvis scoops under and pulls away from the wall, the vertebrae just above the pelvis will touch the wall. Keep moving the pelvis forward.

4. One by one, allow each vertebra to touch the wall and then to move forward, following the pelvis. Continue all the way up to the neck vertebrae (the middle of the neck will not touch the wall) and finally the head. By the time the head reaches back toward the wall, the pelvis is far forward and is ready to reverse itself.

5. Now tilt the pelvis back again, reaching for the wall as the head leans all the way back. As your rear end touches the wall again, your head tilts forward.

6. Do the undulation from the pelvis up several times, feeling the bump, bump, bump of the vertebrae against the wall. Notice any areas of your back that have difficulty articulating themselves. Let the wave move up slowly or quickly.

7. Now move a couple of feet away from the wall, and try the whole exercise again with an imaginary wall behind you.

---

lands, your pelvis moves forward, and then the rest of your body follows like a whip. You can try this standing up, or hanging over from the waist. Don't think too much. Just let the energy move through you.

Now you can play with the undulations, pelvis up and head down. Allow the undulations to move you forward and back. Try them diagonally, side to side. Try the undulations along your arms from the shoulder to the fingertips. Play with imagery: undulations that begin with a shove in the face or a pull in the pelvis. If you find yourself feeling stiff in this work, try the undulation more quickly and easily and less as a "studied" exercise. You may even want to try relaxing and letting

---

The Undulation from the Head Down (2.2)

1. Begin by letting your head fall forward toward your chest.
2. Then lift from the back of the head so that your face turns upward, pulling your neck and then your upper back first forward and then back as the head continues to lead.
3. Allow the wave to move down your back as the head moves back.
4. When the wave reaches your pelvis, the head is ready to start forward again.
5. Let the movement pass like a wave from your head all the way to your feet. Let it actually move you around the room.

---

someone else move your hips, allowing the wave of that movement simply to move itself through you.

The undulations form the core of the Cat exercises but the Cat is not performed standing, so before we try it out, we will examine how the undulations work when you're down on all fours in the movement called the **Cat-Cow** (2.3).

And finally, there is one more undulation from the pelvis up that will help you articulate the lower spine, the **Inchworm** (2.4).

DIGESTING THE WORK—THE HUNKER

Before we go on to study the Cat, we should talk for a moment about what to do when you finish this—or any—exercise.

The human mind operates with several different kinds of memory: working memory, short-term memory, and long-term memory. If you want to remember a number you find in the telephone book while you walk to the phone, you can concentrate on it as you move by using your "working memory." But unless you make an effort to "memorize" the number, it will quickly vanish from your mind. The process of "memorization," of

Cat-Cow into the Undulation (2.3)

1. Get down on your hands and knees. Relax your back and your neck.

2. Arch your back up in the middle, bringing your head and your pelvis toward each other below.

3. Reverse the arch so that the head lifts up and the pelvis tilts backward. This alternation is the Cat-Cow.

4. Now, instead of reversing the arch all at once, tilt the pelvis first and then allow the change of direction to move along the back up to the head.

5. Then tilt the pelvis the other way and let the shift again move up to the head. This is the Undulation from the Pelvis Up.

6. Now, begin the change of direction with your head, allowing each lifting or lowering of the head to move from the head, through the neck, down along the back to the pelvis. This is the Undulation from the Head Down.

7. Now, allow your whole body to move forward and back with the undulation, bending the elbows as the chest moves with the concave back. Try this with the undulation beginning in the pelvis and with the undulation beginning with the head.

8. Now try it with the knees off the ground. This movement will become the center of the Cat.

cementing the information in your long-term memory, is often accomplished by associating the new information with older information and storing it in categories that you can later access by means of reassociation. Scientists don't yet know quite how the brain accomplishes this feat, but it has been found that permanent learning progresses best if the mind first concentrates on new material and then is given some down-time, time to assimilate what it has taken in.

When you are engaging in acting exercises, you may find yourself stumbling upon material—images, emotions, gestures, or sounds—that are very new to you. And it is important that you take time after this intense work to let this new information gel. Sometimes you may find that it is only in allowing

The Inchworm (2.4)

(This version works well done with a partner, with one person walking her fingers up the vertebra of the other, helping her partner feel each part of the back and coaching him not to skip any sections.)

1. Lie down on the floor on your stomach. Place your hands palm-down on the floor near your shoulders.
2. Begin by lifting the pelvis high in the air. Then let the pelvis reverse its direction, tilting forward, while it pulls the lumbar vertebrae upward.
3. As the pelvis returns to the floor, allow the undulation to move like a sliding hump up your back.
4. When the wave reaches your shoulders, push with your hands to allow the wave to travel up to the neck and head. If you are doing the undulation properly, you will move forward like an inchworm.

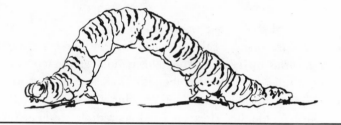

this breathing space after the work is done that the power of what you have just accomplished strikes you. Sometimes it is just a matter of appreciating the work you have done. Sometimes it may help to write down your thoughts in a journal, right then, while they are fresh. But in any case, it is important that you don't go out into the hall to talk to someone, or have a cigarette, or drink coffee until you have digested your work—because all these extra inputs can overlay and cloud the experience you have just had, in much the same way as leaping out of bed to answer the telephone will often wipe away your dreams.

At the end of every exercise or training session, Grotowski counseled actors to squat in a "hunker," allowing their arms and head to hang down while they digested the work. But this position doesn't work for everyone, especially those with short hamstring muscles. I myself sometimes kneel instead, sitting on my calves and putting my forehead on the floor. Some people just sit. What is important is that you allow yourself real privacy, taking a neutral position that permits you to compare how you feel now with how you have felt after other exercises. During this private time just permit yourself to feel what you are feeling and to notice what you are thinking. This process is an integral part of the work.

THE CAT

On the third day of our workshop in 1967, Ryszard Cieślak walked to the center of the floor and lay down on his stomach with his arms by his side. Then slowly he began to move: first his head lifted from the floor, then his torso, and then his whole body rose on his hands and feet, gyrating, flowing, undulating, twisting, and kicking. He moved with incredible power and fluidity, never leaving his spot on the floor, but performing a series of movements that involved his whole body with wondrous energy and precision. After six minutes or so, the energy ebbed, Cieślak's body slowed down, and finally he returned to his prone starting position. Then Grotowski turned to us and said: *"Maintenant, faites le même."* (Now all of you, do the same.) Of course, none of us had any idea what to do, but we were dutiful (and somewhat terrified), so all lay down on the floor to attempt what we had seen.

After many years of teaching this work, I have not found a better way to begin than by demonstrating this exercise and then just asking people to do what they have seen. Of course, there is no way you can actually learn the details of the exercise in this way, but by plunging into the unknown with no certainty of what you "should" be doing, whatever you discover in the process is uniquely *yours*. And that lesson is more important than the details of the exercise. So when I teach this work I refrain from even telling students that it is called the Cat because even hearing that name can restrict what people think they should be finding. I simply demonstrate the form and then ask people to try out what they have seen. After everyone has finished, I gather the group together and ask each actor to describe his or her experience. (If you would like to try entering the Cat without further preconceptions, you should turn now to the directions at the end of this section [2.5], and then return to read the intervening paragraphs.)

As I demonstrate the Cat for my acting class, I am careful to include all the "elements" of the exercise, but at some point the energy of the exercise takes over, and I find myself executing a rather more sly and sensual version of the Cat than I had planned. When I stop, I hunker for a minute and then turn to the group and say, "Your turn." They silently find places to lie down on the floor and then start to move. When they have all finished, we gather again in our circle, and I ask each person in turn to tell us in a few words about his or her experience doing the exercise. Their comments vary enormously.

Veronica is sitting to my left and is the first to speak. She is still breathing heavily, and her wide forehead is beaded with sweat. She begins: "My arms just hurt so much, I didn't think I could keep doing it. Sometimes I just got into it and didn't think about it. But most of the time I just kept thinking, 'Oh, my arms are so weak. I will never be able to do this.'"

Then Peter reports, "I felt like I was an animal and I was hunting or something . . . hunting or having sex. And I felt a lot of energy, like I wanted to scream, but I didn't know if that was allowed."

"Yes, I wanted to make sound, too," says Sandra, who is sitting next to Peter. "I felt like there were these wings or something coming out of my back, and I was a bat. I was a bat out of hell, and I just wanted to kill everything in my path. But then at the end, just as I was stopping, I felt very sad."

A number of the others report having had images or emotions of one kind or another, and a few describe having encountered fatigue or pain like Veronica's. But then Carlos says, "Maybe I was doing it wrong, but for me it was just like a physical thing, you know? I mean I was just very aware of my muscles. I didn't have any of this imagery or emotion or whatever. Is that wrong?"

"Well," I say, "there are a lot of issues being raised here, so when everyone has finished speaking, I'll respond to that. But we still have one more person to speak."

The last person in the circle is Maria, who has rarely said anything at all in class. Although she is the same age as all the others, there is something particularly girlish about her, as if she has not yet grown to accept the full female figure she has developed. Privately she has confided to me that she grew up in a strict Catholic family and lived in Spain until she was eight years old, and that she finds some of the work in this class almost frightening. Now, as she speaks in the circle, her voice is quiet and high with just a hint of a Spanish accent. "I just kept worrying if I was doing it right. I couldn't remember what it was you did, so I kept thinking, 'Am I doing things in the right order?' And then I thought, 'Maybe some of these people have done this exercise before. How do they remember all the parts?' Then, for a while I forgot all that, and I was just moving. But then I noticed that everyone else was doing those kicks already, and I didn't know if I should change."

"Okay," I say, "I shall try to respond to several of the things that people have said, but before I do, I want you to take note of what just happened, because it is more important than anything I say. You all did an exercise. And in spite of the fact that you all did the same exercise, you had very different experiences. In our work, that fact is essential.

"This exercise is called the Cat. It is a structure that fills itself with your energy and 'contains' your experience. Over the next few days I will teach you the technical elements of the Cat, but even when you know all the parts, the exercise remains *your* event. There is no one thing that is *supposed* to happen to you during this exercise. Whatever you find in it *is* what you find.

"Veronica, you said that your arms hurt. That's fine. The Cat does require a lot of pushing with the arms, and the difficulty you encounter will depend on the weight distribution in your body, as well as how strong your arms are. After you do this work for a while, you will find your body getting stronger, and that will be gratifying. But remember that **the *purpose* of this work is not to turn you into a gymnast; the purpose is to help you use the body to get in touch with your inner life and feelings.** So if after one minute your body starts making you feel frustrated or angry, that's not a problem; that's an advantage! Someone else who has been doing fifty push-ups a day for the past five years may have to do the Cat for ten minutes before he encounters that emotion, but you found it very quickly. You're just lucky.

"The Cat is a form that permits you to put that frustration—or any other emotion you encounter—directly into the work, as you did in the Stream-of-Consciousness Warm-up. So the next time when you begin to think, 'My arms are about to give out. This is so frustrating,' at that very moment, try to put that feeling directly into the exercise. If you do, you will find that the Cat acts as a *container* for your inner life. In other words **it is a physical form that evokes thoughts and feelings while at the same time providing safety and permission for their expression.** In fact, the Cat is a very strong and a very safe container; there is no thought or feeling that is too powerful for it to hold. Since it keeps your hands and your feet rooted to the floor, it creates a vehicle through which even an emotion like rage can be safely expressed. All you need to do is let yourself know what you are feeling while it is happening, and give yourself permission to allow that feeling to inhabit the form."

Now I turn to Peter. "You and some others said that emotions arose while you were working. You felt like you were 'hunting or having sex.' Was that okay with you?"

"Oh, sure."

"Were you aware that you closed your eyes while you . . . hunted?"

"Did I?"

"Next time you might keep them open and see who's there."

"But wouldn't I just see the floor then?"

"Well, that's one of the questions we will spend a great deal of time on when we get to the *plastiques*: What happens to imagery when you open your eyes. But for now, just see if you can find out what the difference is when you work with your eyes open or closed."

"And what about making sound?"

"Yes, you and Sandra both had that impulse. The thing about sound is that when you make it, the sound immediately fills the whole room. That means it may affect others, and because you *know* it affects others, making sound adds a certain audience awareness or performance quality to your work. Very subtly it can push you in the direction of doing the work for *them*, or holding back because you know that *they* can hear you. Grotowski always insisted on complete silence in this work, but I think there are also some emotional spaces that are enabled by using the voice. So sometimes we will do this work in silence and other times we will work with sound, and you will find out what difference it makes for you."

"But," says Sandra, "if we are working in silence and I have an impulse to make sound, what should I do?"

"Well, there are two things you can try. One is to put the sound impulse into unvoiced breath, 'screaming' with a relaxed throat on a strong out-breath but without your vocal cords. The other is to try screaming with your hips or your legs instead of with your voice. Remember the story I told you about Leonardo and his impulses. You may find that you can scream very well in another way. I recently worked with a paraplegic actress who could not move her legs but discovered that she could achieve the emotional release of the Cat kicks by 'kicking' with her head.

"But you said another interesting thing, Sandra. You said that at the end of the exercise you felt sad. That is very important. There is often another emotion sort of lying in wait within the emotion you are already feeling, lying in wait for you to ease up your hold on the first emotion so that the second one can show itself. With a little practice, you will start to notice that you do not actually need to wait until the end of an exercise to experience that moment of change. It is actually always available to you. All you need to do is breathe for a moment or relax within the work, and then the next emotion will reveal itself. For instance, if in the midst of feeling like a 'bat out of hell' you ease up on the effort for a moment, you may sense within you the tender feelings you have for the bat's victims. Emotion is not a solid thing. If we loosen our grip on it and allow it full freedom, it will change.

"And now, Maria, you and several others worried if you were doing the exercise right. I think there are two things to say about that. One is simply that this is the first Cat you've done, and there is no reason that you should be able to remember all the things I did. I will go over the details tomorrow. The second is that the degree to which we worry about 'getting the form right' often has to do with our personal relationship to form and to our own 'learning style.' Some people always try to emulate the forms they have been taught, and some people like to break the rules right away. Each of us has his or her own learning style in this regard. What you experience during an exercise is often as much a reflection of that style as it is a reaction to the particular lesson. To explore this question for yourself, try to purposefully break your style: If you are a person who worries about doing things right, try to see what happens if you just trust whatever comes, even if that means breaking the form. If, on the other hand, you are one of those who likes to break the rules, as several of you did today by taking your hands off the floor, you might explore what happens to you if you stick very strictly to the form you have seen. In either case, whatever you find as you explore this kind of habit breaking, put it into the Cat."

Finally I take up Carlos's problem. "You said that the Cat was 'just physical' for you. But how did you feel about its being just physical?"

"Okay, I guess."

"I mean, when you said 'just physical,' it sounded a little pejorative, as if you thought it *should* be something more than just physical."

"No, it was okay. But I didn't have any emotions or 'bat out of hell' or whatever happening to me, you know?"

"But you like doing things that are physical? You like sports or working out?"

Carlos has a very muscular body, and as he responds, he gets a somewhat embarrassed smile on his face. "Yes, I suppose."

"So now I wonder what would happen if, while you were experiencing your 'just physical' Cat, you let yourself have the thoughts you are having now, these thoughts about your body, both the embarrassing ones and the proud ones. Perhaps you would find that 'just physical' is *not* really 'just physical' at all. In fact, that thought, 'It was just physical,' carries with it several contradictory opinions and feelings. On the one hand, it makes you worry a little that you are not having all the groovy 'bat-out-of-hell' imagery that others may be having. On the other hand, it fills you with pride, and/or embarrassment about your body. And all of these various thoughts, opinions, and feelings can be put into the Cat. But to do so you must first let yourself *know* that you are having that rich thought/opinion:

'Oh, this is *just* physical.' And you must allow yourself to experience the inner life of that opinion."

Carlos is shaking his head.

"What is it?" I ask.

"Oh just that I begin to see that there is no way out."

"What do you mean, 'no way out?'"

"That even if I'm thinking that the exercise is not working for me, you are not going to let me use that as an escape hatch."

"You're right," I say.

Note: The best way for you to learn the Cat *is to find someone who has done it before and to have him or her demonstrate it once for you. But if that is not possible, you might work with one other person and have them read these instructions while you do the movements. Before you begin: do some back stretches—whatever works to free the whole back, especially the lower back, for hard work.* **Note:** *if your lower back causes you pain, be careful in this work. Don't risk injuring yourself. If you need to relieve pressure on the lower back, you may try doing the central part of the* Cat *with your knees on the ground.*

The Cat (2.5)

1. Decide how long you will work. Three minutes is a very short Cat; ten minutes is a very long one.

2. Lie down on the floor on your stomach with your arms by your side. Relax for a minute in this position. Close your eyes. Breathe. Let yourself notice what you are thinking and feeling. Let those thoughts and feelings be there and then let them go.

3. Begin by opening your eyes. Let your eyes see what is in front of them. Allow the eyes to look around, to see as far as they can in every direction.

---

4. When your eyes cannot see any farther from that position, allow your head to join in the search. Let the head and neck lift and move, stretching in every direction. Let the face stretch and move also.

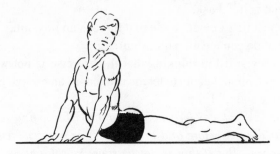

5. When the head and neck have moved as far as they can, bring your hands near the shoulders, place the palms on the floor, and use your arms to lift the upper body so that the eyes, the face, the neck, the chest, and the shoulders can all move up and down, left and right, lifting, twisting, and swinging as far as they can. Let your eyes keep looking while your body moves.

6. When the whole upper body has explored its full range of movement, raise your pelvis and legs off the ground, supporting yourself on your hands and feet. From now until the end of the exercise, the pelvis and knees stay in the air, but you can adjust the distance between the hands and feet. The hands never leave the floor.

7. Make circles with your pelvis. First try flat circles, in which the pelvis stays parallel to the floor. Then allow the pelvis to twist as it circles. Try the circles fast and slow. Allow your head to swing as a counterweight.

8. Now try the Undulation from the Pelvis Up: Beginning with a flat

back, lift your pelvis forward, allowing an undulation to move up the back all the way to your head so that you end up with your pelvis hanging near the floor, your back arched, and your head back. Then bend your knees and your elbows at the same time, pulling the pelvis back until you are almost sitting on your heels. And then push forward until you are back in your starting position. Essentially your pelvis is making a circle—up, forward, down, back—and everything else is along for the ride.

9. Try the Undulation from the Head Down: Begin again with a flat back, but this time lower your head and bend your knees until you are sitting back almost on your heels. Now bend your elbows and lower your chest toward the ground. Allow your head to pull you forward along the floor and then upward as your arms extend, pressing hard with your hands until you are hanging between your arms with your back arched. Now, bring your head down, letting it lead you back to your starting position.

10. Try both of these undulations in different rhythms.

11. The kicks: Let your body turn to one side, your weight on one hand, your hip on that side near but not touching the floor, and the foot turned on its side so that it can carry the weight. Bring the other knee up toward your ear, lifting the foot as if to kick straight out in front of you (see illustration). As the knee reaches toward your body, the flexed foot pulls away, creating an isometric tension. Suddenly the foot wins the battle, kicking into space. Try kicking in a large circle, out, around, and back to the floor. Lift the knee again, and this time try kicking straight backward, allowing the kick to pull the body after it. Repeat to the other side.

12. Twisting undulation: Sit your body back on your heels as you did at the start of the Undulation from the Head Down, but twist to the side so that you are resting your weight on one arm and one foot.

Now push through along the floor as you twist straight so that you end up with your body hanging between your straight arms. Repeat the movement to the other side.

13. Try small back undulations, small kicks, combinations of different parts of the exercise.

14. Continue working with all the parts of your body until you have used up the time you allotted for this exercise.

15. To end, allow the pelvis to return to the floor, then the stomach, the chest, the arms, the neck, and the head. Close your eyes. Breathe.

16. When you have finished, pick yourself up off the floor and find a hunker or another closed, comfortable position in which to digest the work.

17. MOST IMPORTANT: Allow yourself to remember what the experience was like, what thoughts, images, feelings, and opinions you had while doing the exercise. Let yourself know what happened for you.

MORE *EXERCISES CORPORELS*

One of the commonest disturbances in the human being is the dissociation of the upper half of the body from the lower half.   —Alexander Lowen, *Bioenergetics*

There are still places on this planet where people squat or kneel or sit cross-legged on the floor. And there are cultures in which one must crawl through low doorways in order to enter a house. But in our culture we rediscover these "primitive" ways of relating to the ground only when we are camping, swimming, or making love—or when we need to check the muffler. The rest of the time we live as if standing up or sitting on chairs were the only ways to stay awake. But our bodies remember a time, early in our lives, when we knew how to leap and crawl and roll, and they contain many emotions and memories, fears and joys that abide within nonvertical relationships to the earth.

The *exercises corporels* serve to relieve us of our cultural habits of sitting and standing, and in so doing they grant the lower halves of our bodies the freedom to move, to sense, to feel, and to express a much greater range of emotional life. This is a freedom that we lost with our toilet training (which taught us to maintain constant tension in our sphincter muscles), and with our socialization (which taught us to hide our genitals), and with all the lessons about sitting up straight in our chairs, staying clean, and keeping our hands where they belong. So, for years, all the excitement, fear, and anger relating to the energies below our waists has been suppressed, guarded by our predilection for doing all our acting (and living) with our legs underneath us. The *exercises corporels* reawaken the life in our lower bodies by turning us upside down and freeing our legs and pelvis from their assigned roles as guardians of our propriety and porters of our weight.

Because working upside down is so new and unusual for most of us, it has two real dangers. The first is the obvious physical danger: our muscles are not used to supporting us upside down, so we must undertake these exercises carefully, taking whatever time we need to discover our balance. Remember, this is not the Olympics; you get no extra points for speed of execution or elegance. You are not performing here, you are striving to discover the effect of this work on you.

The *exercises corporels* include the Headstands, Backbends, and Rolls, leading up to the **Tiger Leaps.** As you begin these exercises, remember the lesson you learned in the Stream-of-Consiousness Warm-up: The important thing is to "put everything into the work"; there is no such thing as a "mistake." When you are doing a headstand, the process of getting up into the headstand (and the process of "falling" out of it) are as much a "part of the work" as the headstand itself.

The second danger is more subtle. The excitement of accomplishing a headstand for the first time can be very exhilarating: finding your balance, being upside down, feeling like an acrobat can be so much fun that you can be distracted from the real purpose of this work—the experiencing and the expression of image and emotion. Many of those who studied with Grotowski in the 1960s became enthralled by the gymnastic possibilities of the work and lost sight of its acting goals. So as you begin this work allow yourself to experience the exhilaration you find in these exercises—this energy is definitely part of the work, too—but also keep your attention on what the exercises do *for you as an actor*, not just as an acrobat.

Note: *All this work should be practiced first on exercise mats and with a partner to "spot" you!*

THE FORWARD AND BACKWARD ROLLS

The Forward and Backward Rolls (2.6) (2.7) are basically somersaults—like those you did as a child. They permit you to cover space without depending on your legs for locomotion. And they make it possible for you to exit from a headstand safely and with complete control.

Once you are comfortable with the rolls, begin in the Cat position and allow yourself to roll forward and backward, left

---

The Forward Roll (2.6)

1. To execute a forward roll, kneel or stand at one edge of the mat, and bend over, placing your hands flat on the mat.
2. As you begin to roll forward, fold your legs, tuck your chin in toward your chest, and <u>use your arms</u> to support your weight, letting the back of your head just graze the surface of the mat.
3. Allow the full weight of your body to come down onto the mat as your shoulders touch, and permit your momentum to roll you forward, keeping your legs folded until your feet meet the mat.
4. Work for smoothness, silence, and control, then increase your speed.
5. Try rolls from kneeling, squatting, and standing positions.

The Backward Roll (2.7)

1. Stand at the edge of the mat, facing away from it.
2. Quickly lower yourself into a squat and then let the momentum of sitting roll you backward. Or simply begin in a squat and roll backward.
3. With your hands near your ears to push, allow yourself to roll slightly to one side or the other so that you roll over the shoulder rather than the top of the head.
4. Bring your feet under you as you come over the shoulder.
5. Try the backward roll to both sides, then try it over the top of the head.

---

and right, permitting impulse and momentum to control your movements. Keep using your eyes, and keep noticing what you think and feel.

THE HEADSTANDS

Now we move on to the next group of *exercises corporels*, the Headstands. Grotowski taught several headstands:

- The **Shoulder Stand,** on the back of the neck, with legs and arms extended into the air (2.8).
- The **Tripod Headstand** with two hands and the head on the floor (2.9).
- The **Straight-arm Headstand,** with the backs of the hands on the floor, forming a very large triangle (2.10).
- The **Elbow Headstand,** with the elbows on the floor and the hands holding the top of the head (2.11).
- The **Ear Stand,** with the side of the face and one shoulder against the floor and the body twisted in a spiral (2.12).
- The **Handstand,** first with the feet against a wall, and then walking on the hands (2.13).

All of these headstands can be fun to explore, but the one you will probably find yourself using the most is the **Shoulder Stand,** which frees up both your arms and your legs to work. It is also the easiest position to assume without instruction, so if you are doing this work on your own, you may want to explore just this one position to begin with.

The rest of the headstands should be undertaken only with the assistance of a partner.

The Shoulder Stand (2.8)

1. Lie on your back and raise your legs in the air and then up over your head (as in the yoga "plow" position).

2. Reach up into the air with your feet, searching for a balance point. Don't strain your neck; the weight is resting primarily on your shoulders.

3. To help you find your balance, you can place your elbows on the floor and your hands on your lower back.

4. Once you have found your balance, reach up with your hands also so that all four limbs are free to move.

5. Move your hands and feet while maintaining your balance.

6. Roll down, vertebra by vertebra, silently and with control.

Tripod and Straight-Arm Headstands (2.9) (2.10)

1. Place your two hands palm-down on the mat, and place your head on the mat far enough out of line with them so that the three points of contact create an equilateral triangle.

2. Make sure that your lower arms are perpendicular to the floor and that your elbows form a right angle between the upper and lower arms.

3. Test your balance, pushing forward with your feet while feeling what it is like to carry more of the weight on your head or more on your hands.

4. Walk your knees up toward your elbows, and then, one at a time, place each knee on an elbow.

5. Stop. Do not immediately extend your legs. Just feel the balance on the hands and head, and then come back down. Silently.

6. When you can do that much with control, purposefully come down by pushing your weight over the back of your head while tucking your chin and "falling" into a forward roll.

7. Now that you can come down with control in either direction, return to the knees on elbows position and extend one thigh into the air, leaving the knee bent (in other words, straighten the hip joint but leave the heel down near your buttocks).

8. Now extend the other thigh equally.

9. One at a time, unfold the knees so that your legs extend up into the air.

10. At each stage, make sure that you are in control of your balance and that you could silently roll down.

11. Once you are all the way up, try arching your back so that your chest moves forward toward your hands while your feet compensate by reaching backward. Then try moving your legs around in the air, testing your balance.

12. Practice getting up and down slowly and quickly. Practice "falling" out of the headstand into silent rolls.

13. The **Straight-Arm Headstand** is similar to the tripod, but instead you extend your arms and put your weight on the back of your hands (see illustration).

The Elbow Headstand (2.11)

1. Join the fingers of your hands loosely together and place the crown of your head in your hands.

2. Put your head on the floor, with your forehead and the backs of your hands on the ground.

3. Place your elbows on the floor about one foot apart. Be careful not to spread the elbows wide, because doing so will destabilize your foundation.

4. Walk your knees up toward your armpits, lifting your pelvis as high as possible before trying to take your feet off the ground.

5. Lift your feet, keeping your legs curled up. You are now in the headstand, but curled up like a fetus.

6. Slowly uncurl your legs one at a time.

7. The more weight you carry on your elbows, the less is on your neck. You may need to adjust your head position. Eventually you may be able to lift your head up off the floor entirely.

The Ear Stand (2.12)

1. Kneeling, place one cheek, shoulder, and arm on the ground. The elbow of the arm is bent, and the back of the hand rests in front of your face.

2. Place the other hand, palm-down, in the space between the first hand and your forehead. The elbow of the second arm extends straight up in the air (see illustration).

3. Now, walk your lower body around toward the raised elbow, twisting at the waist as far as you can go.

4. Place both knees up on the raised elbow and rest in this position, becoming used to the twist.

5. Now slowly extend the legs up into the air, up over your head.

6. Another method of entering the ear stand is to go up into the shoulder stand, and then to shift the weight of your legs toward one side while reaching one hand across to join the other on the side toward which you are turning. Slowly roll your weight onto that cheek, ear and shoulder, twisting your waist as you do.

The Handstand (2.13)

1. Place a mat up against a wall, and put your hands down on the mat about shoulder-width apart and a little more than one foot from the wall (farther if you are tall).

2. Gently take a few practice kicks up in the air and then kick all the way up so that your feet rest against the wall.

3. Arch your back so that your body bows away from the wall. Lift your head backward so that your face is pointing down toward the floor.

4. Test your balance by pushing with your toes to find center.

5. Take your feet away from the wall if you can.

6. Try walking away from the wall on your hands.

7. If you start to fall, remember your rolls.

THE BACKBENDS

Note: Before you attempt any backbends, be sure your back is limber. Do some stretches in each direction to prepare, and do not bend any farther than is comfortable for you.

Ryszard Cieślak taught backbends in two ways. In the first, he would stand with his back facing a wall and his feet about two or three feet from the wall. Then he would lean over back-

ward and walk his fingers gently down the wall to the floor.
Then, keeping all his weight supported entirely by his arch and
by his legs, he would gently walk his fingers back up the wall
until he was standing again. Be really careful if you try this.

The second method is the **Kneeling Backbend** (2.14).

Like the Headstands, a Backbend is exciting to accomplish,
and as with the Headstands, what is really important about the
Backbend is not its gymnastic virtuosity, but what it can do to
your inner life. The real power of a Backbend as an acting tool
lies in how it opens you across the chest. After we have studied
the *plastiques* you will find a section entitled "The Bodily Emotions" in which I discuss the inner life of this form.

Once you have accomplished the headstands and backbends, allow yourself to play with them, not as still positions
but as passing moments in the midst of rolls, crawls, stands,
and squats. Remember that the purpose of doing a headstand is
not mastering the ability to hold a perfect position, but rather
having the opportunity to explore what happens to you while
you are upside down or while you struggle with the problem of
balance. If you start to "fall" out of a headstand, the important
thing is not to fight it, but to "use" the fall and to play with the
energy of the roll. In fact, that is not a bad way to think of all of
the *exercises corporels*: they are not yoga *asanas* but rather containers of an energy that is always changing, always leading
you on to something new. When you start to fall out of a headstand, it should be as if your body declared, "What do you
mean, 'fall'? I *meant* to roll." In the next chapter we will learn
how to allow a "River" of movements to flow through our whole
body. But now that you have gained some confidence in your
headstands and rolls, you can try a first River of *corporels*. Just
begin with the Cat, and then allow the forms you've been studying to flow one into the next with no pauses. Use the rolls as
transitions, treating every "mistake" as if it were part of the
work.

The Kneeling Backbend (2.14)

1. Kneel "high" with your whole body vertical from knee to head.

2. Relax and release your neck so that your head falls gently backward.

3. As you allow your upper back to lean farther and farther backward, counterbalance this movement by bringing the hips forward.

4. Keep releasing the muscles of the chest and stomach, supporting yourself with the strength of your thigh muscles (not with the abdominals).

5. Slowly allow yourself to lean backward, **but only far enough so that you can always bring yourself back to vertical using the thigh muscles.**

6. Play with the backbend, moving up and down, releasing the upper body. Try reaching your arms gently above you.

7. Try to come down by maintaining your arch while you roll forward so that your thighs, your hips, your stomach, and your chest form a curve down which you roll (see illustration). **Be sure to turn your head to the side so that your chin does not hit the floor.**

TIGER LEAPS

*It would be disastrous for an acrobat to go off wool gath-
ering just before he performs a* salto mortale *or other neck-
risking stunt! . . . He must jump, come what may. This is
exactly what an actor must do when he comes to the culminating point of his part.*

—Stanislavski, *Building a Character*

The most exciting and most revealing of all the *exercises corporels* are the Tiger Leaps (2.15). Although at the outset they
seem to be the clearest example of the external, "acrobatic"
nature of Grotowski's work, in practice the Tiger Leaps reveal
the way in which the outward, physical nature of this work is in
fact an external manifestation and a tangible representation of
an inner, emotional process.

To teach the Tiger Leaps in our 1967 workshop, Ryszard
Cieślak placed the tumbling mats in a long row down the middle of the studio and then stood in the middle while we actors
lined up at the end. Each of us would then run straight toward
Cieślak and leap directly at his face; then just in time he would
duck out of the way, just low enough so that we could sail over
him and land in a forward roll.

With my acting class, I begin the exercise a little more cau-
tiously. We line up the mats and start by walking down this
pathway one after the other in silence. As we begin, the line of
mats evokes a certain excitement and/or terror among the students. There are even a few nervous giggles, so I tell everyone
that we will be working in silence—in part to help people with
their concentration, and in part because these giggles are actually the early signs of the fear and excitement that must be
used within the work itself. Next we add a single somersault as
we go. Each of us walks, rolls, stands, and walks again. The
somersault is not an isolated event; it is part of the walk. On
our next walk, we make a very small dive, letting go of the floor

with our feet a split second before our weight lands on our hands.

Some of the people in the line are clearly nervous. Veronica stops for a moment to place her hands on the floor before she rolls. "Try walking more slowly, but not stopping at all," I suggest. "See if you can experience the emotion of that moment when you want to hesitate. Let yourself feel the feeling but still keep going."

Sandra is jumping a short distance, but she is landing on her head each time she dives. "Try imagining that what you are doing is jumping off your feet and onto your hands; then use the strength of your arms to let yourself down onto the back of your shoulders. It is all one movement, but use your arms!"

Carlos is in his element, running down the mats, sailing into each roll, and then bounding up loudly onto his feet. "Fine," I say, "we will be leaping in a minute. But first see if you can land and roll in absolute silence."

Aisha grimaces, hesitates, and then plunges forward. At the other end of the mats she stands up with a big smile on her face.

Brian is silent, but his eyes keep looking away from the mats, and then they close just before he starts his rolls. I say only, "See what happens if you keep your eyes in the work."

Once again we are engaged in a "purely physical" task, but within this task, each actor is plainly going through waves of excitement and fear as he or she runs down the line of mats. This exterior, physical form is evoking some strong inner experiences.

Then I crouch down in the middle of the mats saying, "Now everyone goes over me. It is no different than what you have just been doing; you are just doing it over my body."

Veronica looks terrified. "But what if I bump into you?"

"I can take it. Even if you just roll right over me, that's fine."

In fact a few people do roll right over my body, while others discover that it is actually very easy to clear me. Still others fly past, high above me.

After a couple of rounds like this, I say, "Okay, now you tell me how high to crouch here. When you start your run, I will be a little higher than you say, but then I'll duck as you take off."

Maria tells me to huddle against the mat. Carlos wants me standing almost upright. The others fall somewhere between. As each leap begins, I duck out of the way, but by the second round, I hardly need to duck at all. Most people are leaping much higher than they thought they could. But each time she starts her run at me, Veronica stops after two steps.

"Right at me!" I tell her, "And scream as you run."

"Oh! I hate this!" she says before she begins.

"Yes, right! And I'm the one that's making you do it! Now, right at me!"

"Oh, I HATE this!" she screams as she comes toward me. I duck just before her hands reach my face. She flies over my body and lands in a perfect roll. The class cheers.

Sandra stalks toward me growling loudly with frustration, and rolls right over me again. Cheers again.

As Carlos runs full speed toward me, I yell at him and he laughs as he flies over my head. So, one by one, each actor encounters his or her personal demon within the exercise. Each one learns how to contain and to use the adrenaline rush he or she encounters in performing this simple physical form. And each one discovers that fear is not something evil that must be denied or overcome. Fear is energy, energy you can use to drive the work.

After the Tiger Leaps, we spend a few minutes in silence, and then I encourage the students to talk about their experience. Some say they loved the exercise and some say they hated it, but no one had a neutral experience today. When all of them have spoken, I add a few comments about fear.

"The trouble with fear is that it has a bad name. We've come to think that there are positive emotions and negative ones, and fear is definitely a negative one. It is an emotion we have been told we would never have if we were brave, and we should never show if we are not. But the surprising thing about fear is that if we acknowledge it and put it into the work, it disappears, or rather it seems to convert itself directly into excitement. But it will not serve to *try* to make the fear disappear. It disappears in the process of naming it, of letting yourself know, 'Okay, this is fear.' It takes real courage to say, 'I am afraid,' so in the act of naming it you are already converting the fear into usable energy.

"In this way, the Tiger Leaps are a wonderful paradigm for all of acting. Ultimately your task as an actor is to allow yourself to come face to face with whatever is difficult for you, and thereby to transform it."

Grotowski put it this way:

> When you perform a somersault in space which you are usually not able to do because it seems impossible, you regain some trust in yourself. . . . It is not knowing how to do things that is necessary, but not hesitating when faced with a challenge. [Quoted in Kumiega, p. 122]

Note: Do not attempt this exercise without someone to spot you and a soft, firm surface on which to land.

Tiger Leaps (2.15)

1. Place tumbling mats in a long line, interconnecting them if possible.

2. Begin by walking down the line of mats in silence. As one person exits from the mats, the next one starts.

3. Add a forward roll in the middle of your walk.

4. Now, let your hands reach out to catch your weight as you let go of the ground with your feet.

5. Add a small dive, allowing your feet to leave the ground a split second before your hands touch. Tuck your chin, catch your weight on your hands, and use the strength of your arms to lower yourself onto your shoulders, with your head just missing contact with the mat. Try to land silently.

6. Move more quickly and dive higher or farther. Place an object or a person in your path to dive over. If you feel some fear, yell as you run toward the obstacle. Reach your arms out as if to attack it as you dive. If the obstacle seems too high, start a little lower.

7. Extend your dive just enough so that you feel the fear and can put it into the work. Be sure to keep your dive controlled and smooth.

Les Exercises Plastiques

PLASTIQUE ISOLATIONS

*Duse had a strange way of smiling. It seemed to come
from the toes. It seemed to move through the body and arrive at the face and mouth and resembled the sun coming
out of the cloud.*

> —Lee Strasberg, *A Dream of Passion*

*To act with the hands, begin with the spine, to act with the
feet, begin in the head or the hands.*

> —Grotowski, in Crawley, *The Stone in the Soup*

The *plastique* exercises served as the core of the work that
Ryszard Cieślak demonstrated in our workshop with Grotowski. At first the exercises seemed to be merely strict physical
forms, movement isolations invested with a sort of "isometric"
energy, as if the body part that moved was being pulled in
two directions at once. But as Cieślak performed them, the
plastiques also drew his attention into the space around him,
as if they were simultaneously exciting his imagination to
see things in the empty air.

When you begin to work with these forms they are simply
physical isolations, movement explorations of one body part at
a time in every direction that part can move. The shoulder, for
example, can move up or down, and forward or back. It can
move in any of these directions, in any order, at any speed, and
with any degree of force. And it can combine several move-

ments into one, moving in a circle: up, forward, down, back. It can move smoothly, or it can move in jerks; it can tremble or slide. And it can hunch, or slump, or shrug.

But as soon as you sense that a lift of the shoulders is a "jerk" or a "slump" or a "shrug," the lift is no longer simply an exploration of movement. It has become an *external* key to an *internal* door, a physical way of asking an image question like, "What am I jerking away from?" or an emotional question like, "What am I slumping about?" or a scenic question like, "Who am I shrugging to?"

And that is not all. Each *plastique* is itself an emotive gesture. When you shrug your shoulders, for instance, you become aware of the feeling that goes with that shrug: "I don't know," or "I don't care." The feeling *inhabits* the shrug itself.

To begin the first lesson in the *exercises plastiques*, the **Plastique Isolations** (3.1), with my class, I stand in front of the group and ask the students to position themselves somewhere in the room where they can see me. I explain that I will go through the isolations from head to toe and that they should begin by simply following what I do. "The first time you do the *plastique* exercises it is useful to let them begin as just a series of body isolations: an exploration of the movement possibilities of each part of the body, so as you work, keep checking in with me to see what I am doing. But if while you work the movements provoke feelings or images, you can allow those things to affect how you are manifesting a particular isolation. As I demonstrate, I will sometimes be following my own associations, so there is no need to do precisely what I do, but use what I am doing as an example or an inspiration."

Note: If you can have someone who knows this work lead you through these plastique *exercises, that is certainly preferable to trying to move while reading the words off the page. If not, try this: work with one other person. One person can read the description while the other one moves.*

The *Plastique* Isolations (3.1)

The eyelids can open and close. They can open partway. One eye can open. One eye can wink. Both eyes can blink. The eyelids can flutter. They can be heavy and keep trying to close. They can snap open.

The eyes can move left or right or up or down. They can move quickly or slowly. They can circle. They can scan the horizon or focus close to the body. They can move below half-shut lids. They can race around, looking for something. They can stare blankly. They can be wide awake or tired. (Through all of the rest of the **plastiques**, the eyes stay engaged. Where and how they focus can change the quality of every other isolation.)

The muscles of **the face and the mouth** can move in every direction possible. Groups of muscles can work together or opposite one another.

The head and neck. The head can slide forward or back or left or right while remaining upright. It can tilt left or right or forward or back. And it can roll around. It can also turn left and right. It can move quickly or slowly. It can shake or wobble or nod or twist.

The shoulders. One shoulder can move up, down, forward, or back. Then it can move in any combination of these directions. It can move in circles, connecting each direction, and the circles can be in either direction and in different rhythms. The movements can be smooth or broken, sudden or gradual. Then there is the other shoulder. And there are the two shoulders together: both forward, both backward, one forward while the other goes back, one suddenly up while the other moves slowly down, circles in the same direction, circles in opposite directions, and so forth.

Each elbow can move out from the body or in toward it. It can move left or right. It can pull backward or reach forward. Each elbow can circle clockwise or counterclockwise. It can rock left and right. The elbows can move together; they can press toward each other or stretch away from each other. They can fly, or swing or pound or dig or caress.

The wrists can lift or circle. They can move left or right, in staccato or in gentle movements. They can pull away from each other with tension or with ease. They can move up and down in a constant rhythm. They can push away from the body or slide in toward it.

The hands and fingers can claw, punch, twist, or caress. They can close as if to grab suddenly, or grasp finger by finger. They can undulate: wrist, palm, first knuckle, second, third. They can push, pull, lift, tickle, or poke.

The shoulders, arms, hands, and fingers can undulate from the shoulder outward. The shoulders, arms, hands, and fingers can stretch up for something out of reach. They can push through the air, or punch, or claw. They can pull against one another. One hand can pull while the other pushes. The fingers can type, play the piano, tickle, or scratch. They can fly. And the arms, hands, and fingers can receive. They can open to the sunlight; they can accept the rain. They can reach out for help. They can hang in despair.

The chest can slide forward and back while remaining upright (be sure it is the chest that is working now, not the shoulders). It can slide right or left (try reaching with the arm and hand, pulling the chest to the side). The chest can circle by moving progressively in all four directions. And it can tilt forward and backward, left and right. Then the chest and arms can work together, or opposite one another. The arms, hands, and the chest can all reach upward, yearning for something beyond reach. The chest can shake, shimmy, or twist. It can inflate and deflate. It can collapse.

The back can push, lift, twist, or wriggle. The arms and back together can lift.

The pelvis can tilt forward or backward, or left or right. It can slide back and forth quickly or slowly. It can circle. It can move on its own or in relation to the arms. The pelvis can push suddenly or move smoothly. It can ride or bump or twist.

The whole upper body can undulate from the pelvis upward. It can lift a heavy weight from the floor to the sky. It can undulate from the head downward. It can shimmy, shake, tremble, whip, flail, undress, hug, enclose, or fly.

(To extend the *plastiques* down through the legs, you can continue to stand, but it can be helpful to sit or lie on the floor so that the legs are completely free to move.)

The knees can lift in each direction. They can circle clockwise and counterclockwise. They can push toward each other or pull away.

The ankles and feet can circle, rub, and kick. They can push forward or back. And they can shake, scratch, and caress.

Stand back up again.

The legs can walk, run, jump, and kick. (Try running in place.) And working with the eyes, the legs can run away from something behind you, or run toward something in front of you, jump up for something above you, or leap away from something below you.

THE *PLASTIQUE* RIVER

*Any time an actor thinks he is merely exercising or train-
ing his muscles, he is cheating himself. These are acting
disciplines. Every instant of every discipline, the actor
must be expressing the emotion of some situation, according to his own bodily interpretation.*

—Tadashi Suzuki, quoted in Brandon, "Training at the Wasela
Little Theatre: The Suzuki Method," *TDR*, 1978

*If during creation we hide the things that function in our
personal lives, you may be sure that our creativity will
fall.*

—Grotowski, *TDR*, Fall 1968

Now that you have studied the *plastiques* as technical, physical isolations, leading yourself consciously from one body part
to the next, the next step is to allow the *plastiques* to do the
leading. To enter a *plastique* **River**, you begin anywhere, with
any *plastique*, and then simply allow the movement of your
body to lead on to the next *plastique* and the next. Don't worry if
your River does not "flow" evenly. If at any point you have no
impulse at all, just start somewhere new. Try large movements
that push you through space and small ones that articulate one
small body part. Try fast movements and slow. Try sticking with
one *plastique* for thirty seconds, searching for small variations
and new details. And try shifting quickly from one body part to
another.

Throughout the River, keep your eyes open and keep using
them in the work. For instance, while you are working with your
shoulder, see what changes for you if you look backward over
the shoulder. While you are making pelvic circles, try focusing
your eyes near your body or far away. While you are working
with your lips, see what happens if you look sideways with your
eyes half-closed. If a feeling or an image occurs to you, trust it.

Each *plastique* is a conversation, a movement that contains a dynamic, two-way pull, a simultaneous desire to move toward and away. This doubleness need not be tension filled; the movement itself may be quite gentle. But even in the gentlest movement there is some life, some energy of resistance, like the resistance that velvet gives your fingers as they move across a piece of cloth.

After I have led my acting class once through the *plastiques*, I demonstrate a *plastique* River for them. I begin with one isolation and then allow the impulses and images that arise to lead me from one movement to another. When I finish, I remind the students not to copy me, and then I tell them to work on their own for ten minutes. After they have finished their Rivers, they take a few minutes to digest their experience. Then we gather to talk.

Until today, Joan has been taking this physical approach to acting in stride. She has spoken very little, but the bitterness she expressed about her previous acting teachers has not prevented her from throwing herself fully into each exercise. But today, after her first River of *plastiques*, the words burst out of her as if a dam had broken. "I hated that! I feel as though I'm just doing things with my body, and, hey, I can dance. I've danced for years. I can do those things. But *nothing* is happening. And I don't see what it has to do with acting or scenes or whatever."

"It sounds to me as though there is a lot happening for you," I respond.

"Oh, don't give me psychology now. Yeah, a lot would be 'happening' for me if I banged my head against a wall, too."

"*Touché.* But the purpose of this work is to allow emotions to happen to you. You probably wouldn't bang your head against the wall just to find tears."

"You don't understand. There is a lot happening for me *now* because there was nothing happening for me *then*, in the exercise. The exercise didn't work for me. That's what I'm saying." As she speaks, Joan removes the barrette that always holds her hair tight. She shakes her head, and for the first time, her long red hair spills down her shoulders.

"Okay. And when did you start to realize that?"

"When? About one minute after we started. I could see it was working for others—which is fine. But it just didn't do anything for me."

"So what did you do when you realized that it wasn't working for you?"

"Do? I just kept trying."

"And what if you stopped?"

"Stopped what? Stopped doing the exercise? You mean just dropped out of it?"

"Maybe. I mean what would it be like to let yourself know that you hate what you're doing, and you're angry at the teacher for telling you to do it, and—"

"I don't understand."

"A central purpose of all this work is to provide you with containers for your emotional life. That's what the *plastiques* are, containers, forms that both *evoke* and *contain* emotional life. You were just very lucky today."

"Lucky!?" Joan looks exasperated.

"Yes. The *plastiques* evoked a lot of emotion in you, and not only at the end. In fact, you say you began to have this reaction one minute into the work. The problem was that you did not find the way to put that emotion into the *plastiques* themselves. The anger just kept building up because you had not found the container or expresser that your anger needed. Your expertise at playing the hardworking student enabled you to keep your anger just barely under control, until, when we sat down, the pressure cooker exploded."

"But this emotion isn't *in* the work. It is *about* the work."

"Exactly."

"So," said Joan, looking confused but intrigued, "what should I do?"

"Well, how would you feel if I asked you to begin the work again, right now?"

"I don't know. I guess I would feel pissed at you for telling me to, and pissed at myself for bringing the whole thing up and getting myself in trouble."

"Great."

"Great?"

"Yes, because the *plastique* work is designed to provide very good containers for all that piss."

"Very funny."

"No, really. Here, stand up with me."

"Oh, god," says Joan, but she stands up, picks up the barrette, and starts to put up her hair.

"Let it be," I say. "Let's begin with the *plastique* called wringing the teacher's neck. Here's my neck, now I'm going to tell you to start your exercises again. And you're going to wring my neck."

"Really?"

"Yes . . . no. You're going to wring my neck out here, about two inches in front of the neck itself, in the air. Okay?"

"But what if I don't *feel* like wringing your neck?"

"Don't worry. I'll take care of that. So, ready?"

"I guess so," Joan said, sounding dubious.

"So, let's start our *plastiques* again," I said, beginning to move my body. "What's the matter? Too hard for you?"

"No."

"You're too tired to work?"

"No, I am not tired."

"You sound a little pissed."

"I am. You're trying to manipulate me and I feel like a fool and—"

"Good," I said. "Now wring!"

Joan begins to twist the air near my neck, first tentatively, and then with more and more force. At first I continue to taunt her, but then, as her energy rises, I encourage her to put her whole body into the work: "Good. And let your legs work, too." She starts to kick the air, some of her kicks almost making contact. "Fine! Yes! But be precise with those *plastiques*! Kick at a spot exactly two inches away from me, but right where it hurts!" As her kicks land in the air near my groin, I allow myself to fall backward, and then I roll out of the game.

"Now let yourself *see* me still there. Know who you are kicking, listen to what *your imaginary partner* is saying to you, and be precise with where you aim your kicks. Allow the image to change if it starts to. Maybe there are some other teacher images you'd like to kick around a little. Good! And now try working with other body parts. Yes. Good. Let yourself win and lose. If the image disappears, trust what comes next."

After Joan has worked for about five minutes I tell her to rest. And after she has caught her breath, I reopen our dialogue.

"There is probably a whole lot more anger where that came from. You've been a terribly good student for years, so you may have quite a bit of emotion to work with in relation to teachers. After years of dance classes, strangling the teacher is probably not a bad place to begin. And even though I told everyone to keep their hair out of their eyes, maybe for you it will be useful to break a few rules in that regard too."

Joan looks a little stunned, but her face has a certain calm the class has not seen before.

"Is something wrong?" I ask.

"No. It's just that I have never thought of that kind of thing as part of my work before. I thought it was something to 'get over' or to 'leave outside the studio.' You know?"

"Yes I do. But it just seems a pity that you should have to exclude such a powerful source of energy simply because it appears dressed in an improper opinion. The feeling 'I hate this exercise' is a clear impulse; what it needs in order to be harnessed into the work is a form, a muscular container, a *plastique*, that will allow you to explore its energy safely. In this case, I invented this *plastique* of strangling the teacher. It seemed a likely guess. But whatever you are feeling, your job is to search through your physical vocabulary to find a form that allows that feeling to exit from your body and to start turning itself into art."

But my explanation to Joan seems to have confused Sandra. "I don't understand. Are you saying that *every* strong gesture is a *plastique*? I thought the isolations you taught us were the *plastiques*."

"Yes and no. The isolations we studied are a neutral vocabulary with which to begin, but there is nothing sacred about the particular movements I demonstrated. **What makes something a *plastique* is that the movement is specific, that it is filled with life, and that it is related to an image.** The image turns each *plastique* into a conversation, a dialogue between two energies. Even the movement of one finger, or of an eye, even a completely *internal* movement could be a *plastique* if it is imbued with emotion and connected to an image."

IMAGE? WHAT IMAGE?

If [acting students] go blank, I tell them to describe the blank and cherish it because some of the greatest scenes in dramatic literature have occurred when people went blank. Lear says, "I will do such things / what they are I know not yet / but they shall be the terrors of the earth."
    —Jeff Corey, in Mekler, *The New Generation of Acting Teachers*

As you practice the *plastiques* it may occur to you that these *plastique* exercises embody both of our warm-up forms. They incorporate the Body Part Warm-up because they help us relate to each part of our bodies, reminding us to pay attention to any part we may have been ignoring. And they include the Stream-of-Consciousness Warm-up because they serve as external containers for whatever feelings we are experiencing inside. So now that you have worked with these forms, you can add both the *corporels* and the *plastiques* to your warm-ups. Let them lead you into physical choices beyond your habitual range. Let them push you off your feet, turn you upside down, and open your body to the space around you. Let them help you discover needs, gifts, desires, and images even as you stretch and awaken your muscles.

In my class, the next day's warm-up makes it apparent that the *plastiques* have indeed affected how the students approach their bodies. When they warm up their feet, for instance, they are no longer simply sitting on the floor giving themselves foot massages; they are running or kicking and reacting to whatever their feet encounter. And, as they do, they are constantly discovering new ways in which a warm-up is more than a purely physical activity. This new freedom has also engendered two problems that commonly hamper actors when they first work with the *plastiques*: *eye focus* and *touch*.

EYE FOCUS

After the warm-up, Sandra quickly brings up the eye focus problem. "What if I don't *see* any images when I'm using *plastiques*?"

"Well," I respond, "what is your experience?"

"It's more like ... energy moving through my body, or maybe impulses. But you keep saying, 'use your eyes,' and when I do, there is nothing there to see."

"And what is that like for you?"

"What do you mean?"

"I mean what does this lack of images feel like? Is it like, 'Why are all these other people having images, and I'm not?' Or is it more like, 'Where are my images? Why don't I have any images?' Or like, 'Why am I locked in this dark imageless world?'"

"I don't know," she says, shrugging her shoulders, "I guess it's more like, 'Where are my images?'"

"There," I say, "you are already beginning a *plastique* with your shoulders. Let yourself say that again."

"Where are my images?" Sandra repeats, shrugging her shoulders again.

"And now let your whole body join those shoulders."

"I don't understand."

"What I mean is that you have to take the situation seriously." As I explain what I mean to Sandra, I begin with a shoulder shrug, but then I look upward to the left and right, pushing through the air with my hands. "Where are my images? Why am I alone? Where have my images gone?

"That thought of yours—'I don't have any images'—is itself a strong image. But, like the thought Joan had yesterday, 'I hate this exercise,' it is an image that comes wearing a disguise. Joan's 'I hate this exercise' appeared wearing the label 'This thought is not part of the work.' Your 'Where are my images' is disguised as the opinion 'This is not an image.' The trick is to challenge that label rather than allowing this opinion to knock you out of the work.

"Unfortunately the word *image* implies that you must *see* something. But actually images come in the form of all kinds of sensations. There are some people who hallucinate easily. But many of us just have a *feeling*, a *sense*, or maybe even an *idea*."

"But," Sandra continues, "that's just it. You keep saying 'use your eyes.' How are we supposed to use our eyes if there is nothing to see?"

"Well, 'use your eyes' does not necessarily mean 'seeing,' or even looking directly at the image. For instance, if I am running, and I feel as though there is something behind me, I can look back over my shoulder, like this. But I can also run with my eyes forward like this, just darting glances to the sides in fear of what is chasing me. Remember how 'Find what the group wants to do' did not mean, 'Force Sandra to do what everyone else is doing'? It meant 'Pay attention to Sandra, even if she is doing something different.' Well, in the same way, 'Use your eyes' means *pay attention* to what your eyes are doing and include them in the work. It does not mean that you will always actually *see* something. On the other hand, when we get to the scene work, you may be surprised to find that you actually *do* see more than you expected. But this is an important question. During the next few lessons we will experiment with some more exercises that expand the definition of what seeing means."

TOUCH

The other difficulty I had noticed in the students' work was the problem of touch. Since none of them mention it, I bring it up myself. "While you were doing your Rivers, some of you were literally touching things with your hands: the walls, or the floor, or your own bodies. Of course, when you are doing scene work, you need to touch real objects and real people. But at this point I suggest that you be very careful with touch for two reasons: First, the real object can give your fingers (or whatever part of you is doing the touching) such strong feedback that it may wipe out any image you might encounter. If you are imagining that you are digging in the dirt, for instance, but the floor keeps telling your fingers, 'This is wood,' it can make it harder for your image world to assert itself.

"The other danger is that the real object can make you hold back your impulses. If, for instance, you have the impulse to hit someone or something, and you try to explore that impulse by hitting a wall, your arm muscles will automatically hold back your punch before it makes contact with the wall in order to save your knuckles. The result will be that you never get the release of energy you would find if you could let your arm strike out with all your strength.

"So, for both reasons, it is more effective to move your image a few inches back, above the floor or in front of the wall, so that your body can fully explore its impulse life.

"The case of touching yourself is similar, but here there is the added danger that the imagery with which you are working can become turned inward. A couple of you had moments in your Rivers when it seemed as though you were being held, but as you worked, you sometimes put your arms around yourselves. But the quality of being held is that you *receive* the holding, which is very different from *doing* the holding. When we are held, our bodies do not pull in; they expand out against the holder. Of course, it is easier to simply hold yourself, and it may seem immediately comforting. But in the end, if you can discover the sensation of letting yourself be held by another, that is a much more powerful experience."

THE PUSHING EXERCISE

The elements of these physical exercises are pretexts *for association and not the other way around—we should not call up an association in order to find a sensible way of doing the exercises, but the exercise[s] should, themselves, trigger memories, persons and places that activate our bodies and emotions.*
—Grotowski, in Crawley, *The Stone in the Soup*

The questions my students have raised about using their eyes actually point to a central conundrum in acting: How can you experience images, memories, or fantasies while remaining present to the world? How can you "see" your dreams while you are active and awake? Some actor training methods suggest that you turn inward to remember forgotten sensations and memories, but in our physical approach to acting you search for your image life as if it were here, in the world around you, as if the impulses that course through your body are, in fact, reactions to outer stimuli.

To help students experience this interplay between inner impulse and outer images, I created the **Pushing Exercise** (3.2) as an initiation into *plastique* Rivers. In the Pushing Exercise, half of the group begins as passive "receivers" of impulses, closing their eyes and allowing the other half of the group to move their bodies. After the receivers have studied how their body reacted when it was actually moved from the outside, they permit themselves to "receive" the impulses of *imaginary* partners. Finally they open their eyes to let themselves "see" the imaginary forces that are moving them.

In my class, when the first group of receivers begins to work with their eyes open, I notice that many of them are not allowing their eyes actually to focus on the imaginary partners who are moving them; an arm flies out to the side, but the eyes stare forward into space. To correct this problem, I reenter the work occasionally and give some of the actors strong impulses from the outside: a pull on an arm, a push on the shoulder. "Look! It's me!" I say. "You can see me. That's right, you can look at my hand holding your arm. But now try looking right at my face."

When I grab Carlos, he yanks against my pull with cold determination, his eyes staring down at my hand on his arm, but the moment he looks up at my face, his own face becomes alive. He grimaces at me with a vicious smile. "Yes," I say, "That's right. Now, let the 'invisible ones' do the same thing to you. And look right at them, too." I turn him loose to "react" to his own imagination.

I pull on Aisha's arm and she lets me drag her across the room. "What happens," I ask, "if you fight back? You don't have to be a passive recipient of this stuff. As long as the impulse is *initiated* by the image, there is nothing wrong with engaging in the battle." Suddenly she is fully engaged, fighting, kicking, and pulling away with all her strength. "Good. Now do the same thing with the imaginary one," I say, pointing at the vacant air beside me.

By this time people are being dragged, pushed, and chased all over the room. I need only say, "Keep letting yourself be surprised, and look for variation: for big shoves and small pokes, for violent and gentle touches, for slow pushes and fast." I allow the work to continue for a few minutes, and then we switch groups.

After everyone has tried the Pushing Exercise, I have them try their *plastique* Rivers again: "This time," I caution, "remember how the Pushing Exercise worked for you. If an impulse moves your body, either allow it to happen to you or fight back, but in either case, allow your eyes to search for what is happening. If at other times there is no clear impulse, simply jump-start your process by initiating a *plastique* on purpose. But even as you do so, immediately treat that movement *as if* it had been initiated from outside. Look to see who or what is doing that *to* you and let yourself react."

The Pushing Exercise (3.2)

Two people can do this exercise. There need not be a group.

1. The group is divided into two halves. Half of the group stands at the side of the room. They will act as coaches. The other half stands evenly distributed in the room. These people will be the receivers. The receivers close their eyes.

2. Those of you with your eyes closed, take a moment to get used to being there, sensing your body, relaxing with your eyes closed.

3. Now the coaches begin to move among the receivers, periodically giving them "impulses." A coach might lift a receiver's arm and let it fall, or gently touch the neck, or push a shoulder. A coach might move one foot, or blow air on a hand, or turn the whole body. It is important that the coaches give the receivers time to recover after each impulse.

4. Those with your eyes closed, your job is just to <u>receive</u> the touch, not to <u>do</u> anything. If someone lifts your arm, let <u>him</u> do the lifting, and when he lets it go, just let it fall back into place. If someone leans your head or your body over, let the movement happen, and then just come back to center. If you need to move your legs to keep your balance, do so just enough to recover. Try not to add or subtract anything from the touch you receive. If you are tickled and a laugh happens, just let it happen—don't try to stifle the laugh or to avoid the tickle. Just keep letting yourself observe what happens to your body and to your inner life as you receive things.

5. The next step is for the coaches to do less and less, to allow the intervals between the touches to become longer and longer. As the coaches do less, the receivers should begin to allow things to "happen" as if from "invisible" impulses.

6. One way to "allow" such things to happen is, right after receiving an actual touch, let exactly the same thing happen to you again, while your body "remembers" what it was like. If nothing seems to "happen," it is all right to "invent" impulses, but, <u>most important,</u> even if you "make it up," as soon as it is happening, treat it just as you would all the "real" surprises: let <u>it</u> move <u>you.</u> Receive the touch.

7. **Those impulses that are initiated by coaches on the outside, are, ultimately, no different from those that are initiated by "invisible partners." And those impulses that are initiated by "invisible partners" are no different from those that are initiated by conscious decision.** They are all movements <u>received from the outside and reacted to from within</u>.

8. As the receivers begin to move more and more on their own, the role of the coaches changes. The receivers may now be moving around the room with their eyes closed, so the coaches, who are no longer giving impulses, must guard the receivers to make sure they do not bump into another actor or a wall.

9. Now, receivers, allow the impulses to come thicker and faster. Even as your body is recovering from one movement, let the next one begin.

10. And now, try to open your eyes, and "see" who or what is doing that to you. If when you open your eyes, the impulses seem to disappear, close your eyes again for a moment, let some big things "happen" to you, and then try opening your eyes again. And when you open your eyes again, really use them to look at what is happening.

IMAGE WALKS

A child can look at a floating twig and see a great ocean liner, and he doesn't have to deny the existence of the twig to do so. He simply transforms his interpretation of what he is seeing. Yet when student actors are asked to visualize a scene, they invariably close their eyes or stare blankly into space, as if the things they might really see around them hindered their ability to pretend. They have lost the

child's ability to contact and accept reality, and then use
it to create an even more vivid illusion.

—Robert Benedetti, *The Actor at Work*

The Pushing Exercise helps to bridge the gap between impulse and image by working from the body to the mind. But we can also cross this chasm in the opposite direction. The **Image Walks** exercise (3.3) suggests the possibility of admitting that any image can motivate the body to react.[1]

***Note:** To try this exercise without a teacher, have a partner call out the images while you work.*

Image Walks (3.3)

1. Walk around the workspace. Notice how you are feeling today. Let go of any tensions you have. Just walk.

2. When an image is called out, just let yourself deal with it. Do whatever you need to do, allowing the image and your fantasy to work on you. Then when the leader says, "Let it go," shake out your body and return to walking.

3. We begin with images related to the floor:
The floor is covered two feet deep in Ping-Pong balls.
The floor is covered with ice.
The floor is three feet deep in mud.

4. Then we add images like
There is a gale force wind blowing from one side of the room.
There is ice cream falling from the sky. It is piling up on the floor.

5. The images start to be stronger:
The floor is covered with hot coals.
The air is full of invisible kisses.
There are bullets flying three feet above the ground.
There are nude bodies lying on the floor.

6. At the end of the exercise, take some time to remember what happened for you, what worked and what did not.

---

1. The Image Walks exercise is based on an acting exercise taught by Kevin Kuhlke.

After the exercise I gather the group to talk about their experience. With this particular group, it is Maria, who is usually so quiet, who responds first. She reports that the only images that worked for her were the "realistic" ones. "I know what it feels like to walk on ice, so my body could believe that one. But when you said we were walking on hot coals, I don't know what that is like, so I didn't believe it."

"So none of the weirder things worked for you, not the ice cream or the bullets or the walls coming in . . . ?"

"No. But when you said the ceiling was coming down, for some reason I believed that. Sometimes I have claustrophobia, so that was real for me."

"Even though the ceiling of the studio was not actually coming down?"

"Yes."

I turn to the others to ask what their experience was.

"For me it was very in and out," says Carlos. "Some things, like the ice cream, seemed real, because I could get into touching it and tasting it. But other things like the bullets or the naked bodies on the floor just felt like bullshit."

Peter and Veronica both say that one image that worked for them was that of the walls moving in.

"And did it seem more real for you when you were just watching the walls or when you were trying to push against them?" I ask.

"When I was watching," responds Veronica.

"Not for me," says Peter. "In fact, I didn't believe it at all until I started to push, and suddenly I actually felt the wall was pushing back."

"And what happened to you with the hot coals?" I ask Peter. "I saw you jump up on a chair and then come back down again."

"Yes, that was very interesting. I don't know why, but the hot coals seemed very real for me. I felt as though my feet were really hurting, so I began by jumping higher and higher, but the higher I jumped, the harder I would land, and the jolt of the landing made the feeling of the heat seem even more real. So then I realized that I could jump up on the chair, and I thought, 'Of course, why didn't I think of that before?' And then when I was up on the chair, for a moment I thought, 'Look at all those stupid people. If there really *were* hot coals on this floor, they would all be fighting to get on this chair.' But then, since I was standing on the chair and I didn't have any contact with the coals anymore, I lost all the sense of the heat, and I realized that I would have to get back down onto the coals to believe in them again."

"So what did you do?"

"Well, I thought that if I just got down to the floor again, I would feel stupid, like why would I do that? I had to make up an excuse, so I imagined that the flames were getting higher around my chair, so I would have to get off there, and then, as I ran across the floor the coals were burning my feet again, so then I jumped on Brian's back."

"Which was great for me," says Brian. "I mean, then there were two things going on for me, the heat and this idiot on my back, holding me down so I couldn't even jump off the coals anymore."

"Right," I say, "and Peter, you were absolutely right about needing to get down from the chair. In fact, this situation raises a very important truth about acting: **As an actor, you are always responsible for two opposite things**: you are responsible for what some acting teachers call '**playing your action**'—in this case, getting off the coals—but at the same time, you are also responsible for **maintaining the obstacle**'—in this case, feeling the heat of coals themselves. If you are too clever for your own good, you will kill the game. If you stay up on the chair, it becomes harder for you to believe in the heat of the coals. So on the one hand as the character whose feet are hot you want to get the hell off the floor. But on the other hand, as the intelligent actor who wants to keep the image alive you need to find a way to work that doesn't kill the image for you. This double consciousness is fundamental to acting, and it is a good 'muscle' to start exercising.

"You actually found two good ways to solve this problem. One was just to turn up the flames around the chair. This method, allowing your image work to grow larger or stronger, lets the image run the show so that you have only to react. **The more power you invest in your images, the more they will feed you, and the less you will have to do.**

"The second thing you did was to involve Brian in your reality. Getting on his back transformed the situation into something much more personal and dangerous. And as he said, the problem you gave him was actually a gift, something that made the exercise stronger for him too."

I turn next to Aisha, who has not yet spoken. "It seemed to me that you also made an interesting discovery while working with the image of the nude bodies on the floor. For a while you were doing what others were doing, stepping gingerly over the bodies. But then something changed, no?"

"Yeah," Aisha smiles. "I was just stepping all around them, and then I noticed this one naked guy who was looking at me."

"So you started to get undressed?"

"Well, I figured you would change the image on us before I got too far."

"*Mierda*," says Carlos.

"You mean, shit you missed it?"

"No. I mean, shit, I had that impulse, too, but I didn't dare follow it."

"But I thought you said the other images didn't work for you."

"Well, I didn't really *believe* that there were naked people on the floor. I mean I just had this sort of flash that *if* there *were*, then what I would do is take off my clothes."

"But Carlos, my friend, that's all there is, that flash. When it happens, the trick is to engage yourself in the physical action, because once you dare to follow your impulse, the very fact that you are doing so will imbue your image with reality: *If* I'm taking off my clothes, there *must* be something making me do it. After all, I know I'm not crazy."

"But that's just it!" Carlos says. "It *is* crazy to start taking off your clothes knowing perfectly well that there is nothing there."

"Carlos," I say, "there are many people in this world who would tell you that it would be crazy to take off your clothes even if there *were* someone naked there, especially with all these other real people in the room. If you weren't crazy in that sense, you wouldn't be in theater in the first place. Acting is crazy. Acting is making up stuff that you know perfectly well is not true and then letting yourself believe in it. That's why actors are on stage getting paid while the audience is in the house, paying.

"But, everyone, I want you all to note that what worked for one of you may not have worked at all for someone else. Some of you who have never been closer to a war than a TV set reacted very strongly to the image of the bullets. For others it seemed like playacting. Some people became quite involved in the mud, while others didn't believe it at all. And not only that, some of you who believed the mud found it disgusting, while others enjoyed playing with it. Your job as an actor is to notice what works for you and to do what you need to do—like pushing on the wall or playing with the mud—to help it affect you as strongly as possible."

When I lead this exercise with my students, I use images from my own imagination, images that work for me or have worked for many actors in the past. But if you try the Image Walks, only *you* know what really works for you. In the end, your job as an actor is to identify what affects you strongly, and then to face that material, not try to avoid it. No one else need ever know what images you are using in your work, but *you* know, and **there is no point in struggling with images that are tepid for you. You must always use what really turns you on.**

STICKING WITH IMAGES

Orientals keep on persevering until the problem is solved. But when Europeans come across difficulties, they simply invent a new, easier method. . . . On reflection, I think the possibility of success is probably the same whether you are searching vertically (continuing to dig deeper into the same hole), or horizontally (digging another hole in a different place). It is a matter of whether you prefer to follow an absolute value in believing that the precious stone can only be found in that particular hole, or to make a relative value judgment; wherever you dig, the probability of finding gems is more or less the same.

—Oida, *An Actor Adrift*

The Pushing Exercise and the Image Walks offer two very different gateways into our imaginations. The Pushing Exercise treats the *plastiques* as a series of physical impulses, depending on a constantly shifting flow of energy throughout the body. With the help of the eyes and the questioning mind, you experience these impulses with the specificity and power of emotional imagery: it is not just that your body is moving, but that someone or something is doing something *to* you. In the Image Walks, you come at imagery from the opposite direction: the senses are the source, and the *plastiques* act as catalysts and containers, helping you make your imagery more concrete and ensuring that your whole body reacts as if the images were real.

But in practice, you will find these two methods of entering the work are complementary. And once your River is "flowing," you will often find it impossible to distinguish between the two. The physical impulses and the images just *happen*, and you just *respond*. It no longer matters which came first.

Once again the actors in my class spend fifteen or twenty minutes on their own, exploring a *plastique* River, and this time their work is much more concentrated. Each student seems deep in his or her own world of changing images, pulled this way and that, responding to sensuous or terrifying visions, playing or struggling with unseen partners, his or her body and eyes working in concert.

After the work is over, Veronica raises her hand with a question. This time she is not speaking out of worry. She simply has a practical work issue. "I think I am beginning to understand now," she says. "I mean this time there was no doubt that things were happening. But sometimes I didn't know whether to stay with an image or to move on to something else."

"Well, that is a good question," I say, "but there is no right answer. There are advantages both ways. The advantage to sticking with one image, allowing it to grow and deepen, perhaps even permitting a story to emerge, is that the image can then lead you into very strong material. It teaches you that you can stand a great deal more emotion than you thought you could. And you may find that sticking with a strong image will eventually lead you to a more satisfying exit from that image. Sometimes when exploring anger, for instance, you might have a tendency to close your eyes or move away right after you yell or strike out. If instead you insist on sticking with your imagery and continuing to look right at it, you may find that in the moment after the anger is expressed, something else arises. If you look after you land a punch, for instance, you may see the damage you have done, and that may lead you into a new emotion: Regret? Or sorrow? Or lust to drink the blood? But these strong succeeding emotions will arise only if you let yourself stick with the image long enough.

"On the other hand, there are also dangers that can result from sticking with your imagery. The greatest danger is that you may fail to notice that there are other, equally strong but less familiar, emotions and images that are trying to make themselves known to you. For instance, a common mistake is to become so entranced with the imagery that your hands can touch (and control) in front of you, that you fail to notice that at the same time other impulses are accosting your legs or creeping up your back, impulses over which you have less control. As you reach forward to grapple with the image before you, you may remain unaware that your legs are simultaneously stretching in the opposite direction, and you could be treating that leg stretch as another image. It is not that there is anything wrong with the image you are sticking with in front of you, but since our hands are so good at controlling the world, there is a great temptation to pay more attention to the images in front of us while ignoring those over which we have less control.

"Besides, letting go of one image to follow other possibilities also trains us to keep listening and staying open to all kinds of surprises. If you are open to the surprises your own imagination thrusts upon you, you will also be more open to the surprises that come from your scene partner.

"So what should you do? Stick with imagery or let it constantly change? The answer is that both ways of working are useful. So you should practice both. Perhaps this is the safest advice: **If you notice that your habit is to prefer constant change, then practice sticking with one image. And vice versa. Each way of working will teach you something about yourself, and each will lead you into a different kind of image and emotional life.**"

At the end of the class, Carlos pulls me aside. "Can we talk for a moment?" he asks.

"Sure."

"I didn't want to bring this up in the group just because I know it is very much a personal problem of mine, but I keep feeling as we do this work that I am *pushing*, you know, working with my muscles to make things happen, and just adding to the physical tension I already have."

"You are right," I say. "Tension is a real danger for you, and it can be a danger for anyone when they begin to work with the *plastiques*. On the other hand, it is also a very liberating experience to find that it is okay to work *hard* on stage, and that making a physical effort can actually lead you to strong emotional life."

"Oh yes, it is *so* wonderful for me not to be acting sitting in a chair, you know. For the first time in my life I feel as though my body can *help* me act, not just get in my way. But I also feel as though I am tensing my throat all the time. And sometimes I'm afraid that the *plastiques* just lead me again and again into violent imagery."

"I understand, but that is because up until now we have been using the *plastiques* in a very active way. Tomorrow we will explore what happens when you use the *plastiques* in a more empty way. Ultimately, of course, you must find a way to work fully with your body without creating extra tension. This issue will become even more important when we get to vocal work. But along the way, you will find that both effort and emptiness are valuable."

WORKING WITH TENSION

One cannot be completely relaxed as many theatre schools teach you to be, because to be totally relaxed is to be a limp rag.

—Grotowski, *Les Lettres français*

In many schools of acting, *tension* is a dirty word. Actors are told that they must "get rid of" their tensions. They are made aware that their tense jaws are inhibiting their voices or that their tense shoulders are restricting their movements, and they are instructed that ridding themselves of tension is the necessary first step toward emotional freedom. Stanislavski himself taught that relaxation was the very starting point of actor training, and American Method teachers follow Lee Strasberg in teaching relaxation as *the* fundamental tool in entering affective memory work. Michael Kahn, for instance, says, "I think that relaxation is the key to everything" [Mekler, p. 332].

But other acting teachers disagree. Michael Schulman remarks: "One of the problems with the relaxation technique was that . . . it often led to very de-energized acting because people were working so hard at keeping their bodies relaxed" [Mekler, p. 38]. And Mel Shapiro declares:

> I don't want students to discharge or release their tension, I want them to keep it. They need it to get revved up for what they want. Relaxation exercises make actors look and act anesthetized. Or like the lobotomized victims of some psychic rape. No. This business of relaxing is rubbish. . . . The world is not a Simmons mattress. Whenever an actor tells me he's not "comfortable," I know we're on the right track. Otherwise he's comfortable, the character's comfortable, the audience is comfortable. Let's all go to sleep. [Mekler, p. 380]

Perhaps this argument over the role of tension is so contentious because tension is not simply a physical problem; it is a means by which the body (literally) holds on to its emotional life. Voice teacher Kristin Linklater has noted that simply asking people to relax and breathe deeply is sometimes all that is necessary to evoke tears. But if we think of tension simply as a "problem" to be eliminated, we run the risk of adding an extra negative judgment on top of the tension that already exists: "I know I should relax. I'm a bad person for being tense," and so forth. Moreover, asking people to "give up" or "let go of" their tensions can sometimes result in their simply moving the tensions around or hiding them.

A couple of years ago I worked with a young woman who had studied dance and Method acting for several years. During that time she had been told over and over that tension was a bad thing, and she had learned to perform with apparent softness and gentleness. Yet she seemed unable to reach deep emotions in her acting.

I suspected that her relaxed exterior might be covering other less gentle energies that lay buried within her, so one day, when she seemed stuck in her River work, I suggested that she sit down opposite me on the floor, put the soles of her feet against the soles of mine, and just push. She pushed and I pushed, and when I encouraged her, her strong dance-trained legs were able to push me quickly backward across the floor. But, as she did so, her face flushed with emotion, and by the end of a few minutes of work, she was in tears. At the end of the exercise, I asked her how she felt. She said she felt good, but that she had no idea where the tears had come from.

Eventually this woman might have connected with the feelings she had hidden within her leg muscles by some other route, with an Affective Memory exercise, or even through relaxation, but by actually allowing herself to work with strength and with "tension" against the resistance I provided, she was able to access the stored emotion very quickly. After that day, whenever she seemed stuck in her acting, I needed only to remind her to work with her legs for her to reconnect with the feeling life that lay hidden within them. This young woman did carry "tension" in her legs, but that tension was not "bad" in the sense that she needed to try to get rid of it; it was stored energy that could serve as a source of information. Thinking of it as a "tension problem" had only put the energy further out of her reach.

I am not saying that tension is a good thing. Perennial muscular stress can, indeed, inhibit physical and vocal freedom and hinder your ability to welcome gentle emotions, like sadness, into your body. But every actor must find his or her own pathway to openness. The tensions in our bodies were once acquired for good reasons, so "letting go" of those tensions can mean dealing with the energies they contain and exploring the imagery they provoke. Therefore, when you do a relaxation exercise, you must take the time you need to notice the tension and then, as you let that tension go, allow yourself to experience all the thoughts and emotions that may arise during relaxation. Remember, the purpose of "relaxation" is not to become a "wet rag," but to be able to choose how and where your acting energies flow.

THE CONTAINER AND THE KISS

Memories are always physical reactions. It is our skin which has not forgotten, our eyes which have not forgotten.

—Grotowski, *Towards a Poor Theatre*

Veronica's question about sticking with imagery has led us in a new direction. Until this moment in the work, almost all of our effort has been directed toward opening more and more doors, increasing the number of physical and imagistic possibilities that are available to us. But once we have discovered the *breadth* of imagination that is available in a River of *plastiques*, we can take a first step toward examining its *depth* by narrowing down the choices that arise.

The **Container** (3.4) and the **Kiss** (3.5) exercises call on your ability to stick with one image for an extended period of time. And, at the same time, these exercises can help you navigate a new pathway between *effort* and *effortlessness*, tension and relaxation—the problem that Carlos's question posed.

Both of these exercises should be done in about fifteen or twenty minutes, and both should be carried out in complete silence. I suggest trying the Container exercise first, and then, after a few minutes' rest, progressing right into the Kiss. If you are working in a group, it can be useful to do this work in a semidarkened room.

The Container (3.4)

1. To begin this River, find a safe place on the floor and curl your body into a huddled position. You can be kneeling or lying on your side in any position that allows you to feel as though your body is confined.

2. The premise is that your body is contained by something, something literal. Your work is to "discover" the image by using your body, by pressing outward against the container, trying to find an exit. It is important that you work with all the parts of your body, with the back of your neck and your pelvis and legs as well as with your arms. You are pushing, clawing, biting, scraping, wriggling your way out through the container, discovering as you do just what it is that holds you. There is no right or wrong solution to this problem; what is important is that you engage fully in the struggle, that you let yourself keep trying things, and that you trust whatever you discover. Use your eyes to help you to "see" what is there and to help you be specific.

3. When you have "escaped," or exited, from whatever was holding your body so tightly at first, you have more space, and the exercise continues. You are again in some sort of container; that is, there is some other piece of imagery that you must actively engage. Again you use your full body to work your way out, allowing yourself to accept and to work with all the details of texture, material, or life that you discover.

4. And so on. Each time you exit from one piece of imagery, you find yourself in another, and each time the image "contains" you so that you must actively engage it in order to progress.

5. The most important thing is to keep using all the parts of your body and to trust what you find.

6. Work for fifteen or twenty minutes. And when you have finished, stop, close your eyes, and give yourself some private time to digest what you have encountered.

The Kiss (3.5)

1. To begin the Kiss exercise, again find a safe place on the floor, but this time begin the exercise either in a high kneel or standing—that is, in some position that leaves you open, rather than curled up. While you work you may find yourself moving into other positions, but be careful if you lie down on the floor that you do not collapse or give in completely to gravity.

2. The premise of this exercise is that a kiss is touching your body, and the kiss moves over your skin. You can use your *plastique* isolations to help you be specific about where the kiss is and how it is touching you, but unlike the Container work in which you were <u>engaging</u> the image, here you are <u>opening</u> yourself to it, allowing it to come to you. Your choices are choices of <u>permission</u> rather than of <u>effort</u>. But again, the most important things you need to do are trust what you find, allow what happens to happen, and stay open to receiving the image.

3. Sometimes during this exercise you may feel like closing your eyes. If you do, try to open them again. See if you can allow yourself to actually see your imagery, to be specific about who or what is kissing you.

4. At the end of fifteen or twenty minutes, stop, hunker, and allow yourself to remember your experience.

EFFORT, OPENNESS, AND IMAGERY

Often you must be totally exhausted in order to break down the mind's resistance and begin to act with truth. However, I do not mean that you have to be a masochist. . . . do not always seek sad associations of suffering, of cruelty. Seek also the bright and luminous. Often we can be opened by sensual recollections of beautiful days. . . . This is often more difficult than to penetrate into the dark stretches, since it is a treasure we do not wish to give. But often this brings the possibility of finding confidence in one's work, a relaxation which is not technical but which is founded on the right impulse.

—Grotowski, *Towards a Poor Theatre*

In my acting class, the work on the Container and the Kiss is intense, but these two exercises inspire very different experiences in different actors. Peter is energized by the Container work. His body literally "fights tooth and nail" with the images he encounters, and he seems to relish the details of each task: a hole in the first imaginary container, which he must enlarge with his elbow; a heavy weight on his shoulders in another; and in a third, a living substance that covers his legs and that he must kick away with all his strength. Sandra, on the other hand, seems defeated by her Container images; she is so trapped by her first one that she spends almost the whole time struggling with it, and ends up exhausted.

In her Kiss River, however, Sandra revels in sensual pleasure. Every once in a while, a great smile spreads across her face; sometimes she even laughs. Veronica's Kiss River, on the other hand, seems quite the opposite. She looks uncomfortable; she starts and stops fitfully, and finally she just gives up.

When we stop to talk, there is a long silence. Finally Sandra says, "I *hated* that Container exercise. I didn't understand what to do. I don't know if I have ever felt so angry in my life. And then I just wanted to give up and cry, it seemed so hopeless."

"And what happened at the end?"

"At the end, I was just grateful that it was over. And then I had this strange thought, like 'What was all *that* about?' I mean there was nothing containing me, so what was I so upset about? It was like I had been hypnotized or something. It was very strange. And it occurred to me that this work might be useful someday when I have to play some weird part in a grade B horror film."

"Or maybe Lady Anne in *Richard III*. There are some very good plays that require some terrible imagery, too."

"But that would mean entering that oppressive emotional space night after night, wouldn't it?"

"Yes," I said. "That's what actors do. . . . And what about the Kiss?"

"I'd rather not say."

"It's easier to talk about what's unpleasant than what's pleasurable?"

"Maybe."

"Pleasurable?" says Veronica. "What are you supposed to do if your imagery keeps . . . attacking you? Do you just have to take it?"

"No."

"So what do you do?"

"Well, the basic problem we are confronting here is the problem of sticking with your imagery, of learning that you can, indeed, stand it. But, at the same time, you can use your knowledge of the *plastiques* to help you do so. For instance, you can restrict what part of your body you are working with. I don't know exactly what your experience was, but, for instance, if the kisses you imagine keep transforming into monster kisses, you might find that if you restrict your *plastiques* and their imagery to your feet, then you can live with the monster."

"Okay, but what if I want to find something pleasurable, like Sandra did?"

"Well, you remember the Image Walks we did the other day? Were any of those images pleasant for you?"

"The ice cream. I liked the ice cream. It was pistachio."

"Well, you might just have to begin with pistachio ice cream then, instead of a kiss. What would it be like for you to create a River dealing with ice cream? You know this Kiss image was just the teacher's idea. It's an image that allows many people to be receptive. But if it doesn't work for you, you may have to begin with something else."

"And what if you have the opposite problem?" Carlos asks. "What if it all seems terribly tame or technical?"

"Then maybe you need the opposite solution."

"Meaning?"

"Well, I told Veronica she might restrict the kiss to just her feet. If, on the other hand, you work with the image of a kiss moving gently up the inside of your thighs, it is very likely that you will find much more happening to you."

One way of comparing the Container and the Kiss is to observe that one exercise engages the *outside* of your limbs while the other touches their inner surfaces. In the Container you press outward with the backs of your arms and legs; you kick outward and push with the back of your head. In the Kiss, on the other hand, you expose your inner arms and thighs, and you open your hands to receive. Or, to return to the question of tension and effort, you could say that in the Container exercise the power of the imagery arises in direct proportion to the *effort* with which you work, while in the Kiss you use the *plastiques* with precision and gentleness rather than with effort. Here the *plastiques* interact with imagery not by resisting it but by inviting it in. And the power of the experience depends on your allowing yourself to be open and receive.

So now you can see that the *plastiques* actually function in two ways simultaneously:

• **First they are *initiators*,** keys, specific forms that you can use to open the doors of your image/emotional life. When nothing is happening, you can use a *plastique* to get your engine going. **The *plastiques* are a method by which you can enlist your voluntary muscle system to turn on or to alter your image and emotional world.**

• **But at the same time, the *plastiques* are also *containers*** that allow you to shape the energies of your impulse and image life, muscular controls that permit you to expand or contract or make the gestural forms that disclose your private imagery to the world more specific.

One way to think about the *plastiques* is as external traces of the actor's inner, emotional life. Yet they are not simply emotion-filled movement. They are gestures that call up an image from within us. They exist at the interface between two simultaneous energies, one of which—the image—is treated as if it were external, while the other—the emotional impulse (or reaction to the image)—seems to come from within. Together these twin energies open us to our emotional life while at the same time providing a vehicle for it, a container that makes it safe for us to experience and to express the emotion.

PHYSICAL ACTING AND "SERIOUS" ACTING

*A lot of the people who are doing body work are aware of
the fact that memory is in the muscle, even sense memory.
Therefore, you can trigger it from the outside in as well as
from the inside out.*

—John Strasberg, in Mekler,
The New Generation of Acting Teachers

After class, Joan takes me aside. "I need to speak to you,"
she says with a tone that lets me know something is seriously
bothering her. We arrange to meet during the lunch break.

When we are alone she begins, "I don't want you to misun-
derstand. I like your class, really. I was afraid when I started
this work that I would find it too strenuous or something. But I
don't. I actually enjoy it. And I like finding that my body can do
things I didn't know it could. I even ended up enjoying those
Tiger Leaps. . . ."

"But . . . ?"

"But I just don't see what all this body work has to do with
acting—you know, with doing real plays. I'm afraid that it will
just lead me into habits I don't want."

"Such as?"

"Well, you know, like melodramatic acting, like doing
everything so large that it isn't *real* at all. I'm afraid of that
because that's what I used to do in high school. At the time it
was fun, and then I saw a videotape of myself and I realized
what I had been doing, and I hated it. And when I began to
study serious acting, it was a great relief to find that I could
have *real* feelings and even cry *real* tears, you know."

"And it seems to you that if you do large, full-body work, you
won't have real emotions?"

"Yes."

"I understand. I'd like you to raise this problem in class

tomorrow, because there may be others who are having the same trepidations about this work. But right now I want to assure you that the work we are doing will not require you to give up any technique that already works for you. You studied at the Strasberg Institute, right?"

"Yes."

"And you found that sense memory exercises worked for you?"

"Yes."

"You worked with the famous coffee cup?"

"Yes. And it was wonderful for me the first time I felt I could actually feel the warmth of the cup and taste the coffee."

"And emotional memory, too?"

"Yes. I found that when I really relaxed, it was not hard for me to find strong memories for myself."

"Good. Can you describe for me the room in which you slept as a child?"

"Right now?"

"Yes."

"Well, my bed was against the wall opposite the door." As she speaks, Joan looks off to her left.

"And where was the door?"

"Over there." She gestures to the far left.

"Did your mother ever stand in that doorway?"

After a moment's pause, Joan smiles and says, "Yes, right there, with her hand on the doorknob."

"What's she saying?"

"She's saying, 'Joanie, I am going to tell you one more time to clean up this room. And I swear if it is not clean by four o'clock today, I will go through it myself, and what I put in the garbage will stay in the garbage!'"

"And then what happens?"

"And then I say, 'Get out of my room!' and I slam the door on her. Really hard."

"How hard?"

"Like this," she says, pushing her arms away from her body. "Oh, no!" Joan exclaims, suddenly upset.

"What is it?"

"I just remembered: I caught her fingers in the door. She was really hurt, too." As she tells me this, Joan bites her lip. She seems to be on the edge of tears.

"Could you repeat that?"

"What?"

"How you responded to her."

"I said, 'Get out of my room!'" Joan repeats, but this time she does not seem quite so upset.

"What was different?"

"I don't know."

"Try it again."

Again she yells at her mother, but again she does not seem very moved.

"Perhaps the difference is that you have not been doing the arm gesture. See what happens if you try it with the push on the door."

Joan repeats the line, this time with a little push of her hands, but again she experiences no strong emotion.

"Here," I say, "use my arm as the door. Now push hard as you say the line."

"Get out of my room!" Joan yells as I resist her shove. This time her voice is more vibrant and suddenly she is in tears again.

"Good," I say. "That's it. You see, the work we will be doing is in many ways the same work you call emotional memory and sense memory work. The difference is that we do not do it relaxing in a chair. We do it with our bodies active because **memories are not encoded only in our brains; they are trapped in our muscles, too.** By working with your arms, you reconnect with a part of that memory, not as a past event, but as a living action. What we are doing now is just freeing up our bodies to do that work."

"But does that mean that to find that emotion I have to do that big shoving gesture?"

"Perhaps."

"But what if the scene I am doing is very quiet, or naturalistic? Or what if my character would never make a gesture like that?"

"Ah, but *finding* a gesture is not the same as *performing* it. Just as doing the research for a term paper is not the same as writing it. The work we are studying now is about how to do the research. The writing comes later."

"Okay," Joan says. "You know I'm really not trying to be difficult. But what I just did was a little, ordinary gesture: pushing a door closed. Not a headstand or a leap or writhing on the floor in some imaginary Container. I don't have a problem doing a little gesture like that. But I keep thinking that all of this big body work is . . . too much."

"I understand," I say. "Tomorrow let's begin class with that question."

BAD ACTING

The operetta and vaudeville make the best school for actors. It was not for nothing that our old actors always began their careers in the operetta or in vaudeville. Without overburdening the soul with deep emotions, without attempting the solution of problems too difficult for young actors, the light genre demands a tremendous amount of outward technique.

—Stanislavski, *My Life in Art*

When we speak of the style of Chekhov, we really mean the style of Stanislavski's productions of Chekhov's plays. In fact, Chekhov himself protested about this when he said: "I wrote vaudevilles, and Stanislavski has staged them as sentimental dramas."

—Grotowski, "Le théâtre est une rencontre"

The next day I ask Joan to explain to the class the doubts she had expressed to me privately. Some of the other students respond that they have been so glad to be using their bodies while acting, rather than sitting in chairs, that they have not been worried about where this work was leading. But Carlos agrees with Joan. "I haven't wanted to say it because I know I'm always objecting to things," he begins. "But it's true. The other day I tried to explain to a friend of mine what we are doing in this class, and he said, 'Oh, yeah, I've heard about that work. You take off all your clothes and roll around on the floor.'"

"And what did you tell him?" I ask.

"I joked about the naked bodies image exercises, and I said we hadn't really taken off our clothes . . . yet. But I really couldn't tell him what any of the rolling around had to do with acting a scene. And in the back of my mind I realized that I was afraid that this stuff we've been doing might be good for commedia dell'arte or something, but not for regular American acting. I mean sometimes, like when we're doing the Cat and everyone is kicking violently, I do worry that it's all just . . . well, you know . . . bad acting."

"First of all," I respond, "I need to say that I don't think you are 'always objecting to things.' Your mind hits doubt and you express it. We cannot work here if you do not feel safe expressing your doubts.

"Then, I want to remind you that we *will* get to scene work very soon, and I hope that when we do the connections between this physical preparation and the scene work will become clear. But there is something else that you and Joan are talking about here that bears looking at: the question of *bad acting*. For better or worse we all have some prejudices or at least some opinions about what is *good acting* and what is *bad acting*. So we're going to take a little pause in our training curriculum today to do some good acting . . . and some bad acting."

Everyone looks pleased and excited as I hand out copies of the scripts . . . until they look at the text.

"What *is* this stuff?" Sandra asks.

"I copied it from a love story magazine. We could use some-thing with more substance, but I've found that this sort of junk works well for this exercise. Okay. I need four people. Two of you will do the acting, and two of you will be prompters. You just feed the actors their lines, okay?"

After four students get up to work, I explain the exercise:

• The two prompters will read the lines to the actors, one by one, phrase by phrase, so the actors don't have to worry about memorizing anything.
• We will go through the scene twice. The first time I want the two actors to simply do *bad acting*, the worst acting they can, whatever that means.
• The second time through, do *good acting*.

It takes about half an hour for everyone to try the exercise. During the *bad acting* versions, a few of the students manage to invent really boring, lifeless styles of bad acting, but most of the class overacts enormously, throwing themselves on their knees at moments of pathos, spreading their arms with joy, and speaking loudly with voices full of (false) emotion. The perfor-mances are often absurd and exaggerated, but they are enter-taining and fun to watch.

During the *good acting* versions, however, something remarkable happens. The actors' arms never move. Their bod-ies only occasionally take a few steps, and their voices are barely audible. Every once in a while one or another of them seems to be playing a real emotion. But even then, they play the scene so very tentatively that the performances are only rarely interesting to watch.

After the exercise we sit down to discuss what happened.

Carlos immediately points out that this was an impossible exercise. "You can't do good acting like that, with no prepara-tion."

"I admit it," I say. "It is a false situation . . . although if you ever do a cold reading for an audition, you will be expected to do just that: good acting with no preparation. But even if I agree that the task of doing instant good acting is harder than doing instant bad acting, still you have to admit that most of the time the bad acting was simply much more exciting to watch than the good. Why was that?"

Several students point out that during the bad acting, people used their voices and bodies fully, while in the good acting everyone stood stock still. "If it had been a silent movie or a dance performance," says Sandra, "it would have been even more obvious. The 'good' scenes were all visually boring, even when the acting actually *was* good."

"Well, I know what the difference was for me being up there," adds Brian. "It was really clear: When I was supposed to be 'good,' I kept worrying about whether I was. In the 'bad acting,' there was nothing to lose because if it was 'bad,' that was good. That made it much easier to be free. Especially with my voice. When I had to do the good acting, I could hear how quiet my voice was, but I just didn't dare be really loud because I was afraid it would sound like . . ."

"What?"

"Like acting."

"Yes," I say. "So there are two related issues here: One is the question of judgment. It is very hard to do *anything* creative when you feel you must look over your shoulder all the time worrying about whether what you are doing is good or bad. Judgments often inhibit our work, and the first step toward freeing ourselves from judgment is just to be aware of it. Later in our training we will find some strategies for coping with judgment head-on.

"But there is another issue: somehow we have all learned that anything big or loud or fun on stage is bad."

"But theater isn't just a matter of whether or not something is fun," Carlos protests. "It is also a matter of whether it is believable, whether it seems real."

"You mean to say it isn't real to throw yourself down on your knees when you are pleading, right?"

"Exactly. I mean I'm often pleading . . . but I never throw myself down on my knees."

"Yes," I say, "exactly. We have come to assume that what we don't do on an everyday basis in our lives is not real. But in fact the small, immobile kind of activity that we have come to think of as real is no more realistic than full-body movement is."

To illustrate what I mean, I describe to my class two children I had recently observed. The first was a three-year-old boy I'd watched as he played near a swimming pool. When his mother told him to move away from the edge of the pool, he became furious. He raised his arms over his head, bent from the waist, and hit the ground with his hands. Then he picked up a long stick and heaved it into the pool. And what was he so violently, so "melodramatically" angry about? Was he a king, like Lear, whose daughters had thrown him out into the raging storm? No, he was just a kid whose mother had told him not to get so close to the swimming pool. Yet each of his gestures had been enormous. Each had involved his whole body, and each had been perfectly "melodramatically" and "unrealistically" suited to express his emotions.

The second child was a girl of about seven whom I'd seen waiting at an airport with her mother for the father to arrive. She was dressed in a fancy wide skirt, and as her expectation was building, the open space must have beckoned to her, for she ran to the center of the waiting area and started to spin. And as she spun, she noticed the skirt fanning out around her, and the smile on her face grew even wider. There was nothing extraordinary going on. She was just happy. How strange, it seemed to me, that we don't *all* spin when we feel happy. How strange that we have come to think of that sort of physical emotionality as "unreal."

When I finish these stories I point out to my class that neither of these children was "overacting" when they employed such extravagant full-body movements to express their inner lives. "They were both acting realistically and naturalistically.

It is *we* who have learned to restrict our understanding of what is natural or real."

"But what if you are acting in a naturalistic production," Sandra begins, "and the director doesn't want you expressing your joy by spinning around the middle of the stage?"

"What you will find is that once you've permitted your body its full expressiveness, it is quite easy to cut back on the size of your actions to keep some of that energy inside. The problem we are dealing with here is that we use our *idea* of what is real or natural to interfere with our ability to get in touch with that energy in the first place.

"In our 'bad acting' exercise, what made the 'bad' performances more interesting than the 'good' ones was not the fact that the acting was bad, but the fact that it was full of energy. What made it bad was that its energetic gestures were not filled with emotional truth. So a great deal of our work will be about exactly that: how to fill your work with emotional truth. But we must remain aware that **the task is finding strong emotional life with which to fill our powerful and expressive bodies . . . rather than cutting back on the power of our physical expression to fit within our shrunken sense of truth**.

"Maybe," I say, turning back to Carlos, "your friend was right when he said that what we do here is 'take off all our clothes and roll around on the floor.' But the clothes we take off are not the material ones; they are the cloaks of fear and the veils of judgment we carry that limit our definition of what is *real*."

Keeping your acting small and naturalistic does not make it more real; it just keeps your risks reduced, and your lack of emotion less obvious. But at the same time it carries with it the real danger of making your performance boring. Many American actors have scaled down their sense of what is real to fit within the categories created by film acting: either long-shot physical action scenes with lots of speed and movement, or close-up emotional scenes filled with subtly changing facial expressions. One result of this limitation is that American actors often have a hard time with Shakespeare or with the Greeks. But it is not just these classics that require full-bodied acting on stage. The plays of Edward Albee and Caryl Churchill and Sam Shepard all require actors who can throw their whole bodies into their work.

American acting teachers have started to wrestle with this misunderstanding of realism, and its consequence: disembodied acting. Richard Hornby points out that "Realism . . . is . . . not stylelessness, nor the basis for other styles, but simply one acting style among many" [Hornby, p. 214]. And in his acting book, Sanford Meisner tells an actor who is playing everything very small:

> Begin working on this problem by allowing yourself to overdo it. . . . If you want to throw yourself on the floor and chew a leg of that table, it's fine with me. It's undignified, it's unmanly, it's ungentlemanly—but it's very good for your acting. [Meisner, p. 116]

Of course, this does not mean that *all* physical choices must be large. The following lesson takes us in the opposite direction: using our physical awareness to capture the smallest flickerings of human emotion.

THE "JUST STAND" EXERCISES

Wanting to be an actor means that you agree to be looked at and that it gives you pleasure to exist and feel in front of an audience.

—Andrei Belgrader, in Mekler,
The New Generation of Acting Teachers

Non-action does not mean doing nothing and keeping silent. Let everything be allowed to do what it naturally does, so that its nature will be satisfied.

—Chuang Tzu

We have approached physical acting from several angles. First we looked at the *plastiques* as simple, physical isolations, ways in which to activate one or another body part by voluntary choice. Then we noticed how body movements could be activated by physical impulses that moved from place to place, and we added the eyes and examined how these moving impulses were related to images. We examined what happened when we allowed imagery itself to be the source of our Rivers. Finally, we explored ways in which sticking with imagery and playing with effort and noneffort could affect our experience. This exploration led us into an examination of tension, and we discovered that habitual tensions like raised shoulders or a tight jaw can contain long-hidden emotional life, parts of our experience that we can choose to explore by purposefully engaging the tensions we encounter.

But not all tensions are so deeply ingrained in body rigidities. Many tensions arise in the moment as the result of small, self-protective physical habits. As we sit down in a chair, for instance, perhaps we cross our legs or unconsciously wrap our feet around the chair legs. When we stand, we may hold our hands behind our back or thrust them into our pockets. What are these small obsessions? And can we learn to tap even these eddies of habituated energy and to turn them into sources for our art?

The very first theater game that Viola Spolin teaches at the beginning of her book *Improvisation for the Theater* is an exercise she calls "Exposure." To start this game, Spolin sends half of her acting class on stage, saying to them simply, "You look at us. We'll look at you."

"Those on stage," Spolin writes, "will soon become uncomfortable. . . . When each person on stage has shown some degree of discomfort, [I] give the group that is standing a task to accomplish. Counting is a useful activity, since it requires focus." [Spolin, p. 51]. In this way, Spolin teaches her actors that they can relieve themselves of their fears of "exposure" by becoming "absorbed in what they are doing." The exercise is Spolin's way of introducing actors to Stanislavski's "circle of concentration" through which they learn to exclude distracting stimuli from their awareness.

But recall that in the section called "A Balancing Act" we found that there was another way to achieve this kind of centering, a method of *in*cluding rather than *ex*cluding the energies of distraction. Similarly, there is an opposite way in which to use Spolin's Exposure exercise, a version I call **Just Stand** (3.6 and 3.7).

I start the exercise by telling my class that each actor will stand alone for sixty seconds in front of the group. "You just stand here for a minute, and during that time, **don t try to do anything**. Stay present with us, don't close your eyes or look over our heads. But don't try to *do* anything. I will say 'start,' and sixty seconds later I will say, 'stop.' That's it."

Note: If you the reader want to attempt this exercise, don't read any further until you have done it . . . so you can have the joy of discovery, unalloyed by images of what happened to the actors in my class.

In my acting class, each student takes a turn in front of the

---

Just Stand #1 (3.6)

To do this exercise, you'll need four or five people—enough so that when you stand in front of them, you will feel watched. As each one of you does the exercise, someone else should act as timekeeper.

The directions are just to stand in front of the audience for one minute, and don't try to <u>do</u> anything.

group. And then, when everyone has finished, I ask everyone to gather in groups of four or five to discuss what happened for them. "First talk only about your own experience," I say. "And then, when each one of you has spoken in the first person, you can talk about what you saw in others."

Afterward, when the full group gathers together again, several people report that while they were "just standing" they felt extremely aware of internal sensations.

"My knees," says Sandra. "I kept thinking, 'Can't they all see my knees are shaking?'"

Peter reports, "I could feel my heart beating in my chest."

"I wanted to smile," says Veronica, "but I didn't think I was allowed to."

Carlos believes he has found a flaw in the rules. "It's impossible not to do anything. The more you try to do nothing, the more you have to *do* something to do nothing."

"But I was very careful in my directions," I protest. "I did not say, '*Do nothing.*' What I said was, 'Don't *try* to *do* anything.'"

"You mean it was a setup?"

"Well, to some degree. The thing is that we are so used to *doing* things, that even when given an opportunity to do *nothing*, it is easier for us to interpret that opportunity as a requirement to *do nothing* than a chance not to do anything."

"You could definitely see people trying," points out Aisha. "Sandra, you kept looking like you were going to smile, and then you would suppress it. And Peter, you too."

"I know," says Peter. "And your feet, Aisha."

"My feet, what about my feet?"

"Yeah," says Brian, "I saw that too. Her toes kept going up and down."

"I knew I should have kept my shoes on," Aisha jokes, because today she had actually spent several minutes methodically removing her shoes as part of her warm-up.

"So," I say, "one obvious thing is, there is a great deal going on for you when there is nothing going on. In fact, it actually takes a great deal of energy to do 'nothing.' Stifling giggles, suppressing smiles, hiding twitches, even just standing there when your knees are shaking—all these *non*-activities require energy.

"But the energy you use to *suppress* what is happening to you is energy that is lost to your acting. What would happen if instead of trying to do *nothing*, you simply *allowed* everything that was happening to you to happen? At first you may find that it takes a little effort to do this allowing, because we are all so used to suppressing what is happening to us, but after a while, you will sense how easy it is to just let what happens happen, rather than trying so hard to *do* nothing."

This time as the students work, I coach them from the side. When Veronica's smile begins to show, I encourage her to let the feeling move down through her body. As she does, the smile turns into a grimace, her hands become fists, and then her body seems to push the audience away. When Sandra stands, I urge her to let her knees really shake. As she does, the knees also turn inward, and when I say, "Let your whole body do what your knees are doing," her hands move down her stomach and cover her crotch. Then she lowers her face and starts to look away. "Even as you feel like turning away, peek out at us," I say. "The energy of this gesture comes from seeing that you are

---

Just Stand #2 (3.7)

1. Again stand facing the audience. But this time, if, for instance, you notice that you are beginning to smile, allow that smile to spread across your whole face, to your shoulders, your arms, your stomach, your knees. Let your whole body smile.

2. Then, let it go, return to center, and wait for the next thing to happen.

3. The next thing to happen might be just a sigh, or straightening your clothes, or pushing back your hair. Whatever it is, let it spread through your whole body while keeping your eyes on the audience.

4. Then again, let it go.

5. Notice how each time you let one impulse go, another appears.

6. For a minute or so, let the impulses appear, let them spread, and let them go.

seen." Sandra's invisible knee tremor has been transformed into an icon of embarrassment. When Brian stands, he also begins to smile, but his smile is different from Veronica's; when he allows it to spread, it grows into a sexy invitation. His hips move sideways, his eyes narrow, and his hands beckon. When Aisha works, the little toe wiggle grows into petulant foot stamping. Joan stands quite collectedly at first; she is barely straightening the hem of her shirt. But when I urge her to extend that little gesture of composure, it grows into an enormous effort to pull the shirt all the way down to her feet, covering her whole body.

So, one by one, as the actors explore these minute, everyday patterns of social gestures, the energies that lie hidden within them reveal their inner life: Some smiles prove to be veiled versions of sensual leers; others turn out to be masks for naked aggression. And gestures as offhand as the straightening of a shirt reveal great reservoirs of fear. This *empty* activity of "just standing" in front of an audience turns out to be very *full* indeed.

And this exercise contains a second great surprise: the experience is wonderfully enjoyable for both the audience and the performer. The revelatory act of *showing* "embarrassment" proves to be much less painful than trying to hide it! Now all the energy the actor had used in trying to keep the corners of his mouth from smiling, or his hands from covering his groin, is available for him to work with. At the end of the class, it is Peter who sums up this experience saying, "God, I've always thought that embarrassment and stage fright were the most terrible things that could happen to you on stage. I never thought that they could ever be a positive experience."

Acting teacher Warren Robertson puts it this way:

Energy is neither good nor bad. It is all life. And if you interfere with one kind of energy, you somehow interfere with all of it. . . . The energy behind fear is the same energy we laugh with and cry with. [Mekler, p. 114]

What we are used to calling stage fright is the energy of feeling watched. In other words, it is the essential energy of performance itself. And it is the same substance whether you call it stage fright or just energy. The Just Stand exercise is thus a performance application of our study of "A Balancing Act." It is an aikido way of acting, a way of transforming the powerful energy of fear, an energy we usually oppose as an energy, into a creative source.

After the Just Stand exercise, I have my class enter *plastique* Rivers once again, this time using the energy of everyday gestures and of feeling seen among their sources of inspiration. This time their Rivers are subtler and richer than before, and it is clear that their whole concept of what a *plastique* and a River are has become more inclusive. A *plastique* is no longer just a particular body isolation; it can be any body movement that is filled with emotional awareness. A River may include gymnastic headstands, but it may also contain ordinary, quotidian gestures, nervous habits, and even invisible, interior movements, as long as these elements are connected with imagery.

At the end of the day I recapitulate our work. "You have now seen that your Rivers can find their origins in at least four sources:

1. physical and emotional impulses,
2. image life,
3. mechanical choices, and
4. everyday, unconscious gestures.

"And these sources constantly flow into each other, transforming more and more of your inner life into physical expression, and permitting every moment of your muscular activity to impinge upon your inner being. Now we must add exterior sources, other actors. And then we will be ready to add text."

BODILY EMOTIONS

With faith in your physical actions you will feel emotions, akin to the external life of your part, which possess a logical bond with your soul. . . . Your body is biddable; feelings are capricious. Therefore if you cannot create a human spirit in your part of its own accord, create the physical being of your role.

—Stanislavski, *Creating a Role*

In order to stir an emotion an actor must be capable of finding the muscle to which that emotion is connected. The process requires a great deal of practice, exercise, and experimentation. The actor's body must be trained to achieve the highest degree of sensitivity. Once he has reached that level of psychophysical harmony, a movement of the right muscle will trigger the truthful emotion.

—Sonia Moore, *Stanislavski Revealed*

At this point in our work, our acting curriculum turns aside from the body work itself. But before we abandon the *plastiques*, it may be useful to take a moment to examine the physical-emotional connections that underlie this work.

One hundred years ago William James took up an idea first proposed by Danish physiologist Carl Georg Lange: that "we feel sorry because we cry, angry because we strike, [and] afraid because we tremble" [James, p. 450]. In James's most famous example—running from a bear—he theorized that we first respond physically to danger by starting to run, and only then do we identify the sensation of flight as what we call fear. James's idea that our emotions are the *result* of our physiological reactions rather than the *cause* of them has often been derided by psychologists, but it points to an important fact: that body-movement can, indeed, trigger our emotional life, especially if it is connected with an image—in this case, the bear.

In the 1940s, psychoanalyst Wilhelm Reich went further by suggesting that what psychoanalysts call "repression" (the unconscious forgetting of traumatic memories) operates by employing muscular tension to "hold" emotional memories within our bodies. In his analytic practice, Reich demonstrated that these feelings can be accessed and released by muscular means.

Similarly, in the work we have been studying, the *plastiques* can serve as muscular reminders, provocations, goads that stimulate submerged feelings to surface once again. By observing the images and emotions that pour through us as we work with our bodies, we begin to "know" ourselves, and we can begin to catalogue the particular physical keys that open our personal emotional doorways.

Because each of our histories is different, there is no one gesture that will provoke the same emotional connection for everyone. (This is why François Delsarte could not create a lexicon of standardized gestures that would serve all actors.) But the human body's mechanisms of muscular memory are universal, and since many of us have undergone similar experiences of repression in our lives, many of us have built up similar muscular defense mechanisms. So it is possible to point to some patterns that can serve as signposts during your personal search for body-emotional connections. For instance, many of us were admonished to "be quiet!" when we screamed and stamped our feet as children, so even now gestures of biting and kicking can stimulate the release of our anger. And since almost all of us once had to strain upward toward our mother, most people can locate wellsprings of unrequited yearning by reaching into the air with open arms.

In offering the following hints, I am *not* suggesting that I believe that an actor's central task is to find emotion. In the end, emotional life is not something you *do*; it is something that must happen *to* you. But the following paragraphs are guides for the actor who wishes to use physical means to explore his or her access to particular emotions. They include suggestions gleaned from work with hundreds of actors. But they are not prescriptions. They are merely entry points for your own search.

IN SEARCH OF ANGER

Parents, teachers, cops, and religious figures in our society often teach us to repress or hide our anger. They instill this lesson with two kinds of fear: the external fear that we will be punished for being too loud or too violent, and the inward fear that we will be held accountable if we injure someone with our anger, that is, guilt. Thus for many of us the greatest difficulty we have in expressing anger is feeling safe from both of these forms of retaliation if we unleash the rage we contain. So in order to explore anger we must first create for ourselves an environment that can safely absorb the energy we will be putting out, an environment that can "take it" without striking back. Several physical forms can be used to do this:

• Try any form that provides strong resistance against which the muscles can strain. The Cat, slow motion *plastique* work, and the Container exercise all offer external impediments that can enable us to let go of our internal restraints.

• Often a great deal of anger is stored in the lower body, so kicking or pushing with the legs, like the kicks we do in the Cat, can be very freeing. What allows the Cat kicks to serve this purpose is the combination of built-up isometric tension and the release *toward* a particular image. Another good way to begin releasing this energy in the legs is to push with the soles of your feet against another person's feet.

• Work standing with the knees bent. Bending the knees helps "unlock" the pelvis, which allows the energies in the legs to be felt in the upper body and voice. The "stomping" work taught by Tadashi Suzuki can also empower the aggressive energies of the lower body to flow.

• Work beyond fatigue. If you do the Cat exercise or a *plastique* River beyond the first level of fatigue, the resistance of fatigue can help you access your anger. When you work this way, your anger may begin as frustration at the theater exercise itself, but once the emotion is flowing you will find that other imagery will quickly make itself available to you.

• Work with "angry" text. You may find that simply by speaking a speech filled with rage you can get in touch with feelings that otherwise evade you. The sounds and meanings of the words act as "Containers" for your voice, just as the pressure of gravity "contains" your body in the Cat.

• Work with another person (a friend or a teacher) whom you trust, pushing equally against each other. Begin back to back, simply pushing against each other and then adding sound. Or try sitting on the floor facing each other and pushing with the bottoms of your feet. If one of these positions works, continue to work with your real partner for a while and then move on to working with an "imaginary" partner who gives you resistance against your feet or back.

• Remember: If any of these forms begins to work for you, there is still another important step: to engage your eyes in the work. The eyes are often the final line of defense against knowing what or whom you are angry at. Often when people begin to open themselves to the energy of anger in the body and voice, their eyes will tend to look down or away, or they may even close. If you find this to be true for you, be patient with yourself, but reenter the work and bring your eyes to look in the direction in which your anger is expressing itself. Let yourself *look* to see who is there. Let yourself stay in contact with the image while the emotion flows through you. And then, finally, let yourself experience what comes *after* the anger. Sometimes there is grief or regret. Sometimes joy or relief. Allow yourself to enter this next emotion.

THE AFFINITY OF SORROW AND JOY

A flow of excitation along the front of the body from the heart to the mouth, eyes and hands will give rise to the feeling of longing expressed in an attitude of opening up and reaching out.

—Alexander Lowen, *Bioenergetics*

All children can laugh and cry fully, deeply, and suddenly, but most adults have lost this ability. Deep sorrow and pure joy both require a vulnerability and an openness of heart that most of us have learned to mask as part of the strange process we call "growing up." One of our primary defenses against these watery emotions is to hide our hearts by protecting our chests. Many men learn to tighten their chests specifically to defend themselves against the "weakness" of showing "childish" or "effeminate" emotions. And women, who are more often "permitted" to show vulnerability, may learn to tense their chests out of embarrassment about their breasts (they think their breasts are either too large or too small, and in any case they are an invitation to harassment). And whatever the source of our pectoral defenses, all of these armorings add to our difficulties in accessing tears and joy. Some of us protect our hearts by slightly hunching our shoulders, others by craning forward the neck and head, or by collapsing the center of our chest, into the sternum. Others "overcompensate," men by holding their chests high in military fashion, women by displaying décolletage.

Although joy and sorrow are very different from one another, the same pectoral tensions can block our access to both. Consequently, opening the chest is often the first step in releasing either of these emotions. And, as you can see in the news photos that accompany the text, the natural expressions of powerful joy and of overwhelming grief are remarkably similar.

IN SEARCH OF SORROW:

One place to begin your search is within the Cat. If while you perform the Undulation from the Head Down you press yourself slowly along just above the floor, the force of gravity itself will open your chest. Look upward and work with sound as you move forward. Another doorway into these emotions can be found by exploring the emotional life of the **Open Chest** (3.8).

The Open Chest (3.8)

1. Lean back gently, relax the chest, and reach up and forward with the arms as you did for the Kneeling Backbend (2.14) on page 69. Open your eyes and look up into the distance.

2. Or, to do the same thing standing, center yourself with your weight evenly distributed left and right, forward and back. Let your head rise up gently from the back of the skull. Breathe easily. Relax the jaw. Relax the facial muscles. (Smile for a moment.) Let the shoulders go. Relax the pelvic muscles so that the pelvis is not held back or forward. The knees are not locked.

3. Allow the arms to open and lift forward a few inches. Keep the wrists and elbows relaxed. Let the arms reach, slowly and gently, as if opening to the sky, as if feeling the sunlight or the rain coming to you. As if you were receiving a gift. Allow your gaze to be directed out and slightly upward. Relax across the face. Let your eyes relax so that they have peripheral vision. Breathe. Feel your chest open. Let your chest and your heart relax and open. Let yourself feel what you are feeling. Just feel it.

4. Let your arms reach out, but gently, without extra effort. Gently explore slightly varied angles for the elbows, the wrists, the hands.

5. Now reach out further, as if grasping for an image that is constantly receding into the distance. What or who is there?

6. We have not studied the voice yet, but often sound makes an effective entrée into feelings of sadness we have long locked away. Try whining: working with the eyebrows, placing the voice up in the head resonators, and playing falsetto sound. Find words to speak. (See the "Voice Work" chapter for more details.)

7. Reach with the arms as you play with these sounds.

8. Trust what you find. Be careful not to divert your eyes. If the image seems to recede from you, reach out further toward it.

9. Keep checking that you have not tightened your jaw, that your head is still floating up, that your pelvis is relaxed. Then try reciting some text, any speech that is not angry or defensive.

10. Explore this vocal work while performing the Kneeling Backbend, but without the backbend. Try working with the arms outstretched in front of you. See what happens if you slide the voice up into the head resonators while the chest remains relaxed and open.

IN SEARCH OF JOY

• Try opening and reaching as you did for sorrow, but this time allow the image you yearn for to move *toward* you, rather than away. Open your arms wider to welcome the image. Let it touch you.

• Enter the Kiss exercise, being sure to work only with those body parts that feel entirely safe.

• Working with a partner, take the time you need to relax, and then lie down with your head in your partner's lap. Allow your partner to feed you something very delicious while you do nothing but slowly chew the food, allowing the taste to penetrate your whole body.

One way to think about joy, is that it is not a feeling for you to find, but for you to be found *by*. It will often appear in the moment of relaxation after you have finished working on something else. But when it does arise, you need to notice: "Oh, I feel good about that," and allow yourself to receive it, working with very little tension.

IN SEARCH OF FEAR

Simply running will not produce fear, as William James proposed; but running from a madman waving a knife rarely fails.[2]

—Sonia Moore, *Stanislavski Revealed*

In our world, it is not uncommon for us live with a constant undercurrent of fear. It is one emotion that is actually encouraged by our society: fear of loss (of love, beauty, or youth) is encouraged by the advertising industry, while fear of strangers, fear of violence, and fear of Communists or terrorists are encouraged by the government and the media. The trouble is that while we are schooled to *feel* fear, at the same time we are trained not to *show* that we are feeling it. Therefore, in public (and onstage) many of us may have a hard time finding and showing genuine terror—the kind that Macbeth must experience at the sight of a ghostly dagger.

If you do have a hard time finding fear,

• Try running hard, in place, while periodically looking back over your shoulder to see what may be coming after you.

• Work with any impulses from behind you, things that happen to you that you cannot see.

• Try letting yourself work with images that are larger than you. Let them be absurd, nonsensical, strange. It does not matter if at first you do not "believe" what you are seeing. If you treat it as if it were real, your psyche will react.

• The Kiss exercise, as we mentioned above, can lead you to joy, but because it is so disarming it can also lead you to experience fear. Try beginning the Kiss, and then purposefully allowing the "kiss" to transform into something less benign.

---

2. I am not suggesting that running *creates* fear but that in the absence of a real bear, running serves to help the body recall the sensation of fear *if one also uses the eyes to look for a frightening image approaching from behind.*

Rather than thinking of these exercises as forms to practice in a vacuum, you may find it more useful simply to bear these forms in mind, so that when you find yourself stuck—when working on some text, for instance—you have some tools ready with which to attack the problem.

If you do try any of these suggestions, there are three central things to remember. One is that most emotions occur in layers, one below the other. For many of us, for instance, laughter lies like a thin sheet of ice over a great lake of tears, so if you hit embarrassed laughter (or even a grin) on the way to sadness, don't fight the giggles, give the laughter its space and let it play itself out. You do not need to "break through" to the tears; they will come to you in due time.

The second thing to remember is that our emotions are usually "personified." We do not dream of anger or love but of a person with whom we are angry or in love. Perhaps the reason you cannot "act an emotion" is that emotions are not intransitive verbs, but transitive ones: they rarely arise without a predicate, the *image* of someone at whom they are directed. The idea that emotion is linked with image is central to all work with the *plastiques*.

In one of his short stories, "The Three Dark Magi," the German writer Wolfgang Borchert describes how emotions and desires require images. The young married couple in the story, refugees in the midst of World War II, are freezing in a barn with their child. We listen to the man's thoughts:

> Now she's got her baby and has to freeze, he thought. But he had no one he could hit in the face with his fists because of it. As he opened the door of the stove, another handful of light fell on the sleeping face. The woman said softly: Look, like a halo, do you see? Halo! he thought, and had no one he could hit in the face with his fists.

The anger he feels at his circumstances inhabits the man's hands, just as, in our work, emotion lives within our bodies. But without an image, without a face to hit, that anger cannot express itself.

The third thing to keep in mind in doing this work is *patience*. At some point your body learned to protect you from certain emotions, and it probably did so for good reason. At that time, it must have seemed the only viable way to survive. You have managed well enough with this defense for many years, so it may take time to undo a habit that carries such weight. Don't push yourself into arenas that are simply uncomfortable for you. Another day, when you are listening to a piece of music or reading a book, the emotion you were searching for may suddenly accost you. And when it does, you will be prepared to notice it, to play with it, and to make it welcome in your body.

Listening

PARADOXES OF ACTING

*In every other art, particularly the plastic arts, the creator
and his creative personality, the material, the instrument,
and the work of art which is the end of the whole creative
process are separate one from the other, so that the material, the instrument, and the work itself stand* outside *the
creative personality.* Only in acting are the creative personality, the material, the instrument, and the work of art
itself combined in a single entity, being organically inca-
pable of separation.

—Alexander Tairov, *Notes of a Director*

At the beginning of our next class, Brian makes an observa-
tion: "I've been thinking that what made the last River different for me was not just that I was working with personal
gestures. It was also different because it was the first time I was
working off another person. I mean up to this point all the *plastique* and image work has been about reacting to stuff that is
really going on inside of *me*. But after the Just Stand exercise,
my River included *re*actions. It reminded me that when I studied Meisner technique, the basic lesson was about reacting to
others. So now I am wondering, are we supposed to be reacting
to each other or to our own images, or both?"

"What you are talking about," I begin, "is the third great
paradox of acting. The first paradox we encountered on the very

first day: the paradox of having 'serious fun.' The second paradox was the discovery we made during our warm-up lessons—that an actor must be both *in control* and *out of control* at the same time. This paradox reappears over and over in our art. When you do scene work it appears as the problem of saying memorized text as if you were making it up as you go along. And when we study character, it shows up as the problem of being both yourself and another person at the same time. And what you are describing now is the third great paradox of acting: that as an actor you must pay attention to what is going on *inside* you and what is going on *outside* you simultaneously. Every acting training system proposes a method for dealing with this paradox.

"In Meisner technique, you begin with the listening work and then you add an activity, first a physical activity and later an inner, emotional activity. Then you learn to balance your attention to the internal activity with your attention to your external partner.

"Our physical acting training confronts this paradox in a different way. **In this work you have been learning to see and experience your inner world *as if it were outside*.** So now as we begin to move on to the listening work you do not need to switch back and forth between two separate channels. Your partner is out there, but so is your inner imagery. Both signals come to you as if on the same wavelength, and both are signals to which you must react. In fact, in working on a scene you might say that what you are doing is perceiving your partner *through* your imagery. This process of 'screening' is similar to what some acting methods would refer to as 'substitution.' We will examine this more closely when we get to the Face Tracing exercise.

"So you are absolutely right, up until this point your image world was yours alone, but now, for the first time, you are starting to open yourself to work with signals from the outside. As Brian pointed out, in the Just Stand exercise the source of inspiration for your body work was no longer your own; it was the energy you received from the eyes of the audience. But before we try to combine the inner and outer signals, we will take a little break from our image body work to do an exercise that allows us to concentrate *entirely* on the external signal, entirely on the process of listening itself."

But just as I am about to teach the **I Feel** exercise (4.1), Peter asks with a smile, "And is there a *fourth* great paradox of acting?"

"Ah, yes," I reply, "the fourth great paradox of acting is that an actor must train himself to remain open, vulnerable, enthusiastic, and hopeful, while making a living waiting tables."

I FEEL

There are two basic principles involved here.... "Don't do anything unless something happens to make you do it...." "What you do doesn't depend on you; it depends on the other fellow."
—Sanford Meisner, *Sanford Meisner on Acting*

Like Meisner's Repetition exercise, the I Feel exercise (4.1) helps us to notice that as we listen to another person, our own inner life changes. And as our inner life changes, so does our relationship to and our needs from our partner. In a playscript this change of relationship and needs is called a beat change.[1]

After we play the I Feel game for a few minutes, I stop the game to ask if there are any questions.

Sandra wants to know, "Am I just expressing my *own* feel-

---

1. The word *beat* began as a misinterpretation of Stanislavski's term *bit*, the smallest unit of character action in a script. In our 1967 workshop Grotowski referred to "units of exchange," in which the actor gives something to his partner, to an object, or to some personification, and gets something back [Crawley, I. p. 5].

ings, or am I expressing the feeling that I have in reaction to what my partner said?"

"Yes," I say, "that is exactly the question here. And the answer is that you are simply naming the first thing you feel, whatever its source. Of course, if you really listen to your partner, what you feel will inevitably include your reaction to her. In fact, it is this very confusion that makes acting possible. You feel what *you* are feeling; you listen to your partner, and then you notice that *your* feelings have changed. Even if you are feeling something very powerful, if you really let yourself listen for a moment, your feelings will change."

"And what if they don't?" Joan asks. "What if I notice that I am having the same feeling several times over?"

"Then check that you are not literally holding on somehow, that you have not wrapped your toes around the chair, that you are not slumped down or leaning forward or gripping with your hands. As we have been learning, our muscles can quite literally contain our emotions, and we often unconsciously hold on to what we are feeling by tensing our muscles. Also make sure that when your partner is speaking, you are really taking in what he or she is saying. Another way in which we hold on to an emotion is simply by ignoring the signals that impinge upon us."

"Is it okay if what we come up with is pretty minor?" Brian asks. "I mean, with the *plastiques* I have been getting into some very strong emotions. And in this exercise it seems like I'm just laughing a lot."

"That's just fine. What you are working on here is just the experience of listening itself and noticing how the external signals instantly affect your internal state. Sitting like this in a chair you are deprived of the physical Containers for large emotions, so it is natural that what comes to the surface may seem to be minor. When we add our image and body work back in, you will find that you can have both instantaneous change and powerful emotions at the same time."

I Feel (4.1)

1. Sit in a chair, opposite a partner. Both of you take a moment to relax. Make sure that you are sitting up but not holding yourself stiffly, that you have not wrapped your toes around the chair, and that you are not holding on to the seat.

2. Make eye contact with your partner. If at any point you want to smile or laugh, that's fine, don't stop yourself.

3. Now, one of you says, "I feel ———," and completes the sentence. Just name whatever you are feeling. It may be something deep or something very minor, but whatever it is, you give it a name. If you can't find the right word, or don't want to say it, you can use gibberish.

4. As the first person speaks, the second person listens. Then the second person says, "I feel ———," while the first person listens.

5. The important thing is that after you speak, let go and really listen to the other person. And then, just name the first thing that arises within you.

6. If you say something and your partner does not respond, but you notice that you are feeling another feeling, you do not need to wait. Just name it, and then go on and listen again.

7. After playing for five minutes, stop and discuss with your partner how it went.

THE FIRST CROSSING

Our next exercise is called the **First Crossing** (4.2).[2] You might think of it as being exactly the same as the I Feel exercise, except that instead of speaking words, your vocabulary for expressing what you are feeling is a step: either a step toward or a step away from your partner. Your body stays relaxed and open as in the I Feel exercise, while the legs do the "speaking."

Note: *This exercise depends upon your making eye contact over a distance, so if you need to wear glasses to see your partner clearly at ten paces, put them on.*

Our eyes are very sensitive barometers of our feelings. If in

---

2. Adapted from Linda Putnam's "Slow Crossing" exercise.

the course of doing the First Crossing you try to take steps toward your partner more quickly than you are actually comfortable with, your eyes will automatically break contact for a second, so, to maintain eye contact, you are forced to be accurate about what you are feeling. Within a few minutes, you will probably start to notice that little things, like your partner's facial expression, can radically change your desire to step toward or away. If you feel that your partner is moving toward you too quickly, or that he moved toward you when he really wanted to move away, your body will react to that feeling. If you try to force yourself to step one way when you needed to move the other way, you will sense it immediately.

In other words, **in the First Crossing, *distance* takes on an emotional quality, and emotion itself is felt and expressed in terms of distance.** This translation, from emotion to action and vice versa, underlies all acting. And this sensitivity to spatial relationship can be a very useful tool for actors (see the section on "Viewpoints" on page 190).

The First Crossing (4.2)

1. Begin by going to the opposite side of the room from your partner, establishing a position about fifteen to twenty feet from each other. Turn away from your partner for a minute and check in with yourself: How am I feeling right now? Am I in touch with my body? Do I have any thoughts about this exercise or my partner? Then let these things go, and turn around.

2. When both of you have turned toward each other, make eye contact. The rule is that you maintain eye contact from now until the end of the exercise.

3. Now, one or the other takes a step, just one step, toward or away from the other. And then each of you, notice how you feel.

4. From then on, either person can step toward or away from the other at any time; just be sure that after each step you notice what you are feeling. If your partner moves, check in with yourself: Which way do you want to move now, toward or away?

5. If you don't know which way to move, don't hang out in indecision, just try taking a step toward or away. If you move the "wrong" way, you'll know it immediately; go ahead and step the other way. Risk making mistakes!

6. If at any time, one or the other of you breaks eye contact, both of you return to your starting positions and begin again.

7. If you and your partner get close enough to touch, the rules change: instead of steps, you now search for a way to touch each other that feels safe and comfortable, <u>without breaking eye contact</u> (no hugs). If while searching for a touch you feel you want to step back, do so. And if you and your partner never get close enough to touch, that's fine, just keep taking steps. If you find a satisfactory touch, you may stop the exercise and move to the side of the room to process the exercise with your partner. (Do not cut through another couple's eye contact as you do!)

8. After about fifteen minutes, stop the exercise and talk with your partner.

THE SECOND CROSSING

Sometimes an actor's first experience of doing a Crossing can be very profound. Because establishing eye contact is at once an extremely deep and a very delicate process, maintaining eye contact can cut through all the normal rules of social etiquette until, step by step, the actor and his partner find themselves communicating in an extremely honest way. At the same time, because the Crossing also translates inner experience into simple walking, it can also serve as a practical tool for the creation of stage movement and blocking—a tool to which we shall return when we begin our scene work. But since scenes are not confined to straight lines or continuous eye contact, we need to loosen the rules of the exercise a little.

LISTING 143

The Second Crossing (4.3)

1. This time, begin by standing a little closer to your partner, so that you have as much room to move <u>away</u> from each other as <u>toward</u> one another.

2. As in the First Crossing, allow yourself to feel the impulses to move toward and away from your partner. But now if you feel like moving away, you may actually turn away from your partner. If you want to break eye contact, do so on purpose. You may also take more than one step at a time.

3. If your partner turns her back on you, you may move around in front of her.

4. But be careful with all this freedom. Remember that the primary tasks are to keep noticing your reaction to your partner and to ask yourself, "Which way do I need to move now?" Even if you had the impulse to turn away from your partner, be sure that after you have done so, you let it go, so that you can truly receive what your partner is doing. This means you may need to "listen" with your back. Even when you break eye contact, you must stay as open and sensitive as you were when your eyes were locked with your partner's.

5. You may add more detail. Try changing "level": you will find that looking up to or down on your partner changes things radically. Try sitting, crawling, and lying down as well as standing. Try hand gestures. Eventually you may even add sound. But as you do so, be sure that you are still listening all the time and still letting go to notice "Which way do I need to move now?"

TWO-PERSON *PLASTIQUE* RIVERS

Every agreeable or disagreeable sight makes the body react backward.

—François Delsarte, *Delsarte System of Oratory*

The I Feel game and the Crossings are "empty" forms. They force us to be extremely open and sensitive to everything our partner does, and they make the changes of beat in our scene unmistakable, but they do not give us strong "Containers" for the inner life that they may provoke. The only forms they offer are a simple word or a step forward or away. The problem with this, as Brian discovered during the I Feel exercise, is that this lack of a physical "container" may keep us wading in rather shallow emotions.

But the body work we have momentarily put aside provides tools that allow strong emotions to play upon us as if they were reactions to outside stimuli. So now let us see what happens if we add our physical training to this new, sensitive listening work. As we combine these two approaches, we must allow our physical forms to remain open and receptive, bearing in mind the sort of sensitivity our *plastiques* acquired during the Kiss Rivers.

After my class has experienced the I Feel exercise and the Crossings I divide the students into groups of four, each group sitting around a square of two joined mats. "What we are going to do now," I explain, "are **Round-Robin Rivers** (4.4). One actor will enter the mat and work with *plastiques* and images for about a minute. Then another person will enter, allowing herself to react to the first person's images in space. The two will work together for about five minutes, then the first person will leave, and the second person will follow her own River for a minute. Then a third person will join the second person. And so on. The central challenge in this work is to let yourself see and receive the images with which your partner is working, as if the images were doing the leading and both actors were following their lead."

An alternative way to experience this work is simply to work in couples in the **Partnered Rivers** (4.5).

At the end of the Round-Robin River exercise, each group of four talks among themselves, and then we all gather to speak together. Veronica explains that she had one problem. "Now I am confused about what to do with my eyes," she says. "In the I Feel exercise and in the Crossings it was very clear: I was working with another person, and either I looked at her or I

Round-Robin Rivers (4.4)

1. Four or five actors sit around a double mat, an area of about eight feet by eight feet. One actor begins by entering the workspace and starting a *plastique* River.

2. When the first actor has established a strong connection with constantly changing images, a second person joins by beginning to work with the images established by the first actor.

3. The two then allow the images to change. Permit yourself to be led by the images; remain available to the surprises and changes of direction that occur; use your eyes to see what is there, and employ the *plastiques* to keep the images clear and precise.

4. Don't try to "figure out" what your partner is doing. Just join in the activity and discover it from the inside.

5. Sometimes you will be working opposite each other with the image between you; sometimes both of you will be opposite one image.

6. If the image becomes unclear or is lost, simply start a new *plastique*.

7. Take turns leading and following, but, overall, try to let the images lead while both of you react.

8. The most important thing to remember is that, even at moments when you are fighting hard and using all your strength, let your body react. You are making "choices," yet you are not "controlling" the River.

9. After about three minutes, the first person leaves the mats, and the second person works alone for a minute. Then a third actor joins the second.

10. Continue the Round-Robin until everyone has worked twice, each time with a different partner.

11. When you finish, take a few minutes to discuss the experience with the others in your group.

---

looked away. But when I work with the *plastiques* I am looking for images, images in thin air. So now I don't know which to do. How do I retain my connection with images when I look at my partner?"

"Yes. It's true," I say, "faces, and especially eyes, are extremely powerful. An infant's brain is preprogrammed to recognize the human face above all else, so for most of us looking

---

Partnered Rivers (4.5)

1. Two actors begin *plastique* Rivers, allowing their images to change constantly.

2. When each of you feels that your image worlds are strong, approach each other, allowing your images to enter the space surrounding that of the other actor. Allow yourself to <u>receive</u> the images and impulses of the other. Allow your images to merge. Allow the images to emanate from one or the other or both of you.

3. Whether working with "your" images or those of your partner, be sure you are "following" the images, rather than "inventing" them. Just let the image change on its own, with your permission.

---

into another person's eyes is sort of the emotional equivalent of staring at the sun. Their light is often strong enough to block out any imagery we may be having. So when you start working opposite a real human being, you need to become very precise about how you use your eyes.

"Actually, we experience images all the time. If we quiet down the outside interference (by closing our eyes or turning out the lights) we start to daydream, that is, to experience imagery. Or if we raise the volume on the internal output (by driving for six hours or taking LSD) we may start to hallucinate, that is, to see our daydreams even with our eyes open. But we unconsciously project our daydreams onto the world around us all the time—it's just that we're not aware that we're doing it. Psychologists suggest that our proclivity for projecting is what makes us susceptible to falling in love with people who look like our mothers or fearing people who look foreign. But most of the time we permit the signals of the real world to drown out our awareness of these projections. And there is no signal that is stronger than a human face.

"But in the theater, you can't simply avoid looking at your partner all the time. So, there is a real problem here: how can you take in your scene partner without having the light and energy of his or her eyes overwhelm and drown out your own image world? To answer this question, we shall try an exercise called **Face Tracing**" (4.5).

FACE TRACING

The word "image" is almost inseparably wedded to the sense of sight. . . . But . . . Carl Gustav Jung . . . speaks of it as "semblance." His exemplary case of illusion is not the reflected image, but the dream; and in dream there are sounds, smells, feelings, happenings, intentions, dangers—all sorts of invisible elements—as well as sights, and all are equally unreal by the measures of public fact.
—Susanne K. Langer, *Feeling and Form*

To begin the Face Tracing work, I have each student sit opposite a partner and study that person's face with his eyes and hands. After a couple of minutes, I have the partners switch. After everyone in the class has completed this first part of the exercise, I have each person turn away from his or her partner and face toward empty space, and I ask each of them to try to "see" and "touch" that same face again in space. Finally, I have everyone turn to face a new partner and then repeat the job of seeing and touching the original partner's face while facing the new person.

After the exercise, Joan laments, "I couldn't do it. I couldn't really see Peter's face when I was facing Veronica. It was there in little bits, like I could see his eyebrows, but then I would think, 'Oh, Veronica looks weird with those eyebrows,' and the image would be gone."

"That's fine," I say. "This work is not about training you to hallucinate. It is simply a version of what Uta Hagen might call 'substitution,' employing your natural ability to project while receiving input from your partner. You may not actually see an image, but *in the very act of searching for it*, the image becomes a filter that alters your reaction to your partner. Your moment of 'Veronica looks weird,' is a moment when you are looking at Veronica but receiving more than just what she is giving you.

"The primary lesson to be gained here is the awareness that **what you see often depends on how you use your eyes.** So from now on, when you work with a partner, be aware of exactly how you are using your eyes. Try looking near her face, but not

---

Face Tracing (4.6)

1. Begin by sitting comfortably opposite a partner (either in a chair or on the floor). Sit close enough so that you can reach out and touch your partner's face.

2. Your partner just sits looking at you, while you reach out and study her face by seeing it with your eyes and touching it with your hands. Take a couple of minutes to "learn" that face. Allow yourself to feel all the feelings you have as you do. Meanwhile your partner allows herself to smile or whatever; she need not be a statue.

3. When you have finished, your partner takes her turn "learning" your face.

4. Then when both of you have finished you both turn away so that you are both facing empty space. Now, in that space, try with your hands and eyes to discover that same face in the space in front of you. Take a couple of minutes to see if you can feel and see the face you just learned.

5. Then each of you go sit opposite a new partner and try again to discover the face of your <u>first</u> partner, but this time do so in the space directly in front of the new face. (If two people are trying this exercise alone, begin by tracing a face from memory, in empty space, and then trying to trace that memory face on your partner.)

6. Adjust your eye focus carefully in front of the new face. Try focusing a little above, below, or to the side of the face. Figure out what allows you to "take in" the real face while "seeing" the image at the same time.

7. As you work, allow yourself to experience the contradictions, absurdity, or humor of the task. Remember, **the important thing is not that you can actually hallucinate; it is to learn how you can use your eyes to perceive inner images even as you observe the outer world.**

quite at it. Try focusing on the space between the two of you, filling that space with your imagery. Try looking at your partner out of the corner of your eye. Try looking at her with your eyes relaxed. Try perceiving the 'negative' space around her. Try to see the energy she is emitting. In every case, work consciously with your eyes. They are muscles that you can exercise and control."

Voice Work

A LOSS OF VOICE

The most elementary fault, and that in most urgent need of correction, is the overstraining of the voice because one forgets to speak with the body.
—Grotowski, *Towards a Poor Theatre*

When an infant begins to make sounds, her voice and her body are one. When she cries, she arches her back and throws out her arms. When she laughs, her whole body shakes. Every strong emotion she experiences engages her voice and her body together. Later, as the child begins to learn language, it is with the aid of her eyes and her body that she first comprehends words. Nouns are pointed to, touched, and tasted. And verbs are lived. In *The Magical Child* R. Chilton Pierce maintains that during this learning process the very meaning of words is identical with the physical gesture they represent. *Sit* is not just a word; it is the action of sitting. This relationship is even more evident with emotionally charged language: Strong refusal is not just the word *no;* it is also spitting out the food or striking the floor with the fists. Joy is not just the word *yes;* it is also the hands clapping and the legs jumping up and down. And in dire need, the word *mommy* is the sound that accompanies the outstretched, up-reaching arms.

But as we grow older language becomes no longer an extension of bodily expression but a substitute for it. We learn that when we need to pee, we should not hold our crotch and whine and squirm. Instead we must raise one hand and ask politely, "May I please go to the bathroom?" And when we are joyful about a new toy, we are not supposed to jump up and down screaming, "Yea!" but to smile and say, "Thank you very much." (And then, of course, to make matters worse, we learn that we are to smile and say, "Thank you very much," even when we are not joyful at all.)

Through this process our words become utterly detached from their original, visceral connections, so that by the time we are ready to study acting, we have often thoroughly divorced our bodies and our emotions from our voices and words. Therefore, before we can demand open, expressive language from our voices, we must first exhume the ancient connections we have spent so many years diligently burying within ourselves.

The disconnection between body, voice, and emotion begins at home, but it is not only the result of personal psychological history. It is also a habit strongly reinforced by American culture, which (unlike some others) discourages physical gesture during speech. Northern European traditions have taught many of us to see strength in stoicism, not in expressive gestures; in the stiff upper lip, not in the scream.

Moreover, not only does North American culture prohibit bodily expression; it also restricts variation in the pitch of our voices. The French, Spanish, and Italian languages use pitch changes to emphasize words and create sentence structure. Even British English employs tonal variation. But—with the exception of the accents of the Deep South—American speech, from Down East to the Far West, is extremely "flat" and monotonic. We emphasize words by changing volume and tempo, not by raising or lowering vocal pitch.

And then there is a further restriction of vocal variation by sex. Men are socialized to use their chest resonators and to avoid the high pitches connected with pleading or crying. Women are socialized in the opposite direction, to stay out of touch with the power and the sensuality of their lower resonators. (Thus the male Brooklyn accent is thoroughly "denasalized," while the female Brooklyn accent uses the head resonators.) So in different ways both sexes are encouraged to cut off the vocal connections between their upper and lower bodies.

Vocal constrictions are often more difficult to approach than physical ones because they are more thoroughly hidden. In the lesson "Work Clothes," I suggested that many of us dress our bodies with clothing to cover or reveal those parts of ourselves we wish to hide or to display. But our voices don't have clothes to wear. To keep them from betraying our true feelings we must disguise them from within with muscular restrictions. It is not strange, therefore, that many of us have learned to clench our jaws, to restrict our breathing, and to curtail our vocal range in order to prevent this volatile instrument from playing those notes we do not wish the world to hear.

The connection between our physical tensions on the one hand and our vocal restrictions on the other can be a real problem. At the same time, understanding this connection will allow us to use what we have been learning about our bodies to help us in working with our voices.

Note: The basic elements of the voice work I present here are a very condensed version of the exercises Kristin Linklater describes in her two books, Freeing the Natural Voice *and* Freeing Shakespeare's Voice. *If you have not done basic breath and sound work like that described in* Freeing the Natural Voice, *I recommend that you study those exercises before moving on to the resonator work below.*

CONNECTING THE VOICE AND THE BODY

Speech is music. The text of a part or a play is a melody, an opera, or a symphony.
—Stanislavski, *Building a Character*

Before attempting the Cat and the Backbends, we prepared our backs by performing some stretches. Now, as we start to work on our voices, it is similarly important that we prepare our vocal instruments by connecting with our breath in the **From Breath to Vowel and Pitch** exercise (5.1).

Note: To minimize pelvic tension, all voice warm-ups are best done with an empty bladder.

From Breath to Vowel and Pitch (5.1)

1. For five minutes, perform any aerobic exercise that leaves you breathing hard.

2. Lie down on your back, giving up your physical tension to gravity.

3. Take the time you need to make sure that your legs are relaxed, that your neck is free, and that your jaw is released. Notice how your breath naturally fills your lower abdomen as you breathe. As the exercise proceeds and your breath becomes shallower, continue to allow your lower body to receive the breath in this way.

4. While making sure that your stomach, chest, and neck stay relaxed, wake up your face by moving the facial muscles around, stretching your tongue and lips, and allowing yourself to smile.

5. Open your eyes and allow your breath to exit from your mouth, fountaining up toward the ceiling. Practice adding muscular choice without interfering with the breath itself by lifting the lower lip toward the upper teeth so that the outgoing breath produces a *fff* sound. Then return to allowing the breath to exit from an open mouth.

6. As lightly as you produced the *fff*, now allow sound to occur on the out-breath, beginning with a gentle *hhuuh,* what Linklater calls a "sigh of relief." Let the sound just "ride" on top of the breath that initiates it, as a surfer rides on top of the powerful wave beneath. You do not have to <u>make</u> the sound, but simply <u>allow</u> it to happen.

7. Now let the vowel change. On the same relaxed breath, allow an *oo* to ride (like the *oo* in *hoop*). Then try an *oh* (like the *o* in *cone*). An *ay* (like the *a* in *wave*), and then *eee*. Just let the different vowels happen without trying to change anything else.

8. Notice how the eee sounds higher in pitch than the *oh,* even though you are speaking the same note.[1]

---

1. The ear can distinguish between these vowels because even when they are spoken on the same pitch, the altered mouth and tongue position change the "overtones" that resonate above the note. On the *eee,* the placement of the tongue and the soft palate directs the sound into the small nasal cavities that resonate at a pitch well above the fundamental note. On the *oh,* the sound is directed into the much larger chest resonator. What we call *vowels* are the overtone changes. The *eee* sounds higher than the *oh* just as the same note sounds different when played on an oboe than on a flute.

> 9. Now, as you slide from *oo* to *oh* to *ah* to *ay* to *ee*, allow the pitch to slide up as the vowels suggest. Meanwhile picture the sound sliding up your body from your pelvis to your head. Let the vowel, the pitch, and the resonation all slide together from pelvis to head (from *oo* to *eee*) and from the head back down again (from *eee* to *oo*).
> 10. Relax and return to just breathing.

To eliminate as much physical tension as possible, you have begun your voice warm-up lying down. But to enable your body to participate in the voice exploration (and to act in most plays), you must stand up. However, as you move from lying down to standing up, it is important not to add any unnecessary tensions. While lying on the floor, your body trusts the floor to hold it up, but when you stand, you may try to hold yourself erect, not only against gravity, but also on guard against the world. Standing requires some tension in the back muscles that lever the vertebrae one upon the other. But overcoming gravity does not require that you create tension in the pelvis, the stomach, the chest, the shoulders, or the jaw. These tensions may serve to help you "face" the world, but they can also interfere with your breath and vocal freedom, so your next task is to stand without adding any unnecessary tensions.

Standing Up without Adding Tension (5.2)

> 1. Begin by returning to your relaxed *hhuuh* sound, the "sigh of relief" on each out-breath.
> 2. During the following steps, move only on the in-breath, relaxing in each new position on the out-breath, and exhaling a sigh.
> 3. On one in-breath, roll onto your side, pulling your legs up into a fetal position. Then sigh, checking that your sound is as relaxed and open as it was when you were lying on your back.
> 4. On another breath, use your arms to push yourself onto your knees. Your head is still down, your forehead on the floor. And again, sigh.

5. Next push yourself back onto your feet, and sigh.

6. Then, on several breaths, slowly straighten your legs, and then unroll the vertebrae of your back one by one, beginning with the pelvis and working your way up to the head. As you do, be careful that your stomach stays relaxed, that your shoulders hang freely, and that your jaw does not tighten.

7. Every time you breathe out, stop, relax, and check the vibration with a light sigh. If you seem to have added any tension, halt the straightening process for a moment while you let the tension go.

8. If you notice that at some particular step along the way your voice has become more restricted, return to the previous position, check the sound again, and then progress up again, changing your position in smaller increments, noticing the sources of unnecessary tension.

9. The last thing to do is to let your head float up, making sure your eyes are open, and your jaw is relaxed.

10. Now that you are standing, again let the relaxed sigh happen on your out-breath. Check through your body that you are not holding anything that does not need to be held.

11. Make eye contact with others, smile and check that you are not "zoning out."

Now that we are standing, we shall return to changing the vowels and pitch, but this time we shall use our bodies to help the sound travel to different resonators.

Undulation, Vowels, and Pitch (5.3)

1. Try a slow Undulation from the Pelvis Up as you let the vowels slide again from *oo* to *oh* to *ah* to *ay* to *ee*, noticing which section of the undulation is associated with which pitches. Do this several times.

2. Then try the undulation in the opposite direction, beginning with the head on *eee* and ending with the pelvis or knees on *oo*.

3. Allow the undulations to extend out the arms and down the legs. Feel what vowels vibrate in different parts.

4. Now play with changing pitch, changing vowels and resonation in different body parts, allowing the voice and body to lead and to follow each other until you can feel how they relate. Try working with various *plastique* isolations, noticing how the voice can inhabit the body.

5. Now allow a River of connected sound and movement to pass through you. As a physical impulse slides from one part of the body to another, allow your voice to follow. Then try thinking of the two elements the opposite way: think of changing the vocal pitch and resonator while allowing the body to find a *plastique* movement associated with the part of the body that is resonating. Soon you will find that the voice and the body are operating together: when the arms reach above the head, the voice automatically slides up. When the voice resonates in your back, it is as if you were being pulled backward.[2]

Our exploration of the *plastiques* began as a "mechanical" movement of body parts, but as we progressed it soon became clear that moving our body parts was not just an exterior activity; it was also a pathway to our emotional and image life. Similarly, choices of pitch and resonation may seem at first to be "technical" decisions, but they may also activate hidden psychophysical connections and put you in touch with strong emotional sources. So now that you have built the "technical" connections between voice and body, it is time to see what happens if you allow the sound of your voice to play directly upon your feelings and memories.

As an introduction to sensing sound as an emotive entity, try the simple exploratory exercise I call **The Sounds of Your Own Voice** (5.4).

2. In her book *Freeing Shakespeare's Voice* Kristin Linklater demonstrates how an actor can penetrate into the vibratory content of Shakespeare's language by allowing the voice to rise and fall with the pitch of the vowels Shakespeare provides. When combined with the physical precision of the *plastiques*, this awareness provides a powerful basis for working with Shakespeare, whose use of sound and language can actually activate an actor's emotions and gesture life. A detailed description of this process lies beyond the scope of this book.

The Sounds of Your Own Voice (5.4)

1. At each step of this exercise, search for the image to which you are speaking. Let your voice be a response to the image.
2. Search for the sound of crying. Let yourself play with sound in falsetto. Try whining, pleading, and calling as a child calls to a parent. Try reaching up with your arms as you do so. Permit any feelings or images that arise to play upon you.
3. Try spitting out angry sentences or cursing. As you are doing this, find arm movements to accompany your voice.
4. Try laughing a deep belly laugh while moving your pelvis.
5. Play with any vocal choice that occurs to you, allowing the sound to evoke movement, image, and emotion.

WORKING WITH SOUND IN A GROUP

When working in a group, voice work is never a purely personal exploration. Every sound you make immediately impinges upon everyone else's consciousness, so working with sound forces us to revisit the ensemble questions we first encountered during the Body-Part Warm-up.

The day after I have taught the basic vocal exercises, I suggest to my class that they include the new vocal work in their warm-ups. With the sound prohibition finally removed, some of the actors begin their voice work at the very start of their warm-ups, while others work with their bodies first and only add their voices later. After ten or fifteen minutes the studio has become a dense cacophony of moans, screams, and laughter.

When we gather at the end of the warm-up, Sandra complains, "That was unbearable. That was as bad as that first group warm-up we did. The noise drove me nuts."

"Well, you could have told us to shut up," offers Brian.

"How could I? Everything was so loud, I would have had to scream just to be heard, and that's exactly what I didn't want to do. I didn't want to scream. I wanted quiet."

"Well, one interesting possibility," I suggest, "would be to say 'shhh!' You'll find that the sound *shhh* has the power to cut through almost any other sound."

Sandra thinks about it for a moment. "But wouldn't that still be imposing my will on the others, just like they were doing to me?"

"Well, when you go 'shhh,' they might shut up and they might not. You don't have the power to impose your will. But there is no way to know what their reaction will be if you don't try. You might find that the others just didn't know that you wanted quiet. It might even turn out that they *all* needed quiet and just didn't realize it yet. Maybe when you show them the beauty of silence, they will appreciate your insight."

"Yeah, or maybe they'll tell me to go to hell."

"Yes, maybe they'll tell you to go to hell. There are no guarantees in this work. The only thing that is sure is that if you *don't* risk expressing your needs, those needs will keep rankling inside you."

"Still," she protests, "I don't see why it has to rest with *me*."

"Well, that's true, too. Sound is (obviously) louder than silence. That is another reason that we have waited this long before introducing vocal work. Our eyes are directional and have eyelids, but we have no earlids, so our ears hear everything. As soon as you make even a tiny sound, it can penetrate the work of someone on the other side of the room."

"I don't get what you're saying," says Carlos.

"What I mean is that making sound is like touching someone. It impinges on his or her private space. Therefore, as with touch, **there is a great responsibility on the part of the person who is doing the noisemaking to be aware of the effect of the sound he or she is making. The louder I am, the more I must listen.** If I am screaming, and Sandra says 'shhh' (or even if she just holds her finger to her lips), her sound or gesture must be able to get through to me as loudly as my scream can get through to her. As she said, she shouldn't have to scream to stop the screaming.

"In other words, when doing ensemble work with sound, there is a responsibility on each side: There is the responsibility of those making sound to listen especially hard. And there is the responsibility of those wanting silence to give clear signals to express their needs."

RECEIVING WITH THE VOICE

When we were studying the *plastiques*, we noted that the actor must strike a delicate balance between effort and non-effort, between putting out energy and receiving it. The same balance must also be found in the voice work, although with the voice, the dangers of using too much effort are greater.

Grotowski helped actors expand the use of their vocal resonators by asking them to imagine that the sound they were producing was emanating from "mouths" in different locations on their bodies. In our 1967 workshop he would sometimes thump an actor firmly on the back, exclaiming, *"La bouche ici! La bouche ici!"* (Let your mouth be here!) At other times he would exhort an actor to "Walk with a big stomach, like a cow, and speak to the floor with the mouth at the bottom of your stomach." Or he would say, "Call to the ceiling with the mouth at the top of your head." With such coaxing and hectoring, Grotowski elicited strong and vibrant resonation all over the actors' bodies. But Grotowski's prodding also led some actors to *push* their voices toward the particular body part, rather than simply encouraging them to *allow* it to go there.

Most of us can, with some effort, force our voices to resonate in our legs, pelvis or foreheads. But if we seek these results without taking the time to experience the emotional connections these vibrations produce in us, we are likely to strain our voices and then quickly return to our old habits when we let up on the effort. But if we allow ourselves to experience the images and emotions we encounter as we expand our vocal range, we can begin to truly unlock our vocal blockages. My feeling is that it is very important that vocal work proceed with great safety, gentleness, and patience.

The following two exercises (5.5 and 5.6) offer subtler versions of Grotowski's *"la bouche ici"* resonator work. In each exercise couples work together, one person leading while the second produces sound. The essential thing in both of these exercises is the sense that **it is the silent partner who is doing the work, while the vocal one is merely responding.** The **Sound Massage** exercise (5.5) allows you to explore the body-voice connection with no physical tension at all. I recommend doing this exercise with same-sex partners.

For some, the Sound Massage exercise can be a very moving experience; for others it is simply frustrating. Because it is done in complete relaxation, the fears and tensions that you encounter in doing it often come right to the surface. After a few minutes of this work in my class, Sandra's partner signals me. She is having some difficulty helping Sandra find vibration in her shoulders, so I step in to work with Sandra for a moment.

"How does that feel?" I ask as I press my thumb firmly into the back of her shoulder.

"It hurts."

"Good, but now look at me as you say it."

As her eyes meet mine, I press her shoulder again. "It hurts," she says and suddenly tears well up in her eyes. The quality of her voice changes as the emotion connects with the vibration. I tell her partner to stay in eye contact with Sandra as they work.

Then Maria's partner beckons. She has been trying to help Maria search for vibrations in her abdomen, but Maria keeps giggling. When I place my hand on her side, I can feel the enormous tension she holds in her stomach muscles. "That's enough," I caution her partner. "You can't rush past the giggles. The giggles are important. For now just let her get used to feeling that much."

In this exercise one must work just to the edge of the possible but not try to force the sound where it is not ready to go.

———

The Sound Massage (5.5)

1. One person begins by finding the most open sound that comes from her body with the least effort, a relaxed sigh.

2. Her partner-coach touches the back and chest of the sounding person to find where the vibration is the strongest. (Of course, you will find the strongest vibration in the throat, but we are looking for resonation here, not the source of the sound.)

3. Then the coach moves her touch from that starting point while the sounding person allows herself to respond to the touch with sound.

4. As the coach moves her touch inch by inch across the sounding person's chest, over the shoulders, across the back, up over the head, then along the arms and so on, the sounding person simply allows the pitch, the vowel sounds, and the placement of the sound to slide, as if in answer to the touch. At each place, the coach feels for the vibration answering her touch. If she finds a place where the sound does not vibrate, she may change the quality of her touch by pressing harder or more softly or by moving in another direction.

5. It often helps for the partners to make eye contact with each other, and for the touching person to ask periodically, "How does that feel?" Then, in answer, the other partner may use sound or words. If you stick with making eye contact while this happens, you can facilitate the discovery of the emotional content of the vibration.

6. After working the upper body in a standing position, have the vocalizing partner lie down while you work with the legs.

7. There is no hurry in this work, and there is no need to push the sound into places it does not wish to go. If, for instance, the vibration ceases as the coach moves her touch down from the chest to the stomach, she may find more vibration if she moves her touch down the sides first instead of over the stomach itself. Many people find that as they allow the vibration to enter the lower abdomen, they begin to laugh. If that happens, don't fight it, let the laughter happen. But go gently; if a great deal of emotion or laughter happens, don't try to go any further. There is no need to drive the voice further than it is ready to go. Your body needs to take time to become used to the new vibrations it is experiencing.

8. Give the sounding person some time now to see if she can find the same vibratory and emotional connections on her own. Then switch roles.

Vocal Ribbons (5.6)

1. One partner begins again by finding an open, relaxed sound.

2. Then the silent, "active" partner begins to pull, as if he were drawing invisible ribbons or strings from his partner, beginning with the chest and then moving to other parts of the body.

3. The partner responds by permitting his body to move as if it were really being drawn by his partner's gestures, and he lets sound resonate from his body along the ribbon.

4. The important thing in this exercise is the sense that the silent coach doing the pulling is the one making all the effort, and that the sounding person is simply <u>allowing</u> his voice to respond.

5. If you are the one making sound, spend about ten minutes allowing yourself to respond to your partner, and then try working with an invisible partner, reacting as if to impulses from outside.

6. After both partners have had a turn, combine this technique with the *plastiques*, permitting your imagery to draw voice as well as physical movement from you.

The next exercise is a more active version of this same work. In the **Vocal Ribbons** exercise (5.6), the active partner pulls invisible ribbons of sound from parts of his partner's body, while the speaking partner permits his body and voice to respond to the image of the pulls. Because the Vocal Ribbons is not as purely receptive as a form as is the Sound Massage, it may not lead to the same depth of feeling. On the other hand, since it allows the body to create a more active "Container" for any emotion that may occur, it enables some actors to "stand" strong vibrations in parts of their voice that are beyond their normal range.

CONSONANTS

If vowels are a river and consonants are the banks, it is necessary to reinforce the latter lest there be floods!
—S. M. Volkonski, *The Expressive Word*

As you work with sound, you will quickly discover that vowels and pitch carry with them emotional qualities. If you begin to laugh with a low "ho, ho, ho" but then slide your laughter up to a tittering "he, he, he," the change in emotional quality will be quite plain. Try working with a partner, making eye contact, and allowing gentle laughter to flow out toward each other. You will find that each change in pitch and vowel carries with it striking changes in meaning.

But the emotional qualities of the vowels are general rather than specific. To communicate more precise nuances of meaning, we need the consonants.

In our body work, the *exercises corporels* served to free your body from the vertical. Now, in a similar way, the vowels have freed your voice from monotones. But if the vowels have served as a vocal equivalent of the *corporels*, the consonants are the *plastiques* of sound. The precision that consonants provide can hone the blunt edge of generalized anger into the specific blades of rage or bitterness or sarcasm; or it can refine the primary blue of sadness into the subtle tints of regret or pity or grief.

Of course, there is no such thing as a consonant without a vowel. In every phoneme the vowel provides the vibration that the consonant then makes particular, so the consonant exercise below must be added on top of the vowel/pitch/vibration work that you are already doing.

After working technically with the vowels and the consonants, go back to playing with sound: remembered sound, dream sound, the sounds of other voices, of characters and animals. Play with rhythm, placement, and accent until you can alter your voice as easily as you can lift your shoulders—and until each word you speak can play upon your inner instrument as intimately as the imagery stimulated by your body and eyes.

You may find at first that this sort of playing makes your voice sound "unnatural" or "affected" to you. But experimenting with your voice is no more unnatural than experimenting with blocking or stage movement. Expanding your vocal range

Consonant Exploration (5.7)

1. Begin with whatever vocal relaxation and breath exercises you like. Make sure your stomach, shoulders, throat, and jaw are all relaxed.

2. Allow open sound to vibrate easily on the out-breath; then play with pitch, vowel sounds, and resonation long enough to rediscover that condition in which the sound seems to be <u>happening to you</u>, rather than you making the sound happen.

3. Now begin to add consonants to the vowels. To do this, permit the consonant to shape, to aim, to refine the vowel.

4. Take one consonant at a time and "taste" it. Let yourself feel what it does to the vibration and to the meaning of the vowel sound. Let yourself play with the consonant using different vowels and different pitches. What does the sound make you feel with the consonant placed before the vowel as opposed to after it (*rrrrrraahh* versus *aahrrrr*)?

5. You may work with the consonants in any order, but be sure to include all of them. I begin with the two consonants that are almost vowels: *w* and *y*. Then I progress through the continuant consonants: *r, l,* and *zj* (azure), *th* (*th*is), *v* (and their unvoiced twins: *sh, th* [*th*in], *f*); the nasal consonants: *m, n, ng*; the plosives *g, d, b* (and the voiceless: *k, t, p*).

6. Feel the vibration of the consonants in your mouth; feel what they do to your body. Notice what emotions, what imagery, and what gestures they evoke in you.

and precision involves exercising muscles and resonators long out of use, so take the time you need, and try to have the courage it takes to push beyond the initial strangeness of vocal experimentation. Most of us have developed deep personal attachments to the sound of our own voices, and it can take some time and patience to get beyond the fear—the loss of self—we may experience when speaking beyond our normal vocal range.

It is this fear that underlies the difficulty American actors have in handling the range of sound required by Shakespeare and other playwrights whose words convey as much meaning in their *sound* as in their *signification*. Of course, you *can* act

Shakespeare without great vocal range and precision. But it's a little like playing a Beethoven symphony in a piano transcription. It is still great music, but the performance misses the roar of the timpani and the song of the violins.

"YES-NO" AND GIBBERISH

Try to forget about the "meaning" and the emotional situation, and concentrate on two things only. Firstly, to "sing" the text, making melody out of the words. And then to enjoy exchanging the melody with the other actor.
                                        —Yoshi Oida, *The Invisible Actor*

After doing experiments with vowels and consonants, my acting class is almost ready to apply all of their physical, visual, and sound work to the rehearsal and performance of a text. But before we act a written text, we must first confront some of the problems that are inherent in working with words and language. So I have my students begin by playing a simple verbal improvisation game: **Yes-No** (5.8).

"This is just a pure fun game to start bridging the gap between all the nonverbal work we've been doing and language. You and a partner will stand opposite each other. One person will say yes and the other will say no. You just stick with your yes or your no, trying to convince your partner of your point of view until you feel that you must change, then you switch to the other side. When one person switches, the other must, too. That's it," I say. "Try it."

Everyone is excited to be finally speaking words—"acting" at long last. But in their excitement, most of them seem to forget many of the lessons they have learned during the past month. While they yell yes and no at each other with great energy and conviction, many of the students stand immobile, the physical and vocal variation they have gained suddenly forgotten. When we stop, I point out what I have observed.

The problem, I suggest, is that we are so used to letting the words do all our communicating for us, that when we open our mouth to speak, the lower half of our body suddenly drops out of the work. Our voice returns to its accustomed resonators, and our arms reglue themselves to our sides. So before I ask the class to try the Yes-No game again, I have them take a moment to reconnect with the body and sound work we have been studying, practicing their *plastiques* with full body and voice. Then I have them add one more step: gibberish.

There are many gibberish games we could play. (See Viola Spolin's *Improvisation for the Theater* or other theater games books.) Today I just have the students tell each other a personal story in gibberish trying to communicate as much detail as possible. As they speak nonsense, they gesture broadly, their voices use the full gamut of sound, and their faces are animated.

"Good," I say. "Now let's return to our Yes-No game, but this time I want you to lead yourself into the words step-by-step. You will begin with two-person *plastiques*, then add vowel sounds, and then consonants; then move on to gibberish, and finally, making sure your bodies and voices are still fully engaged, move on to the actual English words *yes* and *no*. Then, if you are able to keep your bodies and voices alive saying yes and no, try using other words to improvise arguments with each other. Just remember: **Words are very complicated** *plastiques*. They contain all the power of your full-body work, in very precise form. Words have all the vibration and pitch possibilities of vowels and all the precision of consonants *plus* meaning, so be sure to keep all those physical and vocal tools active as you slide into ordinary language."

This time no one performs the Yes-No game standing in one place. Each couple moves wildly around the room, people are on their knees, begging, crying, crawling, and fighting. Many of the scenes are comedic, but some seem very serious, and a few hit different styles and genres with each change of yes and no.

At the end I say, "So, as you start to work with language,

Yes-No (5.8)

1. Stand opposite a partner. One of you says yes, and the other says no.

2. Try every way you can to get through to your partner using your one word.

3. Use your voice, your body, your gestures. Argue, plead, cajole, yell, cry—anything to get your partner to agree with you. But, at the same time, listen to your partner (as you did in the I Feel exercise).

4. Let yourself notice when you have come to the end of what you have to say, or when your partner gets through to you. When this happens, swap words.

5. If your partner changes from yes to no or from no to yes, you must change too.

6. Once you are both listening and reacting well to each other, start to improvise text: "Yes, I want you to clean your room right now." "No, Mom, I won't"; or "Yes, I need you to stay with me. I love you." "No, you don't. You're lying." Or whatever. Dare to invent specifics.

7. Even as situation, event, and character emerge, and even as you try as hard as you can to "win," keep listening for that moment when something changes. And always go with the change.

8. Notice how your body choices affect the game: what happens if you go down on your knees? What happens if you turn and walk away? What happens if you touch your partner? And notice what effect your vocal choices have, too.

9. Notice what closes you off from listening or noticing the beat changes. Notice what leaves you open.

10. Try playing the game very strongly, but listening for beat changes on every line or almost every line. What do you have to do, physically and mentally, to play a moment strongly without becoming so attached to what you are doing that you are not really listening? Is it a matter of alternating between doing and listening, or is there a way in which to do and to listen at the same time?

11. Now start over, beginning with your vowel and consonant work. Connect your body with your voice and then extend the phonemes into gibberish. Now start the Yes-No game again, in gibberish, making sure your body and sound work remain full. Then slide back into English.

always remember that words are only the tip of the iceberg. Beneath the words and their meanings lie great mountains of image, emotion, and vibration. Your job as actors is to discover the whole underwater ice floe that supports the verbal peaks the playwright supplies. Many acting systems ask you to accomplish this by studying the words and their meanings and then breaking down the text logically, while sitting at a table. But since our training has been more holistic, we will be approaching the words not just with our minds but also with our voices and bodies at the same time."

As I dismiss the class, I add, "So now we are at the end of our vacation from text. The next time we meet, I want each of you to bring in suggestions for scenes to work on."

Scene Work

CHOOSING A SCENE

I wish we would all read a few more plays and talk less about technique.

—John Strasberg, in Mekler,
The New Generation of Acting Teachers

Plays are not written to be read; they're written to be seen and heard, so play reading is an acquired taste. But if you are an actor, reading plays is a taste worth acquiring, if only because you often have to pick a scene to work on, and it's nice to know you have some choices. I like to ask my students to bring me several suggestions, and then I negotiate with them to find a scene that we both agree will serve the actor's needs.

In order to find a scene to work on, I recommend that you start your search by talking to friends and/or just going to a bookstore, not necessarily to buy new plays, but just to sit on the floor paging through scenes, looking for lines, characters, or situations that excite you.

What scene you choose will depend on the acting-training task you are working on. Different plays and different playwrights offer very different acting problems. So the first question to ask when choosing a scene is, What are you working on at this particular point in your acting work? What *training purpose* is this scene designed to serve? Some skills you may want to focus on are

- listening and reacting
- emotional breadth or depth
- character choice
- style
- poetry and language

Once you've settled on what skill(s) you want to work on, look for a scene that allows you to confront the task head-on, without distracting you by putting other problems in your way. (Shakespeare writes terrific scenes that require skills in all of the above categories. For that reason it is often best to leave Shakespeare for last so that you are not forced to work on all these skills at once. He has waited four hundred years for you; he'll wait another few months.)

Once you have narrowed down your tasks, and you know what challenges you are looking for, find a scene that furnishes you with **exciting, positive,** and **doable** challenges.

- **Exciting**—because if the scene is not fun to do, you won't put your full energy into it. Keep yourself open to scenes you may not have liked a year ago, but don't force yourself to do a scene just because others have told you it's a great scene.
- **Positive**—meaning, avoid scenes that just encourage old acting habits or lead you into emotions you know all too well. Acting training is about expanding your range.
- **Doable**—meaning that there is no point in confusing or frustrating yourself with tasks that distract you from what it is you want to concentrate on. If anger is an exciting challenge for you, choose a play like Churchill's *Top Girls* that allows its characters to fully vent their rage. If you are trying to connect your full body with text for the first time, choose a play with words that make clear, emotional sense for you rather than one with elevated, poetic language. If you are working on emotional freedom, don't choose a Pinter play with tightly wound characters.

At this point in their training, my acting class has been working on listening, so I suggest that they look for scenes that do not require character or "style" work, and that they select scenes in which characters reveal what they feel rather than lying or hiding the truth. The **Scene-Choosing Guidelines** (6.1) are designed for people selecting scenes at this point in their training.

Scene-Choosing Guidelines (6.1)

1. Choose a scene you <u>like</u>, a scene that makes you *feel* something when you read it, a scene with a situation or characters that intrigue you in some way.

2. Find a scene in which both characters react to each other. There are some scenes in which one of the characters seems to be on stage primarily to serve the other character's action or to elicit information or to advance the plot. Such scenes will teach one of the actors very few acting lessons.

3. Find a scene in which each character goes through emotional changes, a scene in which the power shifts several times or the relationship changes. It is this changing of relationship that provides actors with the basic fuel for acting. Scenes in which one actor always has the upper hand provide fewer acting lessons.

4. Choose a scene that is not filled with long speeches. The task of keeping your acting alive while your partner speaks a big paragraph is an interesting one, but our task at this juncture is simple listening and reacting. Most characters have moments when they speak several sentences in a row, but a scene that is composed almost entirely of long speeches will not help with basic listening-reacting skills.

Here are a few cautions on some popular playwrights. Each of these playwrights has written plays that work wonderfully on stage. And each presents acting problems that may or may not serve you at a particular point in your training. See that the playwright you choose fits the task you are confronting and does not present you with pitfalls that might undermine your learning process.

• **Tennessee Williams** is a terrific playwright. His scenes are all well written, with strong acting beats and rich, poetic language. But many of Williams's scenes require strong character work, and as I note in the chapter "Character Work," the specific acting skills required to create character can make other acting tasks more difficult. If right now what you are working on is emotional depth or listening, trying to do character work may be a distraction. On the other hand, when you *do* want to study character technique, Williams's scenes can be a terrific choice.

• **Harold Pinter**'s characters often hide their feelings beneath a veneer of equanimity. To work on a Pinter scene, you must first discover the scene-beneath-the-scene and then cover that scene with a blasé attitude, while still staying alive to your scene partner. This double task can be very exciting *if* you are already adept at playing strong emotions while listening; but such work can prove extremely difficult in early training. A Pinter scene played for what it *seems* to be about can be very boring.

• **David Mamet**'s characters rarely listen to each other. But the actors playing in Mamet's works must still listen to each other's rhythms. A Mamet scene can serve well to train timing and rhythm, but it may feel a little like performing two simultaneous monologues. If you want to work on listening and reacting to other actors, Mamet scenes will probably push you in the wrong direction.

• **Sam Shepard** scenes are full of strong emotion, and Shepard's characters do listen to each other. The caution with Shepard scenes is that sometimes playing the emotional beats in his scenes can require making strong, *arbitrary* acting choices, without worrying about "justification." In working on a Shepard scene, you may find that some of the beats will actually work just as well one way as another; a line of text may play just as well screamed in anger as it does collapsing in tears. What will not work with Shepard is expecting the playwright to help you by making clear the "right" way to say the line.

When you (and your partner) have decided on a scene, cut the scene short enough so that you will have time to work it several times at each rehearsal. If working on six pages of text means that you can only get through the scene once, cut the scene down. The time spent in memorization might also be time you could spend on your acting skills. Remember, you are not working on play production here.

"DROPPING-IN" *PLASTIQUES*

[EVA MEKLER]: Do you believe that students can arouse their emotions by dealing purely with the text?
[MEL SHAPIRO]: Absolutely. When an actress deals with great language like "Gallop apace...," if she concentrates on what she is saying, things will happen to her organically. She doesn't have to substitute a lot of things or put in a subtext. It's there. When Juliet says, "Take him and cut him out in little stars / And he will make the face of heaven so fine / That all the world will be in love with night / And pay no worship to the garish sun"—what an image! The actress only has to realize what she is talking about. And that's the hard part. It means dealing with the obvious, not looking for something psychological.
　　　　　　　—Mekler, *The New Generation of Acting Teachers*

While preparing scenes from Shakespeare, director Tina Packer, voice teacher Kristin Linklater and the faculty of Shakespeare and Company invented a process they call **Dropping-In.** The essence of Dropping-In is that before memorizing their text, the two actors in a scene remain focused on each other while the text is "fed" to each of them by a coach. The coach feeds a word or two from the text along with a provocative question to stimulate the actor's imagination. The actor simply says the text while "breathing the word into the solar-plexus-diaphragm-breath-emotion-sound energy center."

Then the coach may repeat the same word with another question, and the actor says the word again, allowing the new question to provoke new meaning. Then the coach moves on to the next word in the text, eventually stringing together several words in a phrase. The actor simply stays present with his partner while letting the words and questions play upon him even as he speaks [Linklater 1992, p. 36].

In our work the coaches do not need to feed you actual questions along with the text because the *plastiques* themselves keep your questioning process alive. And, when working with text less dense than Shakespeare, the coaches can feed the text a phrase at a time. I have adapted the Dropping-In for my teaching purposes and created the Dropping-In *Plastiques* (6.2).

Sandra and Veronica have selected a scene from Caryl Churchill's *Top Girls*. Veronica is playing Marlene, the sister who left home to live in London. Sandra plays Joyce, the one who stayed at home and raised Marlene's child. In this scene, Marlene is visiting Joyce after many years' absence; as the two sisters talk in Joyce's kitchen, their years of mutual resentment surface in a violent argument. During Sandra and Veronica's very first Dropping-In exercise, the tenor of their characters' rancor reveals itself in their bodies. Their *plastiques* are aggressive, their voices mocking, and as the scene builds, their attacks overlap, and their bodies strike out at each other's attack even before their coaches can feed them their lines. The physical responsiveness they have been studying enables their bodies to react to every word their partner speaks. Not every line makes sense, but the shape and spirit of the scene is already plain.

After the run-through, I suggest that Veronica and Sandra make some notes for themselves on the moments that worked. "If you do the Dropping-In a couple of times," I add, "you will find that certain lines and certain moments seem to come out the same way every time, while other lines do not. You must

Dropping-In *Plastiques* (6.2)

1. The two actors who are beginning to work on a scene select a portion of the scene to work on. It need not be the very beginning of the scene, but it should be a section with short lines rather than long speeches.

2. The actors hand the text to two coaches, showing them where to begin reading, and deciding which coach is going to feed lines to which actor.

3. The coaches move to the side of the room, and the actors begin their warm-up. Each actor begins a *plastique* River, allowing his images and emotions to change constantly. Once their own Rivers are flowing, the two actors begin to work together, as we did in the Round-Robin Rivers, each reacting to the images and movements of his partner.

4. Then they add voice to the body work, making sure that the sound alternates between the two, while they keep their bodies alive and reactive at all times.

5. When the give-and-take of the sound and *plastique* work is flowing well (both actors are able to lead and to follow, and both are using their voices to reach out and touch the partner), then the two coaches begin to feed the actors, not the text, but short sounds of all kinds. The two actors must use these sounds as the vocal component of their give-and-take. (This step of the work accustoms the actors to allowing themselves to be moved by the coached sounds.)

6. When the two actors are able to play off one another while using the coached sounds, the coaches shift to feeding them the text instead. It is important that the coaches feed the actors just short phrases to begin with—one breath's worth at a time. The actors speak the words that the coaches have fed them, allowing the words to play upon their voices, their bodies, and their image life.

7. This process treats the text as if it were as visceral as pure sound and body work, so it is important that the actors trust their impulses, allowing sense and meaning to arise within the impulse rather than trying to <u>make</u> sense of the words. Notice that your impulse— that is, the acting beat—may change several times in the course of one speech. Trust what your body wants to do.

8. At the end of a few pages, the actors pause to remember what they found and to note down any moments that seemed particularly "right."

trust the rightness of the moments that repeat. You will probably find that some of the beats (the shifts of power and need)
and the actions (what your character is trying to get from the
other character) will make themselves clear even by the second
or third run-through. You can then stick with those actions,
treating them as acting choices you have made, and using them
as jumping-off points as you experiment with the lines that are
not yet clear. Later, in rehearsal, you may find that you have to
change some of those early choices, but for now, trust them."

Peter and Joan have chosen a scene from *The Rimers of
Eldritch,* by Lanford Wilson, a teasing scene between two
teenagers, Robert and Eva, which ends in a near rape. Their
first Dropping-In *Plastiques* session is much less clear than
Veronica and Sandra's. As they work, Peter and Joan keep moving their feet all the time while their arms seem strangely with-
drawn from the action. After the run-through, I point this out
and ask them what happened.

"I don't know," says Peter. "I could feel that my arms were
not working."

"The same with me," Joan concurs. "And I could feel my
feet wandering, but I didn't know what to do about it."

"Well, what is this scene about?" I ask.

"Sex."

"And what was happening in your arms? What did they want
to do?"

"Well, sometimes I wanted to grab him. But that didn't seem
right."

"Why not?"

"Well, I remembered what when we were working with the
plastiques you had warned us not to touch. And besides, it
didn't seem to me that the character would actually do that."

"Good," I respond. "I think you have correctly diagnosed
the problem. The first thing to say is, we are no longer working
on the *plastiques*. But you are right, grabbing your partner still

involves confronting certain risks. Let's see how we can face
them and deal with them. Can you remember the moment when
you wanted to grab him?"

"Yes, it was in this section:

EVA: You don't do things like that, you don't even look! I can,
    though; I know.
ROBERT: You don't know anything.
EVA: I DO TOO! I've seen. . . .

"When he said, 'You don't know anything,' he was turned
away from me. And I came up behind him, and I really wanted
to grab his shoulders and turn him."

"Well, if your arms *want* to grab him, you must acknowledge
that impulse. That desire contains a *plastique* that cannot be
ignored. But working with that impulse, there are several possibilities: One is that you actually grab him and see what happens, even if that seems not right for the character. The second
possibility, if you do not feel safe grabbing your partner, is to
use your image work. Let your hands reach out to grab the
space directly in front of him. He will probably pull away, and
then you will have that pull to deal with. And finally, there are
the words themselves. As you say your line, 'I DO TOO!' you
can let the desire in your arms flow into the words so that the
words grab him. **Let your words have fingers.** Ultimately it is
often the words that will contain the energy of your *plastiques*.
But any one of these methods will permit you to use the
impulse you have. What will *not* work is to remove your arms
and their energy from the action. When you do, your legs will
naturally start to wander around with all that extra energy."

Peter and Joan try the Dropping-In *Plastiques* exercise
again, this time giving themselves permission to touch. The
scene suddenly has great electricity even though, in fact, the
two actors touch each other only for a few fleeting moments, as
if each of their bodies were too hot or too sensitive to handle.
"How was that?" I ask when they finish.

"Fine," says Joan. "I think these characters might even touch each other like that."

"Yes," I say, "you will often find out as you work that your preconceptions about what your characters would or would not do dissolve when you trust the work. But if that had not happened here, even if allowing yourselves to touch had not worked, you could have tried again, making another choice. Remember, what you are doing here is experimenting, *allowing your own reactions to surprise you* with the information you need about how to play each line. For that process to work, you must **trust what happens to you without worrying about whether it seems 'right' or 'logical' or 'appropriate' for the character**. Those questions come later. Some of what you discover will not make sense, and as you repeat the scene several times, those 'inaccurate' impulses will fall away. But some of your reactions will make perfect sense right off the bat; they will be acting beats that arise full-blown, with vocal power and gesture, without your having had to do the 'table work' to figure them out."

"But now I don't understand," says Peter. "Are we supposed to be making sense of the words, or are we supposed to be using the words as if they were just sounds?"

"We enter the words with our bodies and voices to connect with them on an unconscious level. But *unconscious* does not mean 'meaningless.' If the playwright is any good, your impulsive choices will converge with the meaning of the words. If you find that what you are doing is meaning-filled, that's fine."

I turn to speak to the whole class. "The experience of wandering during this work is almost always a sign that you are trying to save yourself from some impulse—for example, that your arms really want to pull you one way, but your mind is pulling you another. If you find yourself wandering, you need to make a clear choice, *any* clear choice, and see where it leads you. If your impulse is to walk up to your partner and grab him, try it. When you do, your partner may move away, so then you will need to cross to him again. Or, if you do grab him, he may push you away, and then you will have that push to react to. Remember your impulse is also a gift to your partner.

"On the other hand, if you take a step forward and that choice feels wrong to you, then you can try the opposite and take a step away, but each time do it fully! And if what you are feeling is ambivalence, then move one way on one line, and then the other way on the second line.[1] In any case, if you don't like the choice you have made, you can always try something else, but as long as you wander, all the audience sees is the avoidance."

The next couple to try the Dropping-In *Plastiques* is Aisha and Carlos, who are doing a scene from Shelagh Delaney's *A Taste of Honey*. Aisha's character is Jo, a teenage girl who is trying to ignore her pregnancy. Carlos plays her friend Geof, who urges Jo to face reality and to accept his support. Their Dropping-In is much more quiet and less intensely physical than the other students', and as they find gestures and movements for the lines they are fed, Carlos and Aisha keep steering away from each other.

At the end, Carlos is worried. "Was that okay? You told Joan to touch Peter in their scene, but in our scene it just felt wrong to get too close."

"I think you're right about that scene," I say. "It does contain a great deal of separation, and you'll be able to see even more clearly if that's true when you try the Dropping-In Crossings exercise later in your training. But at this point, there is no more that you can do in this work than to put your whole self into the process, and then *trust* what happens. You found that these two characters often steer away from each other. Trust it."

---

1. It is true that ambivalent people in real life often display stasis, but stasis on stage will not convey the inner conflict as clearly as taking one action and then taking an opposite one.

The last couple to try the Dropping-In *Plastiques* exercise is Brian and Maria, who have chosen a scene from Ariel Dorfman's *Death and the Maiden*. In this scene they portray Gerardo and Paulina, a husband and wife who have lived through a dictatorship and are now trying to rebuild their relationship across the chasm of pain and jealousy that separates them. During the dictatorship Paulina was tortured and Gerardo had an affair. Now each wants the other to tell his/her story.

The problem Brian and Maria encounter is that although their bodies and voices are fully engaged, they seem not to be affecting one another. Rather than allowing the exercise to continue like this, I stop their run-through to explain what I see happening. "You have to be careful," I say, "to direct your energies *at* your scene partner. Maria, even when you say, 'That bitch came out of the bedroom half naked,' you cannot get so lost in your imagery about the bitch that you no longer care about the effect it will have on your husband. Your *plastiques* are weapons of various kinds. But the battle is between the two of you."

"But in the *Taste of Honey* scene you said that the sense of separation was right," Maria points out.

"Yes, characters often say things that are directed toward their own imagery. Still, you must exist in the same world as your partner. There is also the danger of transforming an argument into two parallel monologues."

As soon as Brian and Maria redirect their *plastiques* toward each other, the scene starts to make sense. They find to their surprise that rather than distracting them from their own desires, the resistance offered by the other character actually increases the vehemence of what they have to say to each other.

After everyone has finished the exercise, I turn to the group to say, "For first run-throughs, it seems to me that these scenes went pretty well."

Joan, however, has doubts. "I don't know," she says. "Somehow this way of working seems . . . purposefully illogical. I mean, I like what we're doing. But each of these scenes we just went through was just a bunch of impulses, as if every scene were some kind of fight. I almost feel like to work this way I have to throw my mind out the window."

"Well," I say, "you are really raising two issues here. One is the question of everything looking like a fight. And there *is* a sense in which every dramatic scene ever written can be thought of as a fight of one kind or another, even love scenes. In fact, Shakespeare writes love scenes in *The Taming of the Shrew* and *Richard III* that demonstrate that love scenes *are* fight scenes. What we need to do is expand our idea of what a battle is. The Weapons exercise we will work on in our next class should help us do that.

"But I also want to say something about the second issue you have raised, the issue of logic. **The basis of the technique we are studying here is that often your body will find deep, connected, emotional logic without interference from your mind.** But that does not mean you must 'throw your mind out the window.' There may well be times when you discover that these purely physical methods are not sufficient to help you make the right choices in a scene. And when that happens, it is useful to let your mind help with the search. Why is your character using exactly those words? What does she really want from the other character? But even then, the mind's job is not to figure out how to play the moment, but rather to help you make another physical choice that will further your physical/ emotional search.

"Remember when we were working on the *plastiques*, you sometimes used your mind to help you notice when you had been leaving one or another part of your body out of the work? That insight could jump-start your engine, but once it did, you had to allow the physical process to do its job. The same is true here. For instance, in the *Rimers of Eldritch* scene, Joan knew that *something* was wrong with a particular line, but when she attacked the problem only with her mind, she was stymied by the opinion that her character would not act in a certain way. The solution came not by using her mind to figure out what her character would do, but by using it to help her search for more options. Once she had another option to try—allowing herself to touch—she had to permit her body/impulse mechanism to sense what the right choices were."

THE WEAPONS WORK

The intellectual content of a text is studied everywhere; our task was to concentrate on the aspect of language that had become sadly neglected over the centuries: the vibratory power of its sound.

—Yoshi Oida, *An Actor Adrift*

When you say, "I was *struck* by what he said," or "Her smile *moved* me," you have metaphorically expressed the *physicality of listening*. And just as your body would be moved differently if you were struck by a feather than if you were struck by a bowling ball, so too you will be "moved" differently by different words. In a naturalistic production, you may not be "bowled over" by each line your partner says, yet each line will "*strike*" you in its own peculiar way. **Since the *plastiques* are movements *in reaction* to what we receive, they act as physical metaphors for the act of listening itself.** They make concrete our task as actors to allow ourselves to be "touched" by everything we hear, and they demand that we be *specific* about exactly *how* we are touched.

The next day in class, I return to Joan's first comment. "Yesterday Joan pointed out that each scene was turning into some kind of a fight. Today I'd like to take a moment to look at the ways in which acting is—and is not—about fighting. Remember, after the *Rimers* scene I talked about 'allowing the words to have fingers,' and during the *Death and the Maiden* scene I pointed out that the actors need to direct their lines right *at* each other? Other acting systems talk about 'playing your intention,' that is, allowing the words to be the *means* by which your character gets what he or she wants. Many acting teachers train their students to figure out the proper intention for their characters to pursue at every moment. But in our process an intention is not something that you have to stop and figure out. As long as you listen with your whole body to what your partner is saying to you, and as long as you direct your energy and images toward your scene partner, most intentions will arise on their own, as impulses in your muscles.

"For instance, when you were doing your Round-Robin Rivers two weeks ago, what you wanted from each other was usually quite clear. You did not need to figure out an intention in order to play it. In your impulsive Dropping-In scene work, your vibrant, listening body supplied the intention on its own. **Your impulses** *were* **the subtext**—even though it was the words that were striking your partner. You did not have to think, 'What my character wants on this line is to shake some sense into my partner.' You were shaking him."

To make this physical-verbal translation clearer, I teach my class the **Weapons Work** (6.3 and 6.4). I ask each actor to stand opposite his or her scene partner and start a "conversation" using vowel sounds and full-body gestures, throwing the sounds toward each other as if they were weapons. As they add the consonants, I suggest that they become more and more precise in their movements, allowing each gesture to be linked with a sound, and letting each sound be like a limb or a "weapon" that reaches out to "touch" the partner. After working with vowels and consonants, I have the actors move to gibberish and finally to the words from their text.

The class has great fun doing this work, but they fall into a common trap. As they work, many of the actors lean forward, craning their necks and tightening their jaws, treating every line as if it were an attack.

"What you are experiencing here," I say when we take a break, "are the very dangers that Joan perceived in the

Dropping-In scenes—the dangers of interpreting every stage moment as aggressive and of failing to listen and receive. To remedy this problem, I want you to enter the Weapons Work again, but this time I want you to remember how you used the *plastiques* when you did the Kiss exercise. I want you to expand your idea of what a weapon is to include all kinds of emotional gestures. The important thing is that your words still reach out and touch your partner, but the sensation those touches inflict could be joy or sorrow or sexuality as well as pain."

The Weapons Work #1 (6.3)

This exercise can be done by a group in a circle, or with partners.

1. One actor sends a sound and movement to another, as if the sound and body gesture were an imaginary weapon directed through space. The receiver then aims another sound/gesture/weapon at another actor. One gesture might be like a giant sword, swung from the waist, the next like a series of bullets from the eyes, the next might be imaginary clods of mud kicked with the feet. Each gesture-weapon activates a particular resonator and pitch, and each is aimed to "hit" the partner in a particular place. What you are working on is a variation and range of weapons (not weapon after weapon held in the hands) and on a particular effect (my twelve-foot fingernails and my nasal whine are scraping the skin off your left leg).

2. At the same time, the person who is receiving the blow allows her body to take in the energy of the hit fully and with precision. (The edge of your tongue-whip slices me across the stomach, knocking me down.)

3. Once you are able to keep giving and receiving with changing rhythms and images, the next step is to begin to use the text, one phrase at a time. Each phrase is like a weapon. Each phrase is clearly meant to get through to your partner, and to do so in a very particular way. (With this word that vibrates in my head resonator, I send a laser beam from my eyes into your stomach. With this rumbling sentence, my pelvis vibrates waves of mud to engulf your legs.)

4. Be careful not to strain your voice.

In the second round of the game it becomes clear that a "weapon" can be really any image that emanates from one actor and touches another, and that the core of this exercise is the understanding that **each word contains an action you are doing *to* your partner.** But that action may not be aggressive at all. This time the "weapons" the actors use start to take on the flavors of their particular characters: While the two sisters in the *Top Girls* scene slash at each other, drawing verbal blood, the teenagers in *The Rimers of Eldritch* use their lines to prod, to irritate, and to tickle each other.

The Weapons Work #2 (6.4)

1. First reestablish your giving and receiving with weapons. Make sure your voice and body are working fully.

2. Now begin to enlarge your interpretation of what a weapon is. Could a kiss be a weapon? Could a feather? Could a smile?

3. And what about the "weapon" of just receiving the blow: The sound of hopeless surrender? The gesture of acceptance, of love?

4. Now continue the exercise, finding "weapons" of all flavors. As you do, you may have to turn up your sensitivity too, so that you can be "bowled over" by a smile. Remember how, in the Kiss exercise, even a gentle, invisible image could affect your whole body and emotions.

5. Now go back to your text. Try out each line in several ways: What is it like to say your line as a slap in the face? What is it like to say it as a caress? Or a plea?

6. Notice which weapons seem to have the greatest effect on your partner. Notice which weapons your partner uses that get through to you.

7. After working through about ten lines, stop to talk with each other and to take notes on what worked.

WHAT ABOUT OBJECTIVES AND INTENTIONS?

Let's say someone does a scene and it's just okay. I will often ask the person if he or she has ever gone sailing. He or she might say yes. I will then ask, "How do you get a sailboat to go from one place to another when you can't go in a straight line? It would be no fun or adventure if

you could just go straight. It's all that tacking that makes
sailing fun. That's *the pleasure. If what happens to you*
while you are going from one place to another isn't excit-
ing, isn't a pleasure, simply having arrived at your desti-
nation in a straight line doesn't make any difference. Now
please try doing the scene again as if you are sailing and
you don't know whether you are going to get to your desti-
nation right away or not, but there is a little time to enjoy
the wind and the sun."

—Allen Miller in Mekler,
The New Generation of Acting Teachers

Early in his career, Stanislavski developed the notion that actors should attempt to determine their characters' "objectives," the unspoken motivations that fuel their actions on stage. And many acting training systems today teach acting students that they must be able to figure out, to articulate, and to play the objectives, and/or the intentions of the characters they are playing. Lee Strasberg writes, "The real action of the scene is expressed by the character's intentions" [Strasberg, p. 36]. So actors who come to the study of physical theater from other training systems are sometimes concerned that I don't employ those terms.

I believe that intentions and objectives and the use of "active verbs" can be very useful to an actor, but these practices also hold real dangers. After all, playwrights do not write intentions or objectives. Playwrights write dialogue. Intentions, objectives, and active verbs may aid directors who need to make a play "work" on stage, but they often serve a scene in much the way tracks serve a train: they keep it barreling forward toward some goal, rather oblivious of the scenery, the hills, and the stations along the way. By skillfully aiming the characters' intentions in opposition to one another, a clever director can make every scene into an exciting train wreck. But most good playwrights have already made sure that the characters are operating at cross-purposes. All the actors really have to do is listen and react to each other, and the train wrecks will occur as written, without the director or the actors trying quite so hard.[2]

There are some playwrights, like Harold Pinter or Oscar Wilde, whose characters are so good at obfuscating what they are feeling that it may be useful for you to begin rehearsals of their scenes by physicalizing the unspoken hostility between the characters—rather than playing what they seem to be saying to each other. But once your body is in touch with these underlying impulses, you will not need to worry about playing these hidden intentions. Each lie your character speaks will reveal itself in your physical language.

With most playwrights, even when they write scenes in which the intentions of the characters are not obvious at first, if you allow the text to play upon you, you will usually find that the way in which the character uses his words, the tone of his avoidance or his lies will betray itself in your body and voice. In other words, even when the intention is hidden, it will reveal itself in your impulses. In *Hamlet*, for instance, the prince hides his true feelings from several of the other characters, but his tone and his asides allow the actor (and the audience) to sense a great deal more of what is going on within the character. What makes *Hamlet* exciting is not watching Hamlet ride relentlessly toward his destruction, but rather all the amazing detours he makes on his way there. Playing Hamlet's intentions may smooth out the emotional roller coaster of his tragedy. But who wants to ride a smooth roller coaster?

To put it simply: if you keep your full body open and available, **your character's intentions will arise within you, quite unconsciously, as you react to your own lines as well as your partner's actions and lines, without your needing to figure them out.**

As Grotowski said, "The intention exists even at a muscular

2. Stanislavski was both an acting teacher and a director. Perhaps it was Stanislavski the director, rather than Stanislavski the acting teacher, who developed the idea of the "objective."

level in the body, and is linked to some objective outside you" (Quoted in Richards, p. 95).

BLOCKING AND STAGE MOVEMENT

While every other artist, both in the process of work and after its completion, being separate from the work he is creating, can at any moment physically see it, check it, varying as he chooses the point of view, distance, light— the actor lacks this important resource. In order to compensate for this lack and not be condemned to blindness, he must develop in himself an inner second sight; he must create along-side his own creative ego a second ego, unseen but seeing.

—Alexander Tairov, *Notes of a Director*

Directors are taught that they are responsible for creating a "stage picture" that includes the location of every character on stage and all the *blocking* that moves the characters about. Since most directors assume these responsibilities, many actors may feel that their character's stage movement is not within their control. They are responsible for their character's voice, gestures, and emotions, but the blocking is out of their hands. In a scene-study class, however, you must work without a director, yet the life of a scene can be enormously affected by its staging. So it is important for an actor to realize that he or she *can* make blocking and stage movement decisions that will support the acting of a scene. In fact, the awareness of space and the sensitivity to physical relationships you have been developing in this physical acting training prepare you to do just that.

Blocking serves several purposes:

1. It helps to focus the audience's attention on the action.
2. It creates images that clarify the story.
3. It expresses the changing relationships of the characters.

With the aid of the **Viewpoint** work (see sidebar), an actor can actually create movement to serve *all* these purposes. But even if you do not wish to take on the responsibility for directing the audience's attention or creating clarifying images, you *must* pay attention to the third purpose of blocking—*expressing the relationship between characters.* **The principal engine of this element of blocking is the constantly changing emotional distance between the characters.**

Some lines leave no doubt about the blocking they demand.

The Viewpoints

Over the past fifteen years, as many dancers have begun to integrate sound and text into their choreography, movement teachers Mary Overlie and Wendell Beavers have created a movement training called *Six-Viewpoints* or *Viewpoint Theory*, which allows performers to "invent" stage movement for themselves. By tuning in to the Viewpoints—Space, Time, Shape, Kinetic Awareness, Emotion, and Story—a performer can develop an awareness of the whole stage picture. Like a musician who listens to all the other instruments while she plays, a Viewpoint-trained actor "listens" to the spatial relationships, the various rhythms and shapes each actor is making, and "sees" the group as a whole. The actor's own movement choices then depend on both his internal impulses and his reaction to all of these other elements.

The Viewpoint of Space, for instance, includes an awareness of groupings of bodies on stage, of lines, of empty space, and so on. An actor with Viewpoint training will sense how the movements of all the other actors alter the space as a whole. Sensing the altered picture, the actor will then adjust his own position on stage to rebalance the space, just as a director might.

Similarly, the actor will react to each new rhythm and each change of energy on stage, searching for how his own character's movements can complement those of the others on stage. The Viewpoint-trained actor thus takes responsibility for the whole stage "composition," as a jazz musician takes responsibility for the "composition" of a piece of music.

Anne Bogart and other directors have also employed the Viewpoints to "compose" stage movement and images from a directorial point of view.[3]

---

3. For a fuller explanation of the Viewpoints work, see Michael Bigelow Dixon and Joel A. Smith, ed., *Anne Bogart, Viewpoints*.

You just can't say a line like, "But, I love you. Please, stay with me!" while walking away from your scene partner. As you speak the line, your body will naturally move toward her. Most lines are not quite this obvious, yet the principle remains the same: the physical impulse you feel as you speak the line will impel your body to create blocking. The Crossing exercises have trained you to react physically even to extremely subtle changes of emotional distance. Now you can use your Crossings to help you become your own director.

THE DROPPING-IN CROSSING

I don't believe in chopping the script up into beats and finding them before you work with your scene partner, because beats are often based on what the other person does.
—Michael Kahn, in Mekler,
The New Generation of Acting Teachers

If you add the Dropping-In work to your Crossings work, what emerges will be basic blocking for your scene. In **The Dropping-In Crossing** (6.5), rather than working fully with your body, keep your body fairly relaxed, simply sending all the acting impulses into your legs, interpreting each impulse either as a movement *toward* or as a movement *away* from your partner. It is important in this work that you interpret the Crossing rules loosely: a move away might be anything from lowering your eyes to running across the room. But the essence of the game remains the same: **you let your body tell you what movement each line requires.**

PRIVATE SPACE

The first couple to try these text-driven Crossings is Aisha and Carlos. In their *Taste of Honey* scene, Carlos's character, Geof,

The Dropping-In Crossing (6.5)

1. Begin doing the Second Crossing work with your scene partner. Remember the essence of the work is the question, "<u>Toward</u> or <u>away</u>?" and that changing your level by sitting, crouching, or crawling is also possible.

2. Work silently for a minute and then add your voices as you did when preparing to do the Dropping-In *Plastiques* exercise.

3. When the two of you are working smoothly off each other, have the two coaches begin feeding you alternating sound impulses while you and your scene partner allow the sound to drive your steps.

4. Then have the two coaches "drop-in" short sections of your lines while you keep the Crossing going.

5. Allow yourself to move <u>toward</u> and <u>away</u>, making and breaking eye contact and changing level as the words move you. You may feel the need to move not only on your own lines but also on your partner's lines. See what happens if you trust these impulses also.

6. Do the Crossing while Dropping-In the lines several times. Trust what you discover. Any moves that seem to recur at each run-through are blocking decisions that you can "set," at least for the moment.

is trying to convince his pregnant friend, Jo, that she should prepare for her coming motherhood, but Jo keeps avoiding the subject. The Crossing exercise makes it quite clear that the "problem" the actors had experienced in their Dropping-In *Plastique* work is not their problem but the characters'. Jo and Geof are having a very difficult conversation with one another, and every time one of them gets too personal, the other seems to avoid the subject.

JO: I never thought I'd still be here in the summer. Would you like to be the father of my baby? Geoffrey?

GEOF: Yes, I would. What time is it?

JO: Half-past four by the church clock. Why do you stay here, Geof?

GEOF: Someone's got to look after you. You can't look after yourself.

JO: I think there's going to be a storm. . . .

At the end of the exercise Aisha says to me, "When we were doing the Weapons Work, you said each word we say relates to what we need from our partner. But in this scene we're working on, a lot of my lines are not really *to* my partner at all, so all I wanted to do was to move *away* from him."

"It was the same for me," says Carlos. "With a lot of my lines I just wanted to move away from her too."

"Well," I say, "one thing to remember is that in our Weapons Work we began to see that there are many different kinds of weapons. Turning your back on your partner can be just as much of a weapon as attacking him. But there is more here. One issue we haven't talked about yet is the need for *private space*. When a character turns away from another character it is not *only* an action directed at the partner. It can also be an expression of the character's need for privacy. Or, to put it another way, when you are moving *away* from your scene partner, you are often moving *toward* something else, a memory for instance, or the image of a character who is not on stage.

"You remember that we began this training with an exploration of Safe Space for you, the actor. But safety and privacy are also important to many characters. In fact, in some scenes this need can be *the* driving force. In the scene from *Top Girls* that Sandra and Veronica are working on, for instance, one of the elements that Joyce and Marlene are arguing about is place. The house they are in is Joyce's house in which she is at home, but in which Marlene is out of place. In Williams's *A Streetcar Named Desire*, Blanche DuBois has had to sell everything she has, and she is reduced to living behind a curtain in her sister's house in New Orleans. One could see the whole of *Streetcar* as a clash of two spaces: Blanche's and Stanley's.

"But even with scenes in which the question of space is not so obvious, actors often discover that their characters need some kind of private space in order to explore their personal thoughts and images, or just to get away from the other characters on stage. This is what is going on in your *Taste of Honey* scene. **What the Crossing does is transform psychological needs**

into objective, spatial action. In your *Taste of Honey* scene, the Crossing converts the characters' emotional avoidance into literal withdrawal. The text indicates that Jo looks out the window at the children, and at the weather. But looking out the window is also a way for her to be alone with her thoughts. You will find in many scenes that your characters need moments when they withdraw from the others on stage in order to be closer to their inner reality.

"As you move this scene toward more and more precision, you will probably find that your props can also help you be alone and communicate. Human beings use objects to protect themselves from each other and to speak to each other. This scene contains baby clothes, a glass of milk, and a bar of chocolate, and each object can serve your physical need to pull away or to approach the other character."

When characters withdraw from each other in a naturalistic scene, they often use elements of the set to help them create their private spaces. As an actor, you may need to reverse this process: to give yourself space and props that supply your character with the private space he or she needs. Depending on the piece you are working on, that private space might be a table at which your character has an activity, or it might be a mirror the character looks at, or maybe your character looks out the window.

Keep in mind that even though your *character* needs the space in order to be alone, you, the *actor*, need to share that aloneness with the audience. A downstage private space turns the audience into your confidantes, so by moving your privacy downstage you can often help yourself feel and share emotions that might otherwise lie hidden. Keep in mind that it is very important that you **fill in the downstage wall with imagery,** so that the energy you receive from the audience is filtered through the character's world, like light coming through a scrim.

Beyond the question of private space, the Crossing exercise can also supply you with other useful information. The length of the Crossings you find yourself making will give you a sense of how large the playing space needs to be. The *Top Girls* scene takes place in a small kitchen in which the two characters are in each other's way. The *Rimers of Eldritch* scene, on the other hand, happens in the woods.

Another clue to your blocking may show itself in your impulse to have your eye level above or below that of your scene partner. In a naturalistic scene, characters raise and lower their eye level by standing or sitting down in a chair. If you keep having the impulse to move toward your partner, yet you sense that you never can reach her, it may be that you need there to be a table or some other physical barrier between you and your partner. In other words, if you pay attention to what your body is telling you, the Crossing will actually help you create a set for your scene. A stage set is not just a bunch of furniture invented by a designer to create an illusion for the audience. **A set can be an emanation of the characters' needs, a structure that serves the physical/emotional relationships in the scene.**

And, if your Crossings do not give you all the information you need, remember: the essence of this work is experimentation. Perhaps you know that your scene calls for a bed, but exactly where should the bed be put? Try the scene with the bed in different places. If you place the bed upstage, does that make for more or less eye contact with your partner than if the bed is downstage? Which solution makes the action of the scene stronger for you? Remember, in creating your set, as in all the work you do, your job as an actor is to create those circumstances that will call up within you the strongest, clearest acting beats possible. You can actually facilitate your acting a great deal by creating a set that helps clarify the characters' relationship.

WHAT ABOUT THE
"PRIOR CIRCUMSTANCES"?

*Preparation is that device which permits you to start your
scene or play in a condition of emotional aliveness. . . .
[But it] lasts only for the first moment of the scene, and
then you never know what's going to happen.*
— Sanford Meisner, *Sanford Meisner on Acting*

The Crossings for the *Rimers of Eldritch* and the *Top Girls*
scenes go smoothly. The actors are surprised at how quickly
their scenes make sense and how much of the blocking grows
quite automatically out of the process of listening and responding with their bodies. But when Brian and Maria try the Dropping-In Crossing with their *Death and the Maiden* scene, they
encounter a problem: The scene begins with Maria's character,
Paulina, saying, "I don't understand why." Her line is obviously an answer to something her husband, Gerardo, has said
to her before the written scene begins. But since our Dropping-
In exercise begins with an improvisation, the moment *before*
Maria's line is different in each run-through. The first time the
two run through the lines, Brian happens to be moving toward
Maria just before their coaches start the text. The result is that
Maria's "I don't understand why" seems very defensive. As she
says the line she throws up her hands and backs away from
him. But the second time through, the coaches start feeding the
lines while Brian is moving away from Maria. The result is that
her "I don't understand why" comes out with an angry edge, as
if she were saying, "Why can't you explain it to me?"

After the second run-through, Brian notes this problem.
"How can we ever get that first line right? Everything else is a
reaction to something in the text, but the first line comes out of
nowhere."

"Good," I say. "You've put your finger on another area we
need to talk about: preparation. In fact the problem you

noticed was true for every scene we have done, because our technique up to this point has begun with pure improvisation. When the improvisation happened to end on an appropriate impulse, the first line seemed right; when it did not, it took a couple of lines before the scene made sense. The same was true with the Dropping-In *Plastiques* work. But, in fact, scenes do not come out of nowhere. The *Rimers of Eldritch* scene is the continuation of a scene that occurs earlier in the text. Both the *Top Girls* and the *Taste of Honey* scenes we are seeing are cuttings of longer scenes, so you know exactly what happened before your first lines. But in this *Death and the Maiden* scene, the author has purposefully begun the scene in the middle of an argument between Paulina and Gerardo, yet it is very clear that just before that first line, Gerardo must have asked Paulina to tell him the story of what was done to her. So in all of these scenes the moment before the first line is quite clear. But even if you were doing a scene that began with two characters meeting for the first time, each of those characters *is* coming from somewhere, from something—on stage or off—that happened to each of the characters *before* the first line.

"To remedy this problem, Sanford Meisner and many other acting teachers suggest that you *imagine* the *prior circumstances* to put yourself in the right condition to enter the scene. But when Meisner wants to give an example of effective preparation, the story he tells is not about mental preparation, but about a physical technique:

> In the last century, the English actor William Charles Macready, before playing a certain scene in *The Merchant of Venice*, used to try to shake the iron ladder backstage that was embedded in the brick. He'd try and try, and would get furious because he couldn't budge it. *Then* he went on and played the scene. [Meisner, p. 80]

"Using the work we have been studying here, you can allow yourself not just to imagine but to *experience* the moments that lead you up to your entrance. If you do a Cat while searching for the imagery of these off-stage moments, you will often find that the requisite images will enter your body, evoking the emotional responses you need for that first line on stage. If the Cat doesn't work for you, look for another physical/emotional container that will allow your body to live through the beats that come just before your scene begins."

I end the class with a final admonition to the students to trust what their bodies tell them in the *Plastique* and the Crossing exercises. "If you do not have coaches to feed you the lines, you will have to memorize a few lines at a time. But, as you do, remember to really listen and to trust your reactions. Trust that your impulses are giving you the blocking you need. As you find movements, beats, and blocking that occur the same way each time, start making decisions. Your decisions need not be final decisions, but **look for physical forms that permit you to play *repeatable* acting beats.** If you start needing furniture, make decisions about the set. But if making the scene very naturalistic seems to inhibit your physical listening, go back to the full-body work. The most important thing is that before you present the scene in class, you have worked on the scene enough so that you have answered all the questions you know how to answer on your own. Then, when you share it with us, we can be helpful in moving you on to the next level of questions."

REHEARSING ON YOUR OWN

In English, the word rehearsal *derives from a rehearing. In French, a rehearsal is* la repetition, *and it means what it sounds like—a repetition. My favorite meaning comes from the German* die Probe *which sounds like what a rehearsal ought to be: the probe! I want to probe, to test, to try . . . to adventure!*

—Uta Hagen, *Respect for Acting*

The experience of working on a scene with another actor but without the guidance of a teacher or director can be a difficult one. When you are actually rehearsing a play, most of your rehearsal process, for better or worse, is done in front of the director. (For better, because the director can guide you toward making effective choices, and supply you with props, images, and motivations. For worse, because the director may short-circuit your acting process, pushing you toward choices while you still need to experiment.) But when preparing a scene for a class, you are usually on your own. The suggestions in this section are aimed at helping you work when there is no outside eye to give you feedback.

Different acting training systems propose different rehearsal progressions. Some techniques teach you to work privately on the images and emotions you will need for a scene before you rehearse with your scene partner. Others have you begin with listening and reacting to your partner first, adding your personal preparation later. Some have you begin your work sitting in a chair; others engage your body from the start. Some would have you "analyze" the text carefully before you try to act it; others tell you to let the text play upon you. Of course, the techniques suggested in this book are more of the "get on your feet and save the thinking for later" school. But, **whatever technique you are using, here is the bottom line: there is no way to work on everything at once. The most important thing is to be clear with your scene partner as to *what* you are working on at each rehearsal.** That way, each day you will be able to measure your progress based on what you *have* accomplished, rather than always dreading what you have yet to do.

When you focus on one element of your process, some other element will often slip. Yesterday you felt as though your emotions were very full, but today, while you are adding details of character gesture and work with props, you feel emotionally flat. That is to be expected. Now that you have established some of the blocking and prop work, you can plan another run-through with a warm-up or preparation that will help you rediscover your emotional depth. There is simply no way to do everything at once.

The following suggestions are designed to be helpful no matter what acting technique you practice:

• Let yourself make decisions and set blocking as you go along. Rehearsal is a cumulative process, and one that requires constant readjustment. Once you have discovered, say, the basic emotional beats of a scene and some blocking that works for you, live with those choices for a while and apply yourself to some other task. If, later, you discover that certain choices you made before no longer seem right, you can change them. But if you always try to keep all your options open, never setting anything, you will find it hard to move on.

• At some rehearsals, rehearse the scene by sections. Don't try to run through the whole thing each time. It may feel less satisfying to go over and over the same six lines, but if you try to run through several pages of dialogue each time, it can be very, very hard to remember what you did; and that makes it difficult to make the choices that allow you to repeat what you liked and change what you did not. So go through a short section—perhaps two or three beats—until it feels right, or at least better than before. Then move on to the next section, and then run both sections consecutively.

• Vary your rehearsal tasks and techniques. If for several rehearsals now you've been working while sitting in chairs, try some full-body work—and vice versa. If you've been concentrating on character, try a run-though in which you're just trying to play off your scene partner's rhythms and emotions. Not only does varying the task relieve the tedium; but very often, *not* concentrating on a problem will allow the problem to find a solution on its own. For instance, some emotion that you have been struggling to attain may suddenly show up while you are searching for precision in your use of props or gesture.

• After each run-through, take a moment to remember what you did before you turn to your scene partner and start talking.

A few seconds' pause right after a run-through will help you remember your work, making it much easier to repeat those moments that worked for you.

• *Give yourself positive feedback*. Even after the worst run-through, there is usually at least a line here, a gesture there, or a bit of timing you might want to save. If you let your mind run immediately to what you did *not* like in the scene, you may distract yourself from recognizing the things that *did* work, and you will then have to rediscover them another time.

• Be specific. If a moment worked well for you, be specific about what made it work: Was it your preparation? The character work? Or was it something your partner said or did on the line before? If so, tell him or her, so it can happen again. If a line that worked during the previous run sounded off this time, try to pinpoint exactly what happened differently.

• Remember that you are working on your acting technique, not on performance. The point is for you to learn about what works for you, not to come up with a finished product for a reviewer (or even for the teacher). This work is for you.

With these suggestions in mind, you should be able to create a process that allows you to build on each rehearsal. But there is one more problem that crops up in rehearsals often enough to bear commenting on: how to talk to another actor.

HOW TO TALK TO ANOTHER ACTOR

An actor has no right to mould his partner so as to provide greater possibilities for his own performance.
                    —Grotowski, *Towards a Poor Theatre*

Many arts can be practiced, accomplished, even enjoyed, in complete solitude. People who become painters and poets thrive on working alone. And many musicians enjoy spending endless hours practicing by themselves. But one of the greatest attractions of the theater is that it is a group activity, so the people who are drawn to theater are often those who relish human interaction.

So . . . what do you do if your scene partner is not giving you what you need, or if every time you rehearse, your partner's work style or choices seem to impede rather than aid your own creative process? In rehearsal for a production, you might be able to turn to the director for help—out of earshot of the other actor. But if the two of you are working alone for a scene-study class, what can you do? Should you tell your partner that what she is doing is wrong, or should you make do with whatever she is giving you, even if it doesn't seem to serve the action you thought you were playing?

Neither. Both of these choices are recipes for trouble.

If you try to tell your partner that what she is doing is wrong, then even if you are absolutely right, you are placing yourself in the position of being a teacher or a director. And even if your partner is willing to take your suggestions, she may begin to resent you, and pieces of her resentment will begin to creep into the scene you are working on.

If, on the other hand, you choose not to say anything, it is *you* who may feel resentment. And your own unspoken feelings may begin to poison your work process and infect the scene. Playing a love scene with a scene partner you resent is as bad as kissing a scene partner with bad breath.

So what can you do?

Here's an alternative: **Rather than telling your partner what she should be doing, ask your partner for what you need.** For instance, instead of saying, "You should be angrier on your line," try saying, "This line is not working for me. I think it might help me if you could give me a shove (a sharp look) on the line before. Could we try it that way once?"

And rather than saying, "Your character wouldn't look away from me," try saying, "When you turn away on that line, I seem to lose something. Can we see what happens if you face me?"

Your scene partner may even find that she likes this new way of delivering her line. But even if your partner insists on playing the line "her" way, you will be able to remember hearing her do it "your" way.

The important thing is that you express what you need to express, so that you don't go on feeling unheard, and that you do so without criticizing your partner's work or insisting that you know better than she what the playwright means. You may or may not get what you need on each line, but at least you will feel that you have tried, and the two of you will be able to continue working amicably together. Moreover, once you have dared to make space for honest communication, your partner will also be able to speak more honestly to you.

A final note: If you find yourself on the *receiving* end of poor communication, try explaining, "You may be right, but it would be easier for me to hear you if you could just tell me what it is *you* need."

LISTENING ALL THE TIME

Peter and Joan are the first couple to present their rehearsed scene in front of the class. As preparation, each of them does a physical warm-up, and then they chase each other around the space several times before starting their lines. This preparation serves perfectly to start them off into the *Rimers of Eldritch* scene, which is full of teasing and sexual tension. During the first part of the scene, Peter's character, Robert, seems shy and slightly badgered by Joan's Eva. His discomfort is obvious, and his nervous movements seem well connected with his lines. But as the two of them near the climax of the scene, Peter's actions become unclear. And when, at the end of the scene, Robert has to attack Eva, Peter's gestures are wooden and unbelievable.

When they finish, I ask the two actors to sit quietly for a moment and think about how this run-through went for them.

"Try to remember details of what worked for you and what did not." I give them a couple of minutes of silence, and then I ask them to come downstage and tell us about their experience.

"Oh, I just can't get that last part of the scene to work for me at all," says Peter. "Every time we run it, no matter how well the rest of the scene goes, it doesn't feel right."

"It was the same for me," Joan concurs. "I actually thought most of the scene went well. Ever since we found that warm-up at one rehearsal, the first section of the scene has felt really solid."

"How set is it?" I ask. "Is the blocking the same each time?"

"Well, we didn't exactly set it. But it comes out pretty much the same. I mean I know when he's going to move away from me. And on one line I always reach out toward him, and he always pulls away. The only difference is whether or not I actually touch him."

"Good," I say. "That's exactly how this work progresses. To keep that moment alive from now on, you will need to become more and more precise about how close the two of you are and exactly how you touch."

I turn to the full group and add, "I want to point out that it is very important to note the *positive* things you have to say to yourselves. Don't worry: you won't forget the negative ones if you put off thinking about them for a few minutes. But the positive ones could slip away.

"But now let's get to the problem with the end of the scene. Peter, you said that you've had this problem at every run-through?"

"There are really two problems. One is that I don't really feel like attacking her. For the whole scene Robert has been running away from her, and I don't know how to make that beat change. And the second thing is the violence itself. I mean he's supposed to throw her down on the ground, you know."

"Yeah," Joan says, "I'm not comfortable with that either. I

can feel myself, the actress, pulling away even more than the character."

"Well," I say, "let's take these problems in reverse order. I want you two to work on the fight first. Take a couple of minutes right now to work out the details of the violence with safety; do it in slow motion, which is a good container for violence. As you work, you need to be sure that the slow motion makes it feel entirely safe for you, but at the same time, you must work with energy in your muscles so that when the moment arises in the scene, you know that you've got a container that is strong enough to hold the emotion."

As the two of them work out the physical details of this acting moment, I say a few words to the rest of the class. "I want them to work on this final moment first to remove their concern with this climax before we work on the earlier problems in the scene. If you are afraid that there might be a cliff at the end of the road, you may start applying the brakes long before you get there."

When the actors have worked out the physical details of their violence well enough so that they can repeat it precisely every time, we go back to the problem Peter had leading up to that moment.

"You said you've been running away from her for the whole scene up until that moment, right?" I ask.

"Right."

"And when does that change?"

"Well it must be when I say, 'You don't know what you're talking about even.' Right after that she says, 'Only not here.' So I guess I have to start attacking her then."

"Well," I say, "let's go back several beats earlier and start running the scene up to that point."

Peter and Joan rerun the first section of the scene. I let it run through the lines Peter described:

EVA: You don't do things like that, you don't even look! I can, though; I know.

ROBERT: You don't know anything.

EVA: I DO TOO! I've seen. You think I'm so young because I'm so little. I'm fourteen; I can have babies already; and I've seen cows do it when they're in heat. But you wouldn't do something like that.

ROBERT: Let's go back.

EVA: Let's do. I know how; I can.

ROBERT: When cows are in heat, that's one cow jumping on another; you don't know anything.

EVA: You're ashamed; you're not old enough to.

ROBERT: You don't know what you're talking about.

EVA: Boys have to be older. But I'll bet your brother could anyway. I might as well because she thinks we do anyway. You're the one who doesn't know anything about it.

ROBERT: I should, just to show you—don't—you don't know what you're talking about.

EVA: What?

ROBERT: Anything. Because you don't know anything about it.

EVA: I do too. You're afraid.

ROBERT: You don't know what you're talking about even.

EVA: Only not here.

ROBERT: Why not? What's wrong with here?

"So what is happening to Robert during these lines?" I ask Peter.

"Well, she's teasing me and—"

"And what is happening to *you*, to Robert?"

"He's trying to avoid the subject."

"Which subject?

"Sex."

"What's wrong with sex?"

"It makes him uncomfortable."

"Does it make you uncomfortable?"

Peter lowers his eyes and smiles. "A little. Probably not as uncomfortable as it makes Robert."

"Probably. But if *you* lower your eyes when you think about it, *he's* never going to get that uncomfortable."

"What do you mean?"

"I mean, *you'll* have to look at her more, if you want Robert to get uncomfortable enough to rape her. She is teasing, and your character is trying to avoid the subject. That's right. But you have to be careful that as your *character* pulls away, you, the actor, are not avoiding the subject yourself. What would happen to you if during this section you let yourself really take her in? If, just technically, you don't turn your body away from her quite so much or lift your shoulders when she speaks to you? If, when she starts talking about sex, you let yourself look at her body for a few seconds? Do you understand what I mean?"

"Yes."

We run the scene again. And as it runs, Peter keeps making minor physical adjustments. He looks at Joan several times before moving away from her. He allows her to get closer to him, and on her line, "You're ashamed," he stands quite still as she touches him, then raises his hand towards her for a moment before he pulls away. This time, by the time the scene reaches its climax, Robert's sexual urges have been building inside him for several beats, and he has no problem turning to attack her. The two go through their moment of violence in very slow motion, but even so it has none of the stiffness of their earlier run-through.

"So," I ask them afterward, "how was that?"

"Good," they both say at once. And Joan adds, "And it was a good thing we worked on that fight."

"Of course, in an actual production, how you perform a moment like the fight is an aesthetic and stylistic decision. You might work from slow motion up to naturalistic speed, or you could stage it with the two bodies halfway across the stage from each other. But in any case, the actors will still need to *rehearse* using a form that allows them to experience the emotions of that moment, and experience them safely.

"But I want everyone to note how important it is to keep yourself, the actor, open to your partner, even if your character is pulling away. Remember when we were doing the Just Stand exercise, I had people look through their fingers at the audience even while they were hiding their faces in their hands. It is the same thing here. **Your job is to take in and accept the gifts of pain and sexuality that your partner is giving you, so that you are ready to pay them back when the beat changes.**"

POSITIVE FEEDBACK

Aisha and Carlos present their *Taste of Honey* scene next. To furnish himself with private space, Carlos's character, Geof, is now folding clothes while Jo moves uncomfortably around the room. She slides along the back wall and stares out the window. Every once in a while the two characters come together, but then they quickly separate again. The scene contains sudden moments of strong emotion, but other sections are very contained. When they finish, I ask them how it went.

"I thought it went well," Carlos reports. "After what you said about private space, I found I needed something to do so that I could be both private and busy. The clothes folding works for me."

"I don't know," says Aisha. "I keep feeling so uncomfortable."

"Well," I ask, "can you name any moments you *did* like?"

There is a long pause.

"Moments?"

"Yes, particular lines or actions that seemed right for you?"

Another pause.

"Okay, I guess I liked some of the moments when something strong happened, like when she gets really angry at him. But so much of the time she's like commenting on the kids outside, or saying she wants to commit suicide, or talking about her toothache. Each topic she raises, she just drops it again. I feel like I'm just sliding along the walls."

"Yes," I say, "that's nice."

"Nice? But it makes me feel . . . like something is going on, but I don't know what it is."

"That's right, something *is* going on, and Jo doesn't know what it is. So I think your feeling of 'sliding along the walls' is probably just right. When Geof asks, 'What time is it?' you answer 'Half-past four by the church clock,' so you must have slid up to the window at that point. Maybe he even asks you *because* he sees you slide up to that window. This character of yours is climbing the walls inside herself, so if you are doing your work, *you* are going to feel uncomfortable."

I turn to the whole class. "This is a wonderful example of something that often happens to actors, something you should start being aware of now: Plays grow on you. If you spend half an hour or more inside the reality of a play, you will start feeling like the people in the scene do. Which is good. But it means you also have to be very careful to distinguish between what you are feeling *in* the work and how you are feeling *about* the work. And I warn you, when you start doing strong character work, this problem can become even more acute. As in the previous scene, the actor's job is to embrace even the uncomfortable emotions into which the scene leads you. They are not problems; they are your acting sources."

Turning back to Aisha and Carlos, I add, "This was very good. And I think you were right about the clothes folding. It served your need for privacy well. But for the next time, I want you to examine how those other props in the scene serve your characters. The milk, the book, and the chocolate are not just objects; they are *plastiques*. Next week we'll work on an exercise to help with that."

THE EYES

Try telling someone about an event that just happened to you, and force yourself to keep looking at him while talking. Probably, halfway through your first sentence you will want to look away—not because you don't want to see him, but because while really seeing him you lost contact with the inner objects you were talking about. . . . Actually, while we talk we look intermittently at the person to whom we're talking. . . . In between these moments of eye contact, we contact the inner objects we are dealing with.

—Uta Hagen, *Respect for Acting*

Grotowski tried to remember something: the position of his spine changed, becoming more erect, his head tilted a little down; his hand hung suspended in the air. He said he sensed physically that his memory lay somewhere behind him; in this moment it was for him in some precise place a few feet behind his head. This seemed very important: the memory was precisely located in the space; *and almost imperceptibly, but clearly, his body arched toward this place.*

—Thomas Richards,
At Work with Grotowski on Physical Actions

Brian and Maria present their scene from *Death and the Maiden* next. The beats of the scene are clear, and the blocking makes sense, but on several lines just as her character, Paulina, speaks about what happened to her during the dictatorship Maria closes her eyes. After the run-through, Maria remarks, "I just feel like something more should happen. But I don't know what."

"Were you aware that you sometimes closed your eyes during the scene?" I ask her.

"No."

"Well, let's start running the scene again. And this time, try to let yourself be aware of what happens with your eyes."

They begin:

PAULINA: I told you this already, Gerardo. Wasn't that enough?

GERARDO: Fifteen years ago you started to tell me and then . . .

PAULINA: Did you expect me to keep on talking to you with that bitch there? That bitch came out of your bedroom half naked asking why you were taking so long, and you expect me to—

GERARDO: She wasn't a bitch.

PAULINA: Did she know where I was? Of course she did. A bitch. Fuck a man whose woman wasn't exactly able to defend herself, huh?

"There," I say. "You just closed your eyes. Try that section again and see what happens if you try to keep them open."

Again they run the lines. This time, when she reaches the line, "Did she know where I was?" Maria looks to her left for a moment, suddenly crosses her arms and legs, and then averts her eyes to the right.

"What happened?" I ask. "What was the image?"

"There is no image," she says. "Maybe something is wrong with me, but this whole 'image' thing doesn't make any sense to me. I don't have images."

"That's fine," I say. "Just say your line, 'Did she know where I was?'"

She repeats the line, casting her eyes quickly to the left and then looking away.

"Did you notice where your eyes looked?"

"No."

"Well, what does Paulina mean by her line? Where was she when he was with that bitch?"

"She was being tortured. . . ." Maria pauses, and then adds, "raped." Again her eyes dart left for a moment.

"You were being what?"

"Raped," she repeats, looking away.

"Now, let's see what happens if you move your eyes to the left intentionally while you say the line."

"I was being raped." As she speaks, her eyes shut again.

"Good. But now try it with your eyes open."

"No. I don't want to," she says, suddenly breaking into tears.

"Yes, I know you don't *want* to. One never wants to look at such images."

"There is no image. It's just a *feeling*."

"That's fine," I say. "But it is a feeling that seems to be connected with your looking to the left. *Image* is just my word for it. You can call it anything you like."

"Maybe it was just an accident. Maybe if I had looked somewhere else . . ."

"Okay," I encourage her. "Let's test your idea. Try saying the same thing while looking over there." I point to her right.

"I was being raped," she says, looking to the right.

"And how was that?"

"Different."

"Yes. Now let's try it to the left side again."

"I was . . ." Maria stops. She looks down. "I don't want to."

"Fine," I say. "Let's let it go for now. You may have to take some time, maybe when you are working alone, to make this beat of the scene safe for you to play. The secret of this work is that you do not need to dredge up the emotion. The emotion is there. All you need to do is the physical act, in this case, the technical task of moving your eyes to the left and keeping them open. If you can do that, the acting will take care of itself."

In Kathakali Indian dance, eye gestures are as important and as precise as gestures of the arms and hands. Over centuries of performance these gestures have become stylized. Each gesture has come to have a particular meaning. But behind the stylization lies an original, human, physical-emotional connection. For the Western actor, however, learning precision with the eyes is not a matter of re-creating a historical form. The purpose of this precision is to allow us to capture and use areas of our own emotional life that have previously escaped from our art.

In Maria's struggle we can see how the physical training begins to work on a very subtle level. It is not, after all, simply a matter of making large, dramatic, gymnastic movements, but rather of being dedicated to finding those particular gestures that open us to our own inner worlds. The remarkable thing is that once we have acknowledged that there *is* something there—an image? a feeling? a thought?—we can access the emotional life connected with that image by *mechanically* moving our eyes to the right position.

The essence of our work is the same whether we are working with powerful leg kicks or subtle glances: **By executing precise *physical* choices that we discovered during our training and rehearsal process, we can dependably access our emotional acting sources.** In his book *Creating a Role*, Stanislavski describes his preparation for *Othello* like this:

> When these physical actions have been clearly defined, all that remains for the actor to do is to execute them. (Note that I say execute physical actions, not feel them, because if they are properly carried out the feelings will be generated spontaneously. If you work the other way around and begin by thinking about your feelings and trying to squeeze them out of yourself the result will be distortion and force.) [Stanislavski, 1961, p. 201]

FINDING THE RIGHT GESTURE

Veronica and Sandra's *Top Girls* scene is next. They have added a great deal of detail, and they have established a set for themselves including a table and two chairs. Sandra's character,

Joyce, is now washing dishes while she talks to her sister, Marlene. The activity seems to provide the privacy she needs for those moments when she turns away. Their scene is now full of energy, and the battle between the sisters is clear. During the final section, the lines tumble out, overlapping one another. (The slash mark in the text that follows indicates where the next character's line is meant to overlap the previous one's.)

MARLENE: I've had two abortions, are you interested? Shall I tell you about them? Well, I won't, it's boring, it wasn't a problem. I don't like messy talk about blood / and what a bad time we all had. I

JOYCE: If I hadn't had your baby. The doctor said.

MARLENE: don't want a baby. I don't want to talk about gynaecology.

JOYCE: Then stop trying to get Angie off of me.

MARLENE: I come down here after six years. All night you've been saying I don't come often enough. If I don't come for another six years she'll be twenty-one, will that be OK?

JOYCE: That'll be fine, yes, six years would suit me fine.

MARLENE: I was afraid of this. I only came because I thought you wanted . . . I just want . . .

JOYCE: Don't grizzle, Marlene, for God's sake. Marly? Come on, pet. Love you really. Fucking stop it, will you?

MARLENE: No, let me cry, I like it. . . . I knew I'd cry if I wasn't careful.

The scene has been effective, but the performance seems somehow reserved. At the end, I ask the actresses to tell us how they think the scene went.

"It was okay," Sandra says, "but for some reason, I feel clogged. And then when she cried, something was wrong. I don't know. I just wasn't ready."

"You mean you weren't ready for the next line?"

"Yes, when I said, 'Love you really,' it didn't feel right."

"That's great," I say.

"What's great?"

"What's great is that you are able to be so specific. You're right, we need to work with that moment to figure out what went wrong. But much more important than what we do is the fact that you were able to pinpoint the problem for yourself. When a moment doesn't work, it is likely that something just before that moment is amiss. And if we were not here, if this were a rehearsal you were doing on your own, you would now be able to go back and experiment with that part of the scene to find out what you need."

After the actresses have finished analyzing the scene for themselves, I ask the others in the class for feedback, reminding them first, "What actors need to hear is clear, specific feedback. It is not useful just to say, 'I liked it,' or 'I hated it,' because that doesn't help the actors to understand what they should change. So try to be clear about exactly what worked and what didn't work for you."

Most of the feedback that Veronica and Sandra receive is positive, but several people complain that they just couldn't hear several lines. And all of the students agree that it was right at the climax of the fight that the greatest problem occurred.

"Were you aware that you were whispering?" I ask Sandra.

"Whispering? No, I felt like I was yelling all the time."

"Well, some of those lines we couldn't hear were actually whispered. So let's try that part of the scene again and see what happens."

Joyce is wiping a dish as Marlene yells at her, "If I don't come for another six years she'll be twenty-one, will that be OK?"

Joyce puts down her dish and takes half a step toward Marlene. Then she turns away and says between gritted teeth, "That'll be fine, yes, six years would suit me fine." But we can barely hear her.

"Oh," Sandra says, "I *was* whispering. Jesus, why do I *do* that!" And as she curses, she throws the dish down on the floor of the studio, where it shatters. "Oh, my God," she cries, "I'm sorry." She looks up at Veronica who is staring at her, startled. "Are you all right?"

Before Veronica can answer, I say, "Veronica, go on to your next line, the next line in the script."

"'I only came because I thought you wanted . . . I just want . . .'" She pauses.

"Yes, and now Sandra, what's your line?"

"'Don't grizzle, Marlene, for God's sake. Marly? Come on, pet. Love you really.'" As she says the line, Sandra places her arm around Veronica's shoulder. Both of them are in tears.

"So," I say, "I think maybe you've answered your own question."

"What do you mean?"

"I mean that when you pointed out to yourself that you were not ready to say, 'Love you really,' you were exactly on the right track. You couldn't get to the 'love you' beat because you had not found a safe container for your anger on the lines just before it. The anger you released when you threw the dish was the anger you were holding back by whispering. When you let it go, the tears became possible."

"So what do I have to do, throw dishes?"

"Maybe . . . if you stick with the dishes. But I think you might get a clearer idea of what you need if you two try the scene as two animals."

"With our blocking?" Sandra asks.

"No, forget the blocking for now. I want you both to start doing the Cat exercise, looking for the particular kind of cat you feel like in this part, and when you feel like you're at the peak of your energy, stay on all fours and just start running the lines."

As soon as they have permission to use their whole bodies, Sandra and Veronica are stalking each other, hissing, scratching, spitting, wheeling, and swinging at each other. They crawl over and around the chairs they have on stage. At one point Veronica seems to have Sandra caught on one chair, like a treed cat. And when Sandra gets to her line, "That'll be fine, yes, six years would suit me fine," she snarls it at Veronica.

At the end I ask, "How was that?"

"It was fun," says Veronica. "But I don't think it was the scene."

"Right," Sandra adds. "I mean all the emotions seemed stronger, and I don't think I whispered, but . . . these are two sisters in England, not two panthers."

"Right, so now the question is, How do these sisters stalk and scratch and run after each other . . . in a small kitchen in the English countryside? Tell me, what are you doing here? What do you feel like doing to your sister?"

"I want to kill her."

"Good," I say. "Unfortunately, the playwright seems to want to keep both these characters alive, but your impulse is right. So the question becomes, Is there some way in which you can get that feeling 'I want to kill her' while playing this scene in the kitchen? It seems to me that maybe dishwashing just isn't a strong enough container to hold the amount of emotion you now know this scene requires. If what you are feeling is 'I want to kill her,' you need to find yourself an activity that will allow that murderous impulse to live in your body."

"You mean like a normal, human activity in the kitchen?"

"Well, ultimately that is a performance style question. There is nothing illegal about doing a panther version of this play. But the playwright does mention tea, so she is hinting at normal bipedal human sisters, not panthers. So yes, the question is, can you find a naturalistic activity with which you could contain this pantheric emotion?"

"Such as . . . ?"

"Experiment. That's what your rehearsal is for. But to help you in your search, tomorrow we'll study *plastiques* with real objects."

As the class ends I add one final comment. "The problem that Sandra encountered, the problem of whispering on stage, is quite common. **Whispering is almost always a sign that some very strong emotion is seeking expression, and you need to find a stronger container for it than the one you've got.**"

PLASTIQUES WITH REAL OBJECTS

As I mentioned before, humans are *projective* beings. We fill the world around us with meaning. Not only do we fall in love with people who remind us of other people; we also endow objects (teddy bears, amulets, wedding rings) with "life." In fact, many ancient religions were based on the belief that every object had a spirit. Of course, we modern, rational folks have banished the gods to the heavens, and we manage to keep our tendencies toward animism under control . . . most of the time. Yet every once in a while our magical, animistic tendencies evince themselves. We talk to our plants. Or we throw out our old lovers' gifts. Or we avoid places that "hold" bad memories. And each of these actions is a sign that we still retain our ability to see inanimate objects as filled with life—life that we have projected *onto* them, but that we experience as if we were receiving it *from* them.

Of course, this is exactly the process we have been learning to accomplish with our *plastiques*. Until now, we have studied this projective capacity of the *plastiques* in relation to images in *space*—creating a theater of muscular imagination, a kind of emotive mime. Now, if we can learn to project our images into material objects, this same capacity will help us create the kind of theater we think of as "naturalism." For what we call *naturalism* is simply a set of conventions: a play in which characters talk to each other in everyday prose (loud enough so that hundreds of people can hear), on sets built to look like rooms (with one wall missing), filled with ordinary objects called *props*.

When we were working on the Crossings, we talked about how the set pieces serve as an "emanation of the characters' needs" to avoid or to approach the other character onstage. Similarly, props can serve your emotional acting needs on a smaller scale. Props are not present simply to create the illusion of reality or to keep the actors' hands busy on stage; they can also be "containers" for acting, "animated" repositories of meaning that serve your text and your character in very specific ways. But they can only serve these purposes if you take the time to endow them with life. The **Object *Plastiques*** exercise (6.6) could be seen as a training in animism: learning to experience the material world as alive.

Object *Plastiques* (6.6)

1. Begin by placing a number of objects on the floor in the middle of your workspace. (It is best to begin with large pliable objects like towels, sweatshirts, and so forth, because small, hard things like shoes and notebooks usually lead to too much use of the hands.) Then forget the objects for a while and enter your *plastique* River work, searching especially for that quality of work in which the images are leading you and surprising you. Make sure your whole body is alive and that you are able to receive impulses with your legs, your elbows, your rear end, and the top of your head, as well as with your hands.

2. When your River is flowing hard and fast, take one object from the pile on the floor and treat it as the source of your *plastiques*. Let *it* lead your River. Let it transform you, let it touch you in different places, and let it keep surprising you. Let it attack you, let it make love to you, and let it abandon you.

3. Keep making sure that you are the one on the <u>receiving</u> end, and that it is the object that is <u>doing</u> the work. (Be careful not to use your hands too much, because they tend to put you in control.)

4. As you work, you may find the object calling up emotions, or situations, or even characters within you. That's fine, just be sure as you improvise that you keep allowing the object to be the one doing the inventing.

5. Now, little by little, move toward using the object as what it "really" is—without losing its life. If you are working with a sweatshirt, for instance, allow yourself to put it on, but even as your arms slip into it, let <u>it</u> be touching <u>you</u>, and telling you how to respond. As you do so, you may well find character and scene happening to you. Spend a while with the story that occurs, and then let the object transform. Take it off and let it invent another scene for you.

6. Now you can try this same work with smaller things like books or glasses or forks as well as with sets and furniture. When you sit down in a chair, let it be almost as if the chair were calling to you, pulling you into it.

7. Finally, try this same work with the props in a scene.

WORKING WITH MISTAKES

After another week's rehearsal, the students present their scenes for the class again in the same order: *The Rimers of Eldritch, A Taste of Honey, Death and the Maiden,* and *Top Girls.*

Peter and Joan's *Rimers* gets off to a strong start, and the sexual tension between the two characters is now clear from the beginning. But about thirty seconds into the scene, Peter forgets a line, stops, and turns to Joan saying, "Can we start again?" For a moment Joan seems stunned, but then she goes back to their warm-up chase, and the two of them start over from the top.

The whole scene goes well, though somehow the tone of the relationship between the characters seems much darker than it had before. Some of the lines that had sounded like banter the previous week now have a foreboding quality about them. But the climactic section we had worked on before holds up well, and the violence at the end seems shockingly real.

At the end of the run-through Joan is clearly upset. After sitting alone for a minute, she goes to speak privately to Peter. Then she turns to explain to us: "I really didn't want to start over; it was going so well, so it pissed me off when he stopped the scene for that line."

"And I didn't know that," Peter explains. "I could feel that something was different in the scene, but I thought it was just her character choices. And all the moments we had set still worked. It wasn't until she told me just now that I knew anything was wrong."

"I guess I could have stopped the scene again," Joan explains. "But I thought, 'If I do that, I'll only make it worse.' So I kept going, and as the scene went on, I was surprised to find that I could *use* all my anger at Peter in the lines, even though I knew it was not really *about* the scene. And then I was really glad we had the fight so tightly choreographed. I think otherwise I would have been afraid to continue with that much energy flying around.

"So," she continues, turning to me, "do you think I should have stopped?"

"Not necessarily. There will always be mistakes. In this case, it was possible for both of you to incorporate the energy of his mistake because you had established acting containers strong enough to hold the extra energy. On the other hand, if you had been working this scene for a production, and you and the director had agreed upon an interpretation of the scene, it might have been important to stop because what you did definitely changed the received meaning of the scene. And you could have stopped. If you had, both of you would have had to work through your feelings a little while you prepared to start again, that's all. What would not have worked would have been to ignore what happened.

"Unalterable rules that prescribe what is and is not permissible in all circumstances are useless. A touch that may be perfectly acceptable to one person may be a violation to another. Or if one of the actors has had a rotten day, a gesture, a look, a caress, or a shove that felt safe yesterday may seem too invasive today. The only way to be sure is to keep giving each other clear signals, and to keep checking in, both with yourself and with your partner. I think as long as you are able to come out of the run-through, talk to each other, and understand what happened, you're doing fine."

PAUSES

The psychological pause adds life to the thoughts, phrases, measures. It helps convey the subtextual content of the words.

—Stanislavski, *Building a Character*

Silence has a myriad of meanings. In the theater silence is an absence of words, but never an absence of meaning.
— Sanford Meisner, *Sanford Meisner on Acting*

Aisha and Carlos present their *Taste of Honey* scene next. It is now filled with clear emotional changes, with beats of approach and retreat, and with moments of privacy for each character. And our *plastique* work with real objects has clearly paid off. Each of the props in the scene—the clothes, the milk, the book, and the chocolate—has been invested with life. As Geof approaches Jo with the glass of milk, he holds it out almost like a weapon. When Jo finishes with the book, she throws it down on the bed. At the end of the run-through, both of the actors say they are pleased with how the scene went. Carlos adds, "I'm surprised. This time it felt even better in class than it did in rehearsal. I think the downstage privacy helped. When I faced away from her I almost felt as though the members of the audience were friends I could turn to for help."

"Yeah," Aisha adds, "I only felt sad at the end because I thought, 'I'm sorry it was over so fast.' Do you know what I mean?"

"Yes," I say, "and I think you're right . . . in two ways. First of all, I think that theater requires that you fall in love with each moment, each play, each scene you rehearse, and then that you feel the twinge of sorrow and loss when that event is over. It is a bittersweet sorrow that actors must live through over and over.

"But this scene was also over too fast because you did rush the scene a little, not that you ran the lines too fast, but you both tended to skip over some of the pauses. It's a very common mistake, rushing through the pauses, especially when the pauses are not written into the script.

"In theater (and in life), many important things happen in silences. Sometimes there are large beat changes between one line and the next, and if you rush ahead to the following sentence as written, you may not give yourself the time you need to allow the inner change to take place."

I ask Carlos and Aisha to run a short section of their scene.

JO: Geoffrey, have you got any of that toothache cure?

GEOF: The only cure for the toothache is a visit to the dentist. Drink your milk.

JO: I hate milk. I never thought I'd still be here in the summer. Would you like to be the father of my baby? Geoffrey?

GEOF: Yes, I would. What time is it?

JO: Half-past four by the church clock. Why do you stay here, Geof?

GEOF: Someone's got to look after you. You can't look after yourself.

JO: I think there's going to be a storm. . . .

"There are some real non sequiturs in that, aren't there? Lines like 'Yes, I would like to be the child's father. . . . What time is it?' and, 'Half-past four . . . Why do you stay here?' contain enormous changes of subject. When you played the scene, you ran through those lines as if the first and second halves of the lines were part of the same thoughts. But what happens if you, the actors, are not in such a hurry? What happens if you let yourself feel all the feelings that might happen in the *middle* of those lines? Let's try running that section again."

This time, after Carlos says, "Yes, I would," I interpose a few questions during the pause: "What would that be like for you, Geof? And Jo, how did his, 'Yes, I would' make you feel? Now, Geof, look at her. Can you see what she thinks about what you just said? What is she going to say? Might she say something painful that would destroy the tenderness? What are you going to do about it? Should you say more, or should you change the subject? Okay, now! Say the other half of your line."

"What time is it?"

"Go on, Jo," I say to Aisha.

"Half-past four by the church clock."

"Stop. Look at him. He just turned away from you. Why? Do you know what he's feeling? What do you feel about him now? Is there anything you can do about it? Now, say your line."

"Why do you stay here, Geof?"

Carlos whirls and as he says his line—"Someone's got to look after you."—his vehemence is such that Aisha is visibly shaken. Seeing that, his next line, "You can't look after yourself," is strangely tender this time.

When they stop both actors are brimful of emotion.

"But will the audience ever get all that, all those silent beats?" Aisha asks.

"Literally, no. Feelingly, absolutely. But you must give yourself and them the necessary time."

I turn to the class. "When characters say things like 'What time is it?' they are probably not just setting their watches. In the text of *A Taste of Honey*, some of the pauses are indicated in the script. For instance after Geof's line 'Yes, I would,' the script says, *'Jo stands in the doorway. The children can be heard singing again.'* But in other places, the playwright does not offer such timing suggestions. There are no stage directions between Jo's 'Half-past four by the church clock,' and her 'Why do you stay here, Geof?'

"I am not suggesting that you should fill all of your speeches with pregnant pauses. When actors do that, their performances can become extremely tedious. All I'm saying is that you need not rush on to the next line of the text just because you've got it memorized. Silence sometimes speaks very loudly. The important thing is to listen even to the silence. This is even more true when you are working with a playwright like Pinter or Beckett, in whose plays a great deal of what is going on is unsaid."

"And what about impulses and emotions when there are no lines?" Aisha asks. "I mean, there are lots of movie scenes I can think of where people just start crying or something because of something they see, and there are no lines at all."

"Absolutely," I respond. "Film is such a visual medium that

many of the beats are not in the spoken text at all. To play those moments, which might even be shot out of sequence, you must depend on the kind of image-emotional work we've done earlier in the training. What we're struggling with here, however, is how you can use your ability to notice beat changes to help you create timing within the written text of a play."

DETAILS

When an actor knows a score of physical actions very well, in order to keep it from descending, as time passes one must break the same score down into smaller actions. Instead of letting it simplify, become more general, one should work in the opposite direction: the line of actions must be made more detailed.
>   —Thomas Richards,
>   *At Work with Grotowski on Physical Actions*

To me, the greater the degree of accuracy of the parameters, the greater the freedom of action within.
>   —David Warrilow, quoted in Lassiter,
>   "David Warrilow: Creating Symbol and Cypher," *TDR* 1985

When Brian and Maria bring *Death and the Maiden* back to class, Maria has incorporated the notes from the previous session into the scene. There are now several points in the scene when her character, Paulina, seems riveted by the memory of what happened to her. Her voice is still thin, but now as she mentions her past she stammers and bites her lip. Her hands twist a napkin she is holding, but her eyes remain on the image. We may not know exactly what it is she is seeing, but it is clear that her present reality is built on a traumatic past.

Both actors express satisfaction with their progress, but Brian adds, "As the scene became stronger for us, I became less and less happy with the space. We kept rearranging the room, but it kept feeling too small, or too large. I don't know. Something was wrong with the space."

"Were you aware," I ask him, "that you were very close to her for much of the time?"

"Yes. And I thought maybe that was wrong. So we tried adding some moments in which I cross away. But they seemed wrong, too. Like when I say to her, 'You already forgave me, you forgave me, how many times will we have to go over this? We'll die from so much past, so much pain and resentment. Let's finish it—let's finish that conversation from years ago.' It just feels to me like I can't present any of those lines while moving away from her. They all seemed to call for me to take steps toward her."

"And she . . . ?"

"Right. We tried that too. We tried having her move away."

"Yes," adds Maria, "but it felt wrong to have Paulina pull away from him. I think she's too strong and too angry to do that."

"Okay," I say, "let's just try running that part of the scene. Begin a few lines before that."

The two plunge back into the dialogue, and within a few lines the emotions are again quite full.

PAULINA: While I defend your life, while your name stayed inside me and never left my mouth—Ask him, ask Miranda if I ever so much as whispered your name, while you . . .

GERARDO: You already forgave me, you forgave me, how many times . . .

As he starts his line, Brian turns toward Maria and crosses the space to her side.

"Wait," I say, "let's go back a line. Give him the cue again. But this time, when she speaks, put your whole impulse into just the turn toward her."

They run the lines again. This time Brian turns on his first line, but doesn't move toward her until he begins the second "you forgave me."

"Stop!" I say. "Notice what she just did."

"What did she do?"

"She looked down. Take that in. Let it hit you. You said, 'You forgave me.' In fact you said it twice. And she looked down. How does that affect you?"

"It just makes me pissed. She's not listening to what I'm saying."

"That's fine. But if you are pissed, what do you want to do? Try it again."

They run the lines again. This time, as he speaks his next line, "How many times will we have to go over this," Brian stamps his foot on the ground, turns away, and throws his hands up in the air. Maria looks back at him.

"Now, look at her. She's looking back at you again."

"But it's hopeless," says Brian. "She's not really listening to what I'm saying."

"Yes, exactly. It's hopeless. So let yourself collapse." Brian's knees buckle. "Now, say your line!"

"We'll die from so much past, so much pain and resentment." He holds his arms out toward her.

"Wait," I say. "Let her take that in. There is no hurry. Let each beat have its time." Maria is looking at him now with sadness as he reaches toward her. She makes a slight gesture toward him. "Now!" I say. "No, don't get up. You can move toward her without standing."

Brian slides toward Maria on his knees. "Let's finish it— let's finish that conversation from years ago."

"Right. So how was that?"

"Much better," says Brian. "But . . . but that's so extremely detailed. I mean, she has to look down, and then I stop and I stamp my foot, and she looks up, and . . . Does every moment have to get *that* precise?"

"Yes," I say. "I'm sorry, but it does. The question is not whether you have to get that precise. The question is, Why settle for anything less? You were absolutely right that the whole speech was a cross *toward* her. And she was absolutely right that the simple fix—for her to move away so that you could continue your cross—would not work in this case. But once you start looking at the details, you can find a hundred little turns and details inside the basic cross itself. Inside one overall beat, you found many sub-beats. And take note: the reason you did not notice all those possibilities before is that, like Aisha and Carlos in the *Taste of Honey* scene, you were rushing and not listening in between breaths. **As the strength of your emotions increases, the responsibility to listen hard also increases. The details emerge within the breath spaces."**

PRECISION

The true lesson of the sacred theatre, whether ancient or medieval European, Balinese, or Indian Kathakali, is that spontaneity and discipline, far from weakening each other, mutually reinforce each other. . . . This was not understood by Stanislavski, for whom natural impulses dominate, nor by Brecht, who gave priority to the building of a role.
—Grotowski, *Les Temps modernes*

When Veronica and Sandra present the *Top Girls* scene again, they begin with a strong, physical warm-up, circling each other like the panthers they had discovered in the last class. Then, as they start the text, they translate their feline energy into human gestures. As the scene progresses, Veronica's Marlene keeps pacing and circling, while Sandra's Joyce barricades herself behind the kitchen table, picks up a knife and starts to chop carrots.

JOYCE: You could have lived at home. / Or live
MARLENE: Don't be stupid.
JOYCE: with me and Frank. / You

MARLENE: You never suggested.

JOYCE: said you weren't keeping it. You shouldn't have had it /
if you wasn't

MARLENE: Here we go.

JOYCE: going to keep it. You was the most stupid, / for someone
so clever you was the most stupid, get yourself pregnant,
not go to the doctor, not tell.

MARLENE: You wanted it, you said you were glad. . . .

Each time her anger explodes, Sandra's knife slices through a
carrot. "You said you weren't keeping it. (chop!) You shouldn't
have had it (chop) if you wasn't going to keep it! (chop). You
was the most stupid! (chop), . . ." And then on the line "get
yourself pregnant, not go to the doctor . . ." Sandra thrusts the
carrot up in the air. It is a gesture so appropriate the students in
the audience gasp. A few beats later, when she is saying, "Listen, when Angie was six months I did get pregnant and I lost it
because I was so tired looking after your fucking baby," she
pours water into a pot and then drops the carrots in to boil.

After the scene the other students speak about how "right"
the gestures Sandra found seemed to be. "How did you find
them?" I ask Sandra.

"Well, I couldn't come up with the right things in any
rehearsals. The boiling idea appeared at one rehearsal when I
tried pouring water into a pot just before the tender part of the
scene and I noticed that somehow the sound of the water
helped me feel the tears. But the chopping business happened
the other way. It was after a frustrating rehearsal and a frustrating day, and I went home feeling terrible. So I decided just to
make myself feel better I would make myself some steamed
vegetables and brown rice. Comfort food, you know. But then,
as I was cutting the vegetables in my kitchen, the lines of the
scene just started happening in my head. And the most amazing thing was that once I knew I was on the right track, it
seemed very important that each chop be exactly at the right

moment, you know. I mean it was different if I chopped on the word *most* than if I chopped on the word *stupid*. And suddenly I was aware that there actually was a *best* way to hold the knife, and a *right* moment to pick up the next carrot. It was scary."

"Yes," I agree. "It is a scary discovery and a wonderful one when you start to demand that degree of precision of yourself. The wonderful thing is the perception that that precision is not a restriction to your creativity or your emotional freedom, but the opposite; it is a provocation of the strongest emotions. The scary part is that once you have experienced such precision, you may never be satisfied with less. You will never again be satisfied in doing what they call *stage business*. **There is no such thing as business. Every object you touch must serve the acting itself.**"

"Does that mean that there is *one* right way to play every moment?" Sandra asks. "One best object for each scene? One best activity?"

"Not at all. There are probably hundreds of right ways to play any moment and hundreds of perfect props for a character. But there are definitely wrong choices too."

I fetch a book of Brecht's poetry, and I read the class part of the poem Brecht wrote about his wife, the actress Helene Weigel, choosing her props:

Just as the millet farmer picks out for his trial plot
The heaviest seeds and the poet
The exact words for his verse so
She selects the objects to accompany
Her characters across the stage. The pewter spoon
Which Courage sticks
In the lapel of her Mongolian jacket, the party card
For warm-hearted Vlassova and the fishing net
For the other, Spanish mother or the bronze bowl
For dust-gathering Antigone. Impossible to confuse
The split bag which the working woman carries

For her son's leaflets, with the moneybag
Of the keen tradeswoman. Each item
In her stock is hand picked; straps and belts
Pewter boxes and ammunition pouches; hand picked too
The chicken and the stick which at the end
The old woman twists through the draw-rope
The Basque woman's board on which she bakes her bread
And the Greek woman's board of shame, strapped to her back
With holes for her hands to stick through, the Russian's
Jar of lard, so small in the policeman's hand; all
Selected for age, function and beauty
By the eyes of the knowing
The hands of the bread-baking, net-weaving
Soup-cooking connoisseur
Of reality.   [Brecht, pp. 427–28]

"So it is not that there is only one possible choice. What matters is that the choice is made with care. The precision with which Weigel selects her props is an act that imbues the props with meaning."

"And what if you don't work in the Berliner Ensemble?" asks Sandra. "What if you work in a theater where the designer just invents the props and gives them to you?"

"Then you may have to do exercises like our *Plastiques* with Real Objects on your own time. If you spend the time filling your props with imagery on your own, your effort will pay off during performance."

THE IMPROVISATION AND THE SCORE

And I was able, never to repeat exactly what I had done before, but to improvise again. And the more often we worked that way, the easier and more certain it became that there was a real possibility, to fix something that

*seems impossible to fix . . . something that leads not to
repetition, but to re-improvisation, re-creation.*
—Zbigniew Cynkutis, *Odra* nr II,
in Kumiega, *The Theatre of Grotowski*

*It is extremely difficult to repeat the same emotion over
and over again. You are taking a big risk when you depend on your emotions as the basis for reproducing a
scene when you have a long run. On the other hand, you
can repeat body details in exactly the same way every day.
Working from body shape is useful for actors.*
—Yoshi Oida, *The Invisible Actor*

The discovery that Veronica and Sandra have made is a manifestation of the second paradox of acting: the paradox of freedom and control. Every acting technique insists that actors
must always be in the moment, treating each moment of each
performance as if it were a surprise. At the same time, however,
outside of improvisational forms like commedia dell'arte, acting also requires setting things: the blocking, the timing, and,
of course, the text. At first this may seem to be an impossible
demand. How can an actor perform the same memorized lines
and blocking each night, night after night, and yet keep them
as alive and new as they were when he or she first did them?

What these students discovered is the strange fact that
ratcheting up the demands of precision by insisting that their
gestures be tightly coordinated with their text actually *in-
creased* their experience of freedom and the strength of their
emotional truth. That discovery is similar to the lesson I
learned years before when Grotowski froze my fingers as I
choked Desdemona. Once you have found emotional depth in
your work, external technical precision does not extinguish
your sense of reality, but can actually augment the fullness of
your internal experience.

It is similar to the lesson every child learns when he places his thumb over the end of a hose: the more narrow you make the exit, the farther the water will shoot . . . up to a point. If the opening is *too* small, or if the pressure in the hose is too low, the restriction will cut off the water entirely.

In acting, this restriction occurs when your full body drops out of the work. The vitality of the *plastiques* depends on your every small gesture being merely the visible sign of a current of energy that is flowing through your whole body: each gesture is just the tip of the iceberg. In a naturalistic scene, you must be especially careful when you sit down that you do not lose touch with your lower body. In a cocktail party scene, you must remember that when you lift the wineglass to your lips that gesture began with the sexual heat in your loins. Without the full-body connection, the gesture and the acting moment will die. With it, you can be exquisitely precise about just how and when you sip your wine, for the act of sipping is but the outward lava flow of the volcano within. **If the body is fully engaged, adding restrictions, even extremely precise ones, will tend to expand your imagination, not close it down.**

AN ACROBAT OF THE HEART

It is not sufficient for [the actor] that he be able to put on the image of every one of the passions that fall within the reach of his author, if he have not, beside this, the power of throwing himself readily and easily out of one into another of them.
            —John Hill,
                The Actor, A Treatise on the Art of Playing (1750)

A circus acrobat practices the elements of her trapeze swing for years. For hours and hours she practices the timing, the midair twist, and the grasp of her fingers around her partner's wrists. Eventually all this practice gives her confidence that if she swings at the right moment and twists precisely and grasps hard when her partner's wrists appear in the air in front of her, she will not fall. But even after all this practice, each time she performs, there is still the moment of giving herself up to gravity and momentum: the moment of *letting go* of the trapeze sixty feet above the floor and daring to fly.

To be an actor is to be an acrobat of the heart. No matter what training technique you practice, whether you use a "psychological gesture" or a "sense memory" or a *"plastique,"* all your technique can do for you is get you ready for the moment of letting go. You can control each element of your preparation, you can concentrate on memories or images, you can tense or relax your body, and you can practice your gestures—but all this preparation is just that: preparation. The moment itself is not under your control. In fact, if you try to control it, you will "push" or "act the emotion" or fail to breathe—and, one way or the other, you will "fall" out of the moment itself.

Once the acrobat lets go of her trapeze, she again has choices to make. She cannot alter her momentum as she flies, but she can make use of it. She can choose to do a double flip, or she can choose to execute a twist. And the same is true for the actor. Once the emotion is flowing through you, you can choose to express it with a different tone of voice, or you can alter your timing, or your gesture pattern, or your blocking. In fact such choosing—vocal precision, timing, or character work, stylization, or even song—can, like the acrobat's flip, make the acting moment even more exciting. But **the inner emotional life that vivifies your acting is not something you can control.** Like the acrobat's momentum, it is not something you are *doing*; it is something that is *happening* to you.

It can be terrifying to trust that if you "let go" of an emotion you are experiencing, you will find another emotion waiting to "catch" you. As a result of that terror, you may make a strong gesture with your arms on a certain line, and then, three lines later, find that your arms are still making that same gesture. Or you may react to some strong image or give voice to a powerful emotion, and then get stuck for several lines playing that one beat. But the best playwrights keep changing the beats on you, and it is your job to dare to let go of each one.

Shakespeare, the best playwright of all, can change the direction of your emotional current in the middle of a line. For instance, in the balcony scene Romeo must say:

> *But soft, what light through yonder window breaks?*
> *It is the East, and Juliet is the sun.*
> *Arise, fair sun, and kill the envious moon,*
> *Who is already sick and pale with grief*
> *That thou her maid art far more fair than she.*

As he starts this speech, the actor playing Romeo is illumined by the images of "light," the "East," and the "sun." As he speaks this line, his whole being is filled with feelings of love (although even here, Shakespeare supplies the violent "breaks" when he could have said "shines"). But then, as he speaks his next line, the actor may fall into an inviting trap. After "fair sun," he may be tempted to pronounce "kill" and "envious" and "sick," as if these words were as sweet and love laden as those in the previous two lines. But, in fact, these images convey the fears of death that darken many of the most love-filled moments in this play. The same actor, if he had encountered the line "kill the envious moon" in a play like *Macbeth*, would probably have had no trouble speaking those words with fear and trembling. But here, in order to capture their pain, he must first release Romeo's sweet lovesickness for a moment and risk plunging into the unknown. But to do this, to let go of love—or of any strong emotion that is working for you—is a very hard thing for an actor to do. It requires that for a moment you must face the void, the fear that perhaps nothing at all will fill you, the fear that your acting will be empty. To take that leap requires real courage, like the courage of the acrobat when she lets go of her trapeze.

But holding on to the trapeze will not do. When you reach

the end of an acting beat, you have the wonderful freedom—
and the awful obligation—to fly.

*Note: My acting class has now come to the end of its work on
the first set of scenes. Of course, there is more that could be
done. With more time, each of these scenes could be made more
precise, each action more detailed, and each beat more clearly
delineated. But we stop the work here so that we can move on to
another layer of the acting work, a set of skills that we have not
yet touched upon: character.*

Character Work

Until this point in our work we have studied acting as an art of physical emotion, image, and reaction. But to limit acting to these tasks alone would be like defining painting as an art concerned only with color, shape, and brushstroke. Yet painting is also an art of representation, the art of the two-dimensional representation of (actual or imagined) three-dimensional objects. Similarly, even in this age of deconstructed texts and mixed media, acting is also an art of representation, the (re)presentation on stage of actual or imagined human characters.

In centuries past, many critics and actors viewed the portrayal of character as *the* central task of the actor. These days, although there are some acting teachers (like Uta Hagen) who still consider the study of character an essential part of acting, there are other teachers, writers, and directors (such as David Mamet and Anne Bogart) who deny that character exists.

I believe that character exists, and that character work presents specific difficulties that can interfere with other acting tasks. That is why I have reserved the study of Character Work until after we have completed our work on emotion, impulse, listening, and reacting. (It is important to note that for some actors, character work actually *enables and enlarges* their emotional range. As I said in the introduction, if you find that this is true for you, it may be useful for you to try some character work early in your training.)

Note: *In the realm of emotion and image, our physical approach may seem a radical departure from other actor train-*

ing systems. In the realm of character work, however, there are many acting teachers who employ a physical approach. In particular, I would recommend Michael Chekhov's To the Actor, *on* the technique of acting; *Stanislavski's* Building a Character and Creating a Role; *Uta Hagen's* Respect for Acting; *and the chapters "Elements of Nature" and "Animals" in Moni Yakim's* Creating a Character.

WHY BOTHER?

There are, of course, wonderful actors who have had long and successful careers playing themselves. Cary Grant is a good example; so is Jimmy Stewart. They varied somewhat from part to part, but it was often a small variation of themselves.

—Michael Shulman, in Mekler,
The New Generation of Acting Teachers

There are no parts which can be considered so-called "straight" parts or parts in which the actor always shows his audience the same "type"—himself as he is in private life. . . . the theater as such will never grow and develop if this destructive "himself" attitude, already deeply rooted, is permitted to thrive. . . . How would you evaluate a playwright who in all his plays unfailingly dramatizes himself as the leading character, or a painter who is unable to create anything but self-portraits?

—Michael Chekhov, *To the Actor*

Why bother studying character work?

Nowadays, American theater depends so much on *typecasting* that it is often the director who is doing the character work when he or she casts the play. The situation can be even more extreme in film and television, where casting notices sometimes describe not only the age, sex, race, and "type" of the role being cast, but the particular stars who represent the type the director is looking for. Moreover, there are a good many American actors, especially in film and television, who make good—no, outrageous—incomes without ever having to act *character* at all. Some of these actors can actually play a wide range of emotions and convince us (or themselves at least) that they are playing a different character by altering only their costume or their hair color.

So why study character work? After all, you don't need it to get rich and famous, and you're going to be typecast anyway. So why bother?

Here are four possible answers:

1. The best plays ever written require character work for many of their most exciting roles. It may be possible for a director to typecast Stella or even Stanley Kowalski, but no director could typecast Blanche DuBois, because no actress who actually *was* a Blanche DuBois type would survive in theater long enough to make it to the audition. And how many actors do you know who are like Pozzo or Richard III? If you choose not to learn character work, you are resigning yourself to playing the roles directors see you in—probably the last role they saw you perform. And American theater being what it is, aren't your chances of getting cast already small enough without adding yet another impediment?

2. Meryl Streep and Dustin Hoffman do character work. That is why they get to play such a wonderful variety of roles. Can you imagine Sissy Spacek taking on the full range of Streep's parts? Can you picture Al Pacino attempting Tootsie?

3. What does it mean to "be ourselves" anyway? The fact is that even if we're not aware of it, most of us play several characters each day. We are not the same person on our job as we are with our parents. And we are not the same person with our parents as we are with our lovers. Character is part of life.

4. Character work is enormous fun. In fact, most of us began our acting careers playing characters. We called it make-believe. And when we played, we never made believe we were the younger sister who has to make peace, or the baby of the family whom adults love. Those were the roles we played when we weren't playing. We made believe we were superheroes and princesses and criminals and animals and monsters. The joy of acting lay in going beyond who we were every day, revealing parts of our being that were hidden beneath our quotidian lives.

To be an actor but never to attempt character would be like being a sailor who spends his whole life plying inland water-ways and never confronts the sea.

WHAT IS CHARACTER?

Character is costume.
> —Joan Darling, in Mekler,
> *The New Generation of Acting Teachers*

Certainly the weak would like you to believe that charac-ter is a costume which can be put on or taken off at will. And from time to time we'd all like to believe it. But that doesn't make it true.
> —David Mamet,
> *True and False: Heresy and Common Sense for the Actor*

In our study of the *plastiques*, we found that emotional life and imagery flow through our bodies like a river of liquid energy. This river might flow fast or slow, hot or cold, but it is always moving and changing. In fact, this constant changingness is one of the most essential qualities of the *plastiques*. Our train-ing, therefore, centered on our learning to sense even the smallest changes in the currents of these rivers and on our mastery of the strokes that would help us follow the eddies and counter-currents from one acting moment to the next.

Perhaps, then, we can conceive of character as a frozen ice floe in our river, or maybe as the canyon walls through which the river flows. Character work does not stop the river of emotions, but it bends it, changes its direction and its rhythm, damming up some emotional expressions while opening others. So if our training up until this moment has concentrated on *opening* all the floodgates of our physical and psychic beings, character work now requires the selective *closing* of some channels and the building of new river banks to contain and direct our energies.

You can build these levees in many ways: *externally* (using costume, makeup, and props), *physically* (by changing your body center, movement, and rhythms), *vocally* (by altering your vocal placement, pitch, or accent), and *internally* (by finding character imagery, history, and attitudes).

Different actors find different routes to character work, and the same actor may find different pathways to different characters. For one character you may begin with a clear visual image, for another, perhaps you can hear the voice quite plainly in your head, whereas a third may be a total mystery to you. For a historical personage, you might find inspiration by viewing paintings in a museum. For another character you might be inspired by an animal you see in the zoo. And for another you may need to visit a local bar. So studying character means opening yourself to many approaches, and it requires that you trust your own process.

We shall divide our study of character work into three steps:

1. First there is the pure exploration of character possibilities, getting beyond the habits of your "everyday" voice and body to discover who or what else you can be.

2. Second, there are exercises designed to combine character work with basic acting skills like listening and reacting.

3. And, finally, we shall study some approaches to building a character from written text.

CHARACTER FROM THE BODY

Many actors use a walk, a posture, or a style of gesture as a starting point for their creation [of character]. No amount of intellectual or psychological analysis will replace the actual experiencing of the character which can occur when you begin to adopt his physical traits.
                                   —Robert Benedetti, *The Actor at Work*

The first step toward the creation of character is to open yourself to the widest possible range of choices. As you try out new gestures, voices, and attitudes, you may become aware that you have been so used to playing the character you call "I" that you have lost touch with many of the other beings who lie dormant within you. Your task at this point is to forcefully (and playfully) shake some of these beings awake.

We begin this shaking process with the body, because it is such an obvious tool, and because we have voluntary muscle control over our physical actions. In the **Circus Walks** (7.1) exercise (as with the *plastiques*) we start with a completely external choice, but again, we will quickly discover that our muscular choices evoke thoughts, opinions, emotions, and images— all the seeds of a character—upon which we can then elaborate.

As I lead my class through the Circus Walks, they encounter a few common problems. When their first set of characters (developed by walking on the outsides of their feet) start to converse with each other, they have difficulty standing still. They talk and argue and bicker and joke with each other, but as they do, they continue to move around the space. After the class has let go of these first characters and returned to their "neutral" walks, I point to this problem.

"We began with an adjustment in our feet, so it is natural

Circus Walks (7.1)

1. Begin by simply walking as you normally do. Take a minute to let go of any tensions you feel and to clear your mind.

2. Now, as you continue to walk, change the way your feet meet the ground; for instance, walk on the outside edges of your feet.

3. Allow these new feet to alter the way your legs work. It's not a matter of making a change in your legs, but just of allowing the feet to affect the legs.

4. Now continue making changes all the way up through the body: Allow the pelvis to change to go with the new legs. Then the lower back and stomach; the upper back and chest; the shoulders, the arms, hands, and fingers; the neck, the head, and the face. As you reach each new body part, take the time you need to make sure the change has altered each muscle group, at least a little. The changes may be very small, but they should leave no part unaffected.

5. When your whole body has found its new shape, see if you can stop walking. Can this new body sit, lie down, stand, run, or jump?

6. Now allow the new body to find its breath and voice. Try out the voice alone for a minute, and then let yourself talk with other people. Play with listening and speaking, examining the rhythms and gestures of your character.

7. After a few minutes, let these adjustments go. Shake out your body and return to your neutral walk.

8. Now repeat the exercise, beginning with another "walk": pigeon-toed, or on your heels, or stiff-kneed, and so forth. Each time, take the time you need to allow the changes to penetrate your whole body. Then find a voice.

9. After working with different walks, work on altering any body part: tilt the pelvis back, or cave in the chest, or open the eyes very wide. Then permit the alteration to affect the adjacent body parts until the whole body has changed.

10. You can also begin with a vocal choice (pitch, placement, accent, and rhythm) and then find the body to go with it. Remember to take the time you need to allow the changes to penetrate each part of your body.

that you kept working with your feet in order to maintain the character. But the foot choice is really only a starting point, a seed, for your character. Once you have allowed that choice to penetrate your whole body, it is important that you take the risk of letting go of that starting point. This does not mean that you need to allow your feet to return entirely to their neutral positions, but try to find out how it is that this character maintains him- or herself when he or she is *not* walking. What happens if you stop, if you sit down, if you lie down? As you create your next character, see if you can discover what the essence of the character is so that you can keep being that person without having to walk all the time."

As we progress through more and more physical adjustments, I keep suggesting that the actors discover in each character exactly what it is that they must "hold on" to in order to stay in character and what they can "let go" of. "Once you feel you have found a character for yourself, keep going beyond what you know. If you discovered the character from a slow, lumbering walk, find out if you can stay in character even when your character needs to run or to crawl. If you came to your character from a vocal screech, investigate how this person talks when making love."

The variety of characters that emerge is wonderful. Each round, all the students begin with the same physical adjustment, but then their personal inspirations lead them in very different directions. At the end of the exercise, the group dissolves into excited conversations and pockets of laughter. When we gather to talk, Carlos says, "That was a little eerie. I mean it reminded me of how I used to play when I was a kid. It was fun, you know, just pure fun. So, of course, I started wondering if it was really okay."

"Yes," I respond, "it's a little terrifying that we can get so serious about our acting training sometimes that we forget how much fun acting once was. But having fun is necessary because the joy you are experiencing communicates itself to the audience. It allows them to feel safe watching your character commit murder or to suffer him making a fool of himself because they can sense that even in those moments the *performer* within is having *fun*. So doing things that are fun is actually very important. If you find that character work is fun, that's just one more good reason to do it."

Lee Strasberg's son John puts it this way: "It's a lousy profession to begin with, so you might as well enjoy what you're doing" [Mekler, p. 94].

BASEBALL (THREE-PART CHARACTER)

Tempo-rhythm carries with itself not only external qualities which directly affect our natures, but also our inner content which nourishes our feelings. In this guise tempo-rhythm remains in our memories and may be used for creative purposes. . . . Every human passion, every state of being, every experience has its tempo-rhythms.

—Stanislavski, *Building a Character*

The Circus Walks may help us to recognize the multiplicity of character possibilities that lie hidden within each part of our bodies and voices. But there is more. What happens if we add gesture and rhythm to our character sources? And what happens if, rather than depending on a single source, we combine several sources at once?

The **Baseball** exercise (7.2) requires four people on stage and several more to be an audience. It was dubbed "baseball" by a student who noted that the four actors performing the work stand on stage as if they were on first base, second base, third base, and the pitcher's mound.

When my class plays its first game of Baseball, each actor is challenged to display characteristics completely unlike his normal self. Joan, usually so strong-willed and outspoken, is transformed into a tentative, breathy child. Peter, who is usually placid and altruistic, becomes a foul-mouthed, hyperactive tough. And even the normally tentative Maria becomes a snide bureaucrat.

"So, how was that?" I ask after each actor has had a turn.

"It was fun," says Peter. "I should act like that guy more

Baseball (7.2)

1. One actor stands center stage (on the mound). The other three stand to the left, the right, and upstage of the "pitcher."

2. The center-stage actor turns to the actor on his left (first base), and that actor demonstrates a way of standing, of holding oneself (for instance, slumped over and pigeon-toed, or hips to one side with the chest raised). The central actor then allows his body to copy this stance. When he feels he has got it, he turns to the upstage actor (second base).

3. The upstage actor then speaks with a definite vocal choice. Any choice will do, but it is most interesting and challenging if the vocal choice is clearly not related to the body stance the central actor has taken from the first baseman. The vocal choice should include pitch, intonation, placement, and accent, but it should also take on a tempo and rhythm. The actor in the center then imitates this voice, practicing first with the words he was given but then improvising while maintaining all the characteristics of the vocal choice. Then he checks back for a moment with the first baseman to make sure he has not lost the body he was given. When he feels he has both the body and the voice, he turns to the last actor (the third baseman).

4. The third baseman then demonstrates some simple gesture pattern (with arms, hands, face, or feet), and the actor on the mound imitates it—without losing the body or the voice.

5. Now the "pitcher" takes a moment to check back with all three "basemen" to make sure that he has all the elements, and then he practices maintaining all the elements at once.

6. When he feels he can keep all three elements of his character going at the same time, he asks the audience for a first line.

7. Someone in the audience provides the actor with a phrase, and then, starting with those words, he just begins to improvise, trusting the thoughts, images, and words that come to him. If at any time the pitcher draws a blank, he can always go back to the first line he was given or ask for another line.

8. Meanwhile, the three other actors support his work, reminding him if he starts to lose any physical or vocal element.

9. After each round, the "pitcher" sits down, the "third baseman" moves to the "mound," the "second baseman" to "third," the "first baseman" to "second," and a new actor takes over at "first."

often. But, seriously, I think most of us were so bent out of shape, and so full of twitches and tensions, that we were not just characters; we were grotesques."

"Exactly," I concur. "The first time through this game the choices are often very exaggerated, so we will play the game a second time, and this time after you have acquired your body, your voice, and your gestures, I want you to internalize the physical choices, moving back toward neutral bit by bit so that the character you end up with still has the essence of the external choice, but the outward display of that choice is much less blatant. This time, explore how subtle you can make your gestures without losing the feeling that you are 'in character' and without losing the images and verbal inspiration that the character work evokes in you."

This time through, the actors' characters are much more like people you might see in the street every day, a bit strange, but, for New York at least, not grotesque. But while Joan is working, she notes a different problem. Still in the character of a bitter and wizened crone, she complains, "I keep laughing at myself, he-he, and every time I laugh, the laugh takes me out of being who I am, d'yuh know what I mean? He-he."

"Good," I say. "That's right. Keep playing with it. When you feel yourself slipping out of character, you may have to enlarge some of the body choices again. Your character has become so naked now that your own characteristics are showing through. You have to put back on some of the character armor that the grotesque version gave you."

Joan exaggerates her shoulder tension a little.

"Good," I say. "So how is that now?"

"Well, I ain't laughin' anymore, y'know. But now I feel more like a goddamned groto-scue, or whatever you called it, again."

"That's fine. So now, see what happens if, bit by bit, you ease up on the shoulder tension again, searching for exactly how much you need in order to preserve the character."

Joan's shoulders relax a little.

"That's good," I say. "Much less 'groto-scue.'"

"Are you making fun of me, buster?" the character asks, but as she does, Joan again laughs her own laugh.

"No, not at all. Now take a moment to practice the character's laugh."

"How can I? Nothin's funny now, young man."

"That's fine. Just fake it. You need to practice it enough so that when you do laugh, you have the container ready to hold it. Just as you practiced the fight for the *Rimers* scene."

For a minute Joan explores the laugh, finally hitting on a form that seems right for her character, "heh-heh-heh, heh-heh-heh."

"Good," I interrupt. "Now that's not so 'groto-scue,' is it?"

"You *are* laughing at me, heh-heh-heh!" Joan's character shouts. "You think I'm weird, don't you? Heh-heh-heh! Well, it's *you* that's weird!"

"Exactly!" I exclaim. "Now you have refined the container enough so that you can feed all the energy back into the character without all the extra tension."

When all the students have finished their second round of Baseball, I add two final observations: "I do want to note that when you were coaching from one of the bases, several of you gave the pitcher very strong choices. It was as if you were thinking, 'Well, I can make this choice *really* weird because *I'm* not going to have to play this character.' Especially with some of the vocal choices you made. So as we go on exploring character during the next few days, remember, you can give yourself challenges that are just as weird and exciting as those you gave each other.

"The other thing I want to point to before we leave this exercise is that this game can free you from the need to be so damned inventive all the time. There is a prejudice in our society in favor of individual creativity and the new. In the arts, this prejudice creates a constant need for inventiveness, which ignores the fact that the greatest artists, like Shakespeare, depended on reworking characters, plots, and images that they had plagiarized from others. Remember, it is actually very exciting and creative to plagiarize, to steal ideas, to let yourself be inspired by others rather than having to invent each character from zero yourself."

IMITATION

Peter [Brook] showed us photos of the Ik at particular moments in their daily lives—people eating, laughing, or just sitting. We looked at the image in the photo, and then we imitated the body position and the facial expression. We started from the outside, but little by little we tried to feel what the person in the photo had felt at that particular moment. If you don't attempt to get "inside" the image, you can't really construct a good imitation. Equally, if you really imitate the outside image in detail, your body position will start to generate feelings inside.

—Yoshi Oida, *An Actor Adrift*

It may seem a little obvious, but one of the most straightforward ways to get out of your own habits of voice and body is to get into someone else's. Imitation is one of the ways we began acting when we were children. Of course, since then we have learned to be self-conscious about imitation; we have learned that acting is a finer, deeper, more artistic endeavor than mere imitation and impersonation.

Nonsense.

Of course, imitation on its own can be shallow and trite, but it can be a wonderful first step toward letting go of ourselves. *Not* playing yourself is nearly impossible. Imitating someone else is a positive activity.

I assign my class the **Imitations** exercise (7.3) as homework, asking them to bring in characters developed from people they actually see in the street.

But after I have described the assignment, Joan is worried. "How do you know what a person is really like by just watching their gestures or their walk?"

"You don't. You have to trust your own inspiration. But your inspiration and insight may be based on details you are not even aware of."

By way of illustration, I describe two women I recently saw in a restaurant. A woman of about sixty sat down opposite another woman whom I guessed to be about twenty. They did not resemble each other, but somehow I knew that they were mother and daughter. But then I wondered: *how* did I know? What was it about the ways they were acting that made me so certain?

It was only then that I became aware that the young woman was sitting all the way at the very front edge of her chair, that her whole body leaned in toward the older woman, and the lean brought her closer and also lowered her head so that although she was taller than the older woman she was actually looking slightly upward toward her. The older woman was sitting more stiffly, but she did not lean away from the younger one. And so on. It was all these little, external details that gave me the feeling about the mother-daughter relationship.

I ask the class to do the Imitations exercise and bring two very different characters to the next class—one based on a voice they hear and one based on body gestures they observe.

As you try out this Imitations assignment, the most important thing is to trust your intuition. Look for the details, but dare to guess at what you don't know.

CHARACTER OR CARICATURE

Peter Sellers said that when he got the voice right, "the person takes over," with the walk, gestures, and even the look of the character following almost automatically.
　　　　　—"The Prime Minister of Mirth," *Time*, August 4, 1980

Imitations (7.3)

1. Begin by following someone down the street (at a safe distance) and trying to imitate his walk. Notice how he shifts his weight, swings his arms, holds his head. Let yourself feel what it must be like to live in that body, to walk that way. What do you find yourself thinking and feeling? Trust what you find. Then try again, with another person.

2. Move on to other sources. Try eating the way someone else eats. Notice someone who uses gestures you would never use, and try using those gestures.

3. Listen to a voice that is unlike yours, and try to imitate it exactly: the pitch, the tone, the accent, the words. Begin with the words you heard, and then start to improvise. Trust wherever the words lead you.

4. Build a whole character based on someone you've seen or heard. Let one character begin with a voice you hear and the other begin with body gestures.

The next day, I tell my class to spend some of their warm-up time practicing the characters they have brought in. Then one by one we "interview" the first set of characters. "Where do you live?" we ask. "How old are you?" "Do you have any brothers or sisters?" "What do you do for fun?" As the characters respond, we let their answers lead us to more questions: "Oh, when did you leave there?" "Why?" And so forth.

When Veronica hesitates, searching for an answer to one of the questions, I encourage her to just blurt out whatever comes to her. "Just make it up. The right answer is whatever you say."

Later she explains that she was worried that she might make up something that didn't make sense. "I had thought about my character's history, so some of the questions were easy. But when you asked about what animals I liked, I wasn't prepared, and I was suddenly afraid that I would say something that contradicted something else."

"But this is not a test. A fact of your character's history is not more true because you invented it last night than it is if you invent it as you speak. And if you do contradict yourself, well, maybe you were trying to hide something, or maybe your character tends to lie. Your task here is not to make finished characters but to allow the character you are constructing to open thoughts and feelings within you that are not yours."

"My problem," says Joan, "was that I didn't believe my character was real. It seemed more like a caricature than a character."

"Okay," I say, "and what makes something a caricature rather than a character?"

"Well, it was like she was a type, the *type* who lets the cigarette hang from the corner of her mouth and who talks tough all the time. It gave me that same creepy feeling I had when we started working on the *plastiques*: the feeling that the work led me to the *surface*, you know, to the exterior."

"You're absolutely right. But that is exactly what this exercise is for, to let you see and feel how many more questions there are to answer. If you feel that your character is the type who lets a cigarette hang from the corner of her mouth, then perhaps you need to explore what happens to her when she runs out of cigarettes.

"It is absolutely true that several of the characters we just met seemed thin. I even suspect that a few of them were made up today rather than prepared at all." A few sheepish grins appear. "**What makes a character different from a caricature is detail,** and when you begin, of course you will not have much detail. But it takes time to create detail. If you condemn yourself at the beginning because you do not already have a finished product, you will never let yourself get started. A caricature is to a character as a sketch is to a finished painting. And many artists begin by making pencil sketches before they attempt to add color. The artist may change his mind later, and change the hair color or the gesture of his subject several times before he finishes, but he cannot allow his critical mind to so inhibit his first strokes that he does not dare to begin with a crude sketch. So, in this exercise, or whenever you start to create a new character, if you find your judgment criticizing your work, the important thing is to take that criticism as a spur to the creation of further detail, rather than a condemnation of your first attempts."

ANTI-TYPECASTING

The Sudanese or Cirebonese dancer, regardless of personality, begins by learning a refined character whose slow, measured movement and melodious, centered voice are considered furthest from the ordinary self. By starting with the character which stretches the average performer most, the system tries to enfranchise him/her with the full potential range. . . . The training is designed to give each performer multiple personae, with different vocal, energy, and spatial usages—different "bodies"—so that the performer can ultimately realize that all of the masks of the "other" are merely sides of the eternal self.
        —Kathy Foley,
            "My Bodies: The Performer in West Java," *TDR* 1990

At the opening of the Living Theater's *Paradise Now*, the cast walked through the audience naming all the things they were not permitted to do. "I may not take off my clothes." "I may not smoke marijuana." And so forth. Everything they named was a prohibited act, but something they *could* do if they didn't mind facing the consequences.

One way of looking at the characters we enact in our daily lives is that they are what we have left ourselves after having put away all the facets of our personality that have been "prohibited." I know a young man who builds his body, lives on a strict diet, cuts his hair short, wears severe clothes, and lives in a simple, almost spare, room. He seems to be an extremely controlled and controlling character. But this is the person he has learned to be. When he was very young, he was a very wild kid—and he was often punished for his wildness. Over the years he learned that if he did not tightly contain his wild energy, he would suffer for it. But somewhere within him the wild man still lives.

And it is so with many of us. Over the years we have learned to put away the sides of ourselves that we could not show in public. And that means different sides for different people. Many women in our society have learned that acting loud or powerful is "unladylike." So over the years they have developed quiet voices. Others have discovered that it is not acceptable (or safe) to show their sexuality, so they have learned to act demure. Many men have learned to disguise their fear, to hide their sense of wonder, and to deny their ignorance because looking afraid or innocent or stupid is not permissible for men. And almost all of us have learned to be "nice" in public, saving all our tantrums, our cruelty, and our despair for our closest friends or our private nightmares.

But just because we have hidden these sides of ourselves does not mean that we have destroyed them. Most of us contain within ourselves powerful characters who are quite the opposite of those we display in our daily lives. And, if we ever hope to play Lady Macbeth or Iago, it will serve us to spend some time freeing these illicit selves who lie incarcerated behind the facades of our seemly exteriors. By purposefully seeking to display characteristics that are *unlike* our ordinary selves, we can use character work to encounter and push past our ordinary hesitations.

The **Not I** exercise (7.4) is designed to help you face and explore the characters within you, the parts of yourself that you normally avoid.

Note: *After any strong character exercise, it is important to take time for a* warm-down. *Character work can be like letting genies out of a bottle. You need to take the time to put them back in.*

Not I (7.4)

1. Begin by making a list of adjectives, ways of being in the world that describe sides of yourself that you rarely or never show—descriptors like <u>sexy</u>, or <u>cruel</u>, or <u>stupid</u>, or <u>vulnerable</u>, or <u>peaceful</u>, or <u>joyous</u>, or <u>crazy</u>.

2. Choose one word from your list, some trait that would be interesting and challenging to explore. (It need not be the most difficult trait on your list.)

3. Stand opposite a partner or in front of the group and start by explaining: "I am never . . ."or "I never permit myself to seem . . ." and fill in the blank.

4. Then, little by little, expand on your statement with examples, details, and demonstrations. For instance, "I would never permit myself to act cruel. I mean, if I caught a cute little bunny rabbit, I could never just take it in my hands like this and squeeze its neck, like this, and twist its head off. . . ." Or "I would never come on to another man, even if he looked really sexy, like you do in that tight tee shirt. . . ."

5. As you demonstrate what it is you could never do, just let yourself "imitate" that kind of behavior. It does not matter if at first it seems completely false. That's fine; it <u>is</u> completely false for "you." But as you progress, allow your body work, your gestures, voice, and imagery to take you along for the ride.

6. If you are working with a partner, you might ask your partner to aid your exploration by encouraging you—one way or another. For instance, if you were working on being cruel, it might inspire you to have your partner say either, "No, please, don't!" or "Yes, again, harder!" Experiment to see what sort of help or inspiration gives you greater permission to explore this forbidden side of yourself.

7. If the character that emerges is someone you want to explore, add some detail, invent some words, or tell a story.

8. If, on the other hand, it feels too uncomfortable to work with that character right now, let go of the voice and body you have created. Make sure the character is gone by saying a few words to your audience as the "normal" you.

9. At the end of the exercise, allow yourself some quiet time to reflect on what just happened and to put "yourself" back together.

10. Take a little time to process your experience. If you have worked in front of a group, spend a few minutes alone. If you have done this exercise with a partner, share anything you want with each other.

Warming Down (7.5)

1. Take some time to sense how you feel and what energies and thoughts are pouring through your mind and body. Stay alone for a couple of minutes.

2. Let yourself think about the acting experience you have just had. Allow yourself to have all the thoughts and opinions you are having.

3. Shake out any excess energy you feel. Run, yell, do whatever you need to do to help the character exit from your body and to recognize yourself as you.

4. Think about where you must go after rehearsal, whom you will have to see, what character you need to put on to face the performance called real life.

STANDING IT

A characterization is the mask which hides the actor-individual. Protected by it he can lay bare his soul down to the last intimate detail.

—Stanislavski, *Building a Character*

In my acting class we try the partnered version of the Not I exercise. Many of the students find it difficult, and they spend a long time in conversations with their partners afterward. At the end of the class, Veronica comes over to talk with me.

"Oh, that was so painful," she says. "I just couldn't do it. I felt like I did the first time we tried the Cat, like 'I just can't stand this.'"

"What were you working on?" I ask.

Veronica looks down. "On being pretty," she says. Then she corrects herself: "On being beautiful."

"Is your partner still here?"

"Maria, yes."

After the others leave the room, Veronica begins to work on her "beautiful" character in front of Maria. She begins moving her hips and swinging her hair, and for a moment the glimmer of a smile crosses her face. Maria smiles back at Veronica, and says, "You're beautiful," but as soon as she does, Veronica's smile turns to embarrassment, she lowers her eyes, and she stops working.

"Let's try again," I suggest. "See if you can notice what happens the moment *before* the embarrassment hits, in that split second before you look away."

We try again. Again the same thing happens, although perhaps the smile lasts a moment longer this time.

"Well?" I ask.

"I felt . . . warm. Like electricity."

"And . . ."

"And then I looked away."

"And what would happen if you didn't turn your eyes away?"

"I don't know. I don't know if I could stand it."

"I know what you mean," says Maria. "That's exactly the same thing I felt when we were working on that scene from *Death and the Maiden*, remember? I just felt like I couldn't stand to keep my eyes on that image."

"And what did you do to overcome that problem before you brought that scene back to class?" I ask Maria.

"It was hard. The first time I tried to work on it alone, I just started to cry. All I could think about was that I was angry with you for making me do it. So I decided to do a Cat. In the end I did one very long Cat in which I explored . . . well, it was pretty violent."

"Should I try that?" Veronica asks.

"You might. The Cat provides a safe container for strong emotions like anger and fear. The problem is that the very muscular tension that provided safety for Maria's anger may block the sensations of pleasure you are searching for rather than allowing you to release them."

"So what should I do?"

"Why don't you start your work again, but take it in very slow motion, so that you can notice the moment when the electricity begins. When it does, I want you to just breathe slowly and deeply. If you feel the embarrassment arising, as your eyes start to lower themselves, don't stop them, just slow them down and then try slowly and gently returning them to Maria."

Again Veronica begins to move her hips, but this time much more slowly and gently. Then, as Maria says, "You look beautiful," a glowing smile slowly spreads across Veronica's face. "Very beautiful." Veronica's smile broadens into a grin, then a laugh. "You do, Veronica, you look incredibly beautiful."

"Oh, help!" Veronica says, grinning, her eyes making little, frightened forays toward the ground and then returning to look at Maria.

"Gently now," I say. "No hurry. First just play with your eyes, finding exactly how much you can look at us without losing the electricity. Good. Now take some time to search with your voice and body for containers that allow you to stand this feeling."

"Oh, yes," she says, her voice suddenly lower. "Yes, I am. I am so beautiful, that you *must* keep looking at me." Veronica's vocal placement slides around, the vowels altering their shape. Finally her voice acquires a Hungarian accent, "I am, how do you say? . . . irreseestible."

"Trust it now," I say. "Look for the gestures."

Veronica's fingers slowly brush the hair from her face. "Yes, you!" she says, pointing at me. "You must look at me also." Her hands slide down her sides. "You must all look at me!" She gestures as if to a large crowd. "All of you peeeple herre, must loook at *all* of me." Veronica seems very alluring now, exuding a confidence and a sensuality she has never shown in class.

After a minute or two, I ask Veronica to stop. "How was that?"

"Great."

"And could you stand it?"

"Oh yes, it felt good."

"Now take a minute to remember what you did. You slowed down your reaction enough so that you could notice the separate moments within the reaction. This allowed you to become aware of the feeling of electricity that preceded the embarrassment. Then you found physical and vocal forms, insulators you might say, so that you the actor would not be shocked by the unaccustomed pleasure.

"Like the Cat, or the Kiss, character work is a container. Your slow motion, your lowered voice, your Hungarian accent, and the gestures you used were all specific forms that allowed you to contain your experience—that is, they permitted you to feel the emotional energy of your imagery while at the same time supplying you with a form that insulated you from the embarrassment—the feeling you called 'not being able to stand it.'

"This may be an important area for you to work on, but be gentle with yourself. Do it little by little. Your body is not used to this. It is like an unused muscle that needs to be strengthened bit by bit. If you strain it, it might go into spasm, and then you will feel confirmed in your belief that you can't stand that feeling. **But the fact of the matter is that most of us actually can stand much more of any sensation than we give ourselves credit for.**"

Veronica probably had deep-seated reasons for her embarrassment, reasons that would become clear only in a psychotherapeutic setting. If our aim had been psychotherapy, I might have asked Veronica to look behind her habit, to become aware of its historical roots and to confront these psychic sources. She might have learned to be able to stand being beautiful without needing to dress up her voice in a Hungarian disguise. But this is acting work, not therapy. Our purpose here was therapeutic only by the way. Our primary goal was to broaden Veronica's range of performance possibilities.

In the section called "Acting or Therapy," in the final chapter of this book, we will examine several areas in which acting training is—and is not—contiguous with psychotherapy. At this point I simply want to suggest that during the work, you may sometimes run up against neurotic habits that impede your

artistic progress. When you do, your ability to exercise technical choices can help you overcome these habits. The sensations you "cannot stand" and the inner characters you like to
avoid often contain within them very exciting energies. They
are to theater what bright colors are to painters. If you do not
want to restrict your stage roles to the works of pastel playwrights,
you must find a way to be able to stand strong emotional conditions and to become people very unlike your everyday self. To
expect an actor to play in Shakespeare or Tennessee Williams
plays without enormous emotional range or character stretches
would be like asking Van Gogh to paint the Arles countryside
with the palette of his early "Potato Eater" years.

DRESS-UP

*Clothing so influences my character, is so crucial to me,
that I would find it as impossible to come to a rehearsal
for Blanche in* A Streetcar Named Desire *dressed in slacks
and sneakers as it would be for me to work on* Saint Joan
in a frilly chiffon dress and high-heeled shoes.

—Uta Hagen, *Respect for Acting*

*We often overlook the importance Stanislavski placed on
the externals. Just like the Kabuki actor, he stood in full
costume and make-up before a mirror, fully realizing his
own externals before he considered his characterization
complete.*

—Robert Benedetti, *The Actor at Work*

In *An Actor Prepares*, the student Kostya, Stanislavski's
youthful alter ego, stands before a mirror and learns a lesson
that mask actors from many cultures (and five-year-olds all
over the world) have known for centuries: that costume and
makeup are wonderful aids in the creation of character. Seeing
himself transformed in a mirror enables Kostya to enact a side

of himself he had never before displayed or acknowledged in public.

When you dress up, a part of the change you undergo is physical: high heels and a sheath skirt literally force you to change the way you walk. But part of the change is psychological: the image you see in the mirror, or the look and the touch of the clothing against your skin conjure feelings and thoughts and fantasies within you.

So my next assignment for the class is simple:

> Use costume and makeup to transform yourself so thoroughly that you look and feel like a different person. Come to the next class sufficiently transformed that we don't recognize you.

The next day, some of the students have altered their clothes only a little. They look like themselves but dressed up for Halloween. But several of them are so unrecognizable that I have to figure out who they are by a process of elimination. When all of them have gathered, I suggest that they spend their warm-up time working with the characters they have created, becoming specific about the gestures, the voices, and the internal life these new exteriors inspire.

"Work alone for a while," I say, "until you feel really secure in your character, and then try interacting with others." In a few minutes, all over the studio, *character scenes* start to emerge, tiny conversations and dramas that grow from the interactions of a room full of people who normally might never meet. Because we have previously talked about the need for detail, today's collection of characters consists of more than stereotypes. Sandra's whore eats candy bars and speaks of her concern about her daughter's public school, Brian's stockbroker is a depressive whose mind seems to wander, his hands hanging limply by his side. Aisha's overweight male plainclothes cop bets on football games, and so on. But now there is another step we need to take.

"I want you to become aware that your characters tend toward certain emotional *moods*. Brian, your stockbroker seems sad all the time, even when others are fighting all around him. And Aisha, your cop is constantly picking fights with everyone."

"Yeah? So what!" the cop retorts, "What's wrong with that?"

"Nothing," I say, "nothing at all. But maybe even an angry cop can laugh at a joke once in a while. And even a depressed stockbroker might fall in love.

"It is a common trap in character work to confuse character with mood. Next week we will work specifically with ways to enable unchanging characters to experience changing emotions. But for now, I simply want you to try placing your characters in situations that stretch them beyond what you know about them.

"A straightforward way to expand on the character work you have started is to begin with physical or rhythmic changes, changes that are purely technical and over which you have complete control. If, for instance, you have been working on a character in a standing position, try sitting, or lying down, or running. What do you have to do to enable the character to remain the same person in this new shape? Which muscular choices were essential to the character and which were extra? If the character you've created always seems to move slowly, try moving quickly; to help yourself, give yourself a situation in which the character would *have* to move quickly. What if she had to catch a bus? What if the house were on fire? Then ask yourself: when you move quickly, has the character disappeared? If so, go back to the slower version and try speeding up the action little by little, sensing with each increment what is it that makes the character who she is. Is it possible that her *mind* moves slowly even when her body starts to run?

"Now try changing the psychological situation: How does your character act if he is hungry? How does he talk when he is falling in love? How does he react to the death of a child? Remember the work we did long ago with our Image Walks: your work as an actor is to find images that have strong effects on you."

After the actors have improvised among themselves for a
while, I ask small groups to improvise in extreme situations,
such as a stuck elevator or a shipwreck. As the odd group of
characters sit in the lifeboat, I narrate images and incidents:
"You can see the ship sinking. It's starting to rain. You've been
on the boat for two days and you're running out of water. You
see a shark." And so forth. As I throw new situations at them,
the characters must deal with the difficulties . . . and with each
other. As they do, the actors explore the difficulties of staying
within the characters while facing strong circumstances.

CHARACTERS WHO LISTEN

*Thinking that a character always remains the same while
meeting other characters in the play is a crucial mistake
that even great and experienced actors often make. It is not
true, either on the stage or in everyday life. As you may
have observed, only very stiff, inflexible or extremely con-
ceited characters always remain "themselves" while meeting others. To perform stage characters in such a manner is
monotonous, unreal and resembles a kind of puppetry.
Observe yourself and you will see how differently you in-
stinctively begin to speak, move, think and feel while meeting various people, even if the change others produce in
you is only small or barely noticeable. It is always you
plus somebody else.*

—Michael Chekhov, *To the Actor*

There is no end to the work we could do to expand our character vocabulary with exercises that push us beyond our
physical, vocal, and imagistic habits into the unknown. But
ultimately we must move from the pure pleasure of creating
characters out of thin air to the more difficult problem of creating characters that coincide with the ones written in a playscript. But before we do, it is useful to confront head-on a

problem we have already noticed in our character improvisations: the problem of separating character from mood and emotion.

As I mentioned in the section "The Bodily Emotions," the psychoanalyst Wilhelm Reich suggested that the muscular tensions people acquire as they age are not just the *symptoms* of their psychic histories; they are the very *mechanism* human beings rely on to contain and repress their memories. He referred to these habitual muscular tensions as *character armor.* His view was that in reaction to life experiences each of us creates his own personal armor, and that these constrictions make us who we are. When you make physical choices for your character, however, you must be careful that the character armor you choose is "permeable," that it does not interfere with your own capacity to listen, that it does not "protect" you from exactly the kinds of images and impulses you have been working so diligently to open yourself to.

Because the I Feel and Crossings exercises demand extreme sensitivity to the smallest emotional changes, we can now use them both as barometers of "permeability" for our character work (7.6). If your character armor is blocking your ability to listen, you will find in doing the I Feel exercise that you keep hitting the same feeling over and over again. In the Crossings work your "stuckness" will show up as an impulse to keep stepping in the same direction no matter what your partner does.

One note of caution: If in building a character you use physical tensions or gestures similar to your own habitual tensions, these character armors will tend to interfere with your ability to listen and respond. (For instance, if you are a person who often stores his tension in his shoulders, playing a character with lifted or hunched shoulders will enlist your own best defense systems, making it much harder for you to be receptive.) If, on the other hand, you choose character armor that is very different from your own personal habits, you will probably be more open and available to incoming signals. These forms of armor can be just as "strong" as your accustomed ones, but for you

I Feel and Crossings in Character (7.6)

1. First remind yourself of what the I Feel exercise is like <u>without</u> character. Sit across from a partner and spend a few minutes just playing the game as you remember it. (It might work as well to use the Meisner Repetition exercise or any other exercise based on listening and response.)

2. Then you and your partner spend a few minutes getting in character. Use any of the character exercises that work for you, making sure that you have created a character who is able to sit and make eye contact with your partner.

3. Now, in character, play I Feel.

4. If you find that you are naming one feeling very often, try easing up on some of your character adjustments. Play with the different muscles, vocal choices, or images you have been using to maintain your character. Notice in particular whether you are quite literally "holding on" to your character by wrapping your feet around the legs of your chair or by slumping down and collapsing your chest as you sit.

5. Try to find the degree of effort or tension that is necessary to remain in character without blocking your ability to listen and to react.

6. Laughter is a particularly sensitive barometer of presence and listening. Search for a condition in which your character can laugh naturally—but then make sure that the laugh is in the character's voice, not yours. If you add too much effort, the laugh will die; if you ease up too much, you will laugh in your own voice. Try letting go of the character adjustment and relaxing enough so that laughter just happens to you. Then purposefully, but gently, alter the pitch, placement, or accent of your laugh to match the character's without stifling the laugh.

7. Now, stand up and try the same experiment using the First Crossing exercise.

8. After testing your character work with the I Feel and the Crossing, return to doing an open improvisation with your character. See whether you are now freer to enter a wide range of emotions and more able to react to other characters.

they will be less "opaque" and more permeable to emotional input from other actors.

So, to recapitulate our character work so far, the first problem in entering character work is simply to find ways of pushing yourself beyond your known, everyday habits of voice, body, and emotion, beyond the self that you consider "real," or "normal," or "you."

The second problem is learning to maintain character while, at the same time, staying open to all the listening, reacting, and emotional tasks upon which acting depends.

Now we face the third problem: That of building a character who corresponds to the role written in a play. And the first step in tackling this problem is to select a scene that will present you with an exciting character challenge.

CHARACTER SCENES CHOOSING

When you choose a scene as text for character work, some of the basic guidelines we listed for choosing any scene still apply: It is still important to choose a scene you like, and it is still a good idea to select one in which the characters really listen and react to each other. But in a character scene it is not so important that the power constantly shift between the two characters; an unchanging power relationship between the characters may be a reflection of their character traits.

At the same time, there are several new considerations that are important in choosing scenes for character work. We live in a world filled with prescriptions and proscriptions about who we *can* and *should* be, and character scenes can either reinforce the stereotypes and restrictions we already feel, or they can expand our range of human possibilities. If during our professional careers we find ourselves "typecast" by directors, that will be a constriction of creative freedom with which we must contend. But if we "typecast" ourselves during our own artistic training, that is self-strangulation.

In my acting class, I encourage students to search for character scenes that will expand their personal character range. In this particular class, it takes a bit of juggling to find scenes that will serve everyone's needs. After their work on *Top Girls* and

Rimers of Eldritch, Sandra and Peter both express an interest in playing comedy. Sandra says she wants to play someone sexy, while Peter wants to try a character much older than himself. After some searching they agree that Albee's *Who's Afraid of Virginia Woolf* will present each of them with useful challenges.

Veronica wants to continue the work she had begun in the Not I exercise, so she is looking for a female character whose beauty is central to her self-image. Brian, meanwhile, having played the tense, guilt-ridden Gerardo in *Death and the Maiden*, says he wants to play someone relaxed and powerful. Though they each express some fear about taking on such well-known characters, they accept my suggestion to try Blanche and Stanley in *A Streetcar Named Desire*.

Some of the others, however, have a harder time finding scenes that will satisfy them. My greatest concern is for Maria. Until this point in our work, her progress has been fitful. In the *Death and the Maiden* scene she managed to find a way to confront the images she had tried to avoid, but her final performance in that scene was still tentative, and throughout the training her vocal work has continued to be weak. I'm hoping we can locate a scene that will provide her with a chance to break through whatever has been holding her back, and one that will present her with some way to overcome her vocal tensions. When we meet to talk about her scene choices, I present the problem as I see it.

"I don't know what is making this work so difficult for you, Maria, but it seems to me that you have not yet found the way to connect your voice with the rest of your being."

"I know," she says, casting her eyes downward, "I know. Sometimes I feel almost as though my voice is not *my* voice at all." Maria looks truly frightened. I guess that she is wondering if I am about to ask her to drop out of the work.

"So," I continue, "I found myself wondering whether you have ever done a scene in Spanish."

"No," she says. "Well, once in a Christmas play in church. But no, not in any real theater work."

"But you grew up speaking Spanish at home?"

"Yes, until I went to school. Everybody spoke Spanish. I first learned English from the television. Do you think that matters?"

"That you learned English from television? No. But I do know that there is something special about the connection we all have to the first sounds we heard as children. And returning to those sounds can sometimes help us get in touch with parts of our being we've put away. So I was wondering, have you ever read any Lorca?"

"No." Maria looks down again. "When I learned to read, it was important to me that I be able to read in English."

"Well, I'd like you and Carlos to take a look at *Yerma*, in Spanish. Lorca's characters are powerful and interesting, and his Spanish may lead you to the vocal connections you are looking for."

With a smile, Maria runs over to talk to Carlos.

My suggestion to Aisha, however, evokes a very different reaction. She has come to me saying that all the plays she has ever done have been serious, so she definitely wants to work on a comic scene this time. For a character stretch, she says she would like to tackle playing someone older, but none of the scenes she has been able to find really appeal to her.

"Have you looked at *Paper Dolls* by Elaine Jackson?"

"No. Who is that?"

"She's an African-American playwright."

"You mean because I'm black I should play an African-American character?"

"Not at all, but it's a good comedy with two older women in it, and I have heard you talking about what it is like for you being the only black student in this class. Until now you haven't had the opportunity to put any of those feelings directly into your work."

"Well, that's true. I mean, I would like to find some way to let all these white folks see what the world looks like from this side, you know. . . . No offense."

"No offense."

"But I don't want to typecast myself."

"Of course, but it seems to me that black is not a type any more than female is a type."

"I guess."

"And I think there is something else here: Sometimes we avoid some of the images we hold in our hearts because they seem too clear, too close or too obvious. But one of the greatest values of character scenes is that they give you an opportunity to explore your own hidden desires."

After looking at *Paper Dolls*, Aisha agrees that the part would present her with an exciting challenge. "But what about my scene partner?" she worries. "I don't know if anybody else in this class will want to play an aging African-American beauty queen."

I suggest that she show the script to Joan and see what she says. At the next class, as the students are entering the studio, Aisha and Joan pull me aside.

"Well?" I ask.

"Well," Joan says, "I loved the play . . ."

"But . . . ?"

"But," Joan explains, "I'm worried about creating the voice and gestures for this character because I've never spent any time with anyone like these women."

"Don't you worry about that, girl," Aisha responds, her voice taking on a fresh inflection. "Next Friday night you and I be makin' a little trip uptown."

"Good," I say, turning to the rest of the class, who by now have gathered around our discussion. "One of the things you will all want to do is to expose yourself to images and people who stimulate your imagination about the characters you're playing."

"And what about me?" asks Veronica. "I don't have time right now to visit New Orleans."

"Well, then you may have to make do with some videotapes. You could spend some time watching *Gone with the Wind*."

But something is still troubling Joan. "I just want to be sure it isn't somehow racist for me to be acting this part, you know?"

"Why should it be?" Aisha says. "It wasn't racist when I played that English girl in *A Taste of Honey*."

"I know," says Joan. "I thought about that. But then I thought maybe this is different."

"I think you're both right," I say. "As long as Joan is not playing the role in order to make fun of the character, there is nothing automatically racist about a white woman playing a black character. But we are not operating in a vacuum here. We live in a society in which race relations are not the same in both directions. And we are making theater in the wake of history, including a theatrical tradition in which white actors *did* play black roles in order to denigrate the characters they were portraying. So I think that you are right, Joan, to hesitate, to make sure that neither Aisha nor anyone else feels insulted."

"Damn," says Aisha. "Why should choosing an acting scene be so difficult? Isn't it strange?"

"Not strange," I respond, "with three hundred years of painful racial history on the one hand and a group of truly sensitive people on the other. Not strange at all."

I turn to address the full group. "The first thing you need to do is to read the play you have selected—the whole play, several times—allowing yourself to notice your reactions, especially your reactions to the character you will play. Let yourself have all the opinions you have, positive, negative, and otherwise. You can make notes on your thoughts, but don't do any memorizing yet. Then, to prepare for our first exercise of finding character from text, select a few lines from your character's speeches, lines that seem particularly difficult for you, words that you, yourself, would never say. And come to the next class with a copy of the entire play."

The three exercises (7.8–7.10) in the following sections offer three different ways to begin your search for character choices.[1] Different techniques may work for different actors or

---

1. These exercises are just three possible doorways into character from text. Many other exercises, including animal work, work with costume, and historical research might also be used at this point to inspire character choices.

for the same actor working on different characters. As always, you must remember that the process of experimentation often involves the discovery of many dead ends and wrong turns along the way. But the time you spend eliminating the choices you don't like is not wasted time; the process can help you feel more certain of the choices you do like.

Note: Since character work necessitates being "not you," it is important before you enter these character exercises that you take off any jewelry or other personal accoutrements you wear. And it is useful to take some time in your warm-up to clear out your personal worries of the day so that you can begin the work of becoming someone else as unencumbered as possible by those things that remind you of yourself.

Choosing Scenes for Character Work (7.7)

1. Choose a scene that <u>requires</u> character—a character that you could not play as "yourself." (Many of Tennessee Williams's plays, for instance, only make sense if you create the particular character they require.) Be sure this is true for *both* characters in the scene.

2. Choose a scene that presents you with an <u>exciting</u> and <u>healthy</u> character stretch.

• **Exciting,** meaning a character that opens you to self-images and ways of being in the world that you tend to hide from or avoid in your everyday life. Self-images that you dream about or fear or hold in awe.

• **Healthy,** meaning choices that do not reinforce any negative self-images that you, yourself, commonly fall prey to. Playing a character with similar qualities can undermine your acting freedom.

3. Avoid types you have often played or types that come terribly easily to you. At the same time, don't give yourself such an enormous stretch that you cannot handle it. (Playing the opposite gender, for instance, can be much harder than you think.)

CHARACTER WORD JAM:
THE CINDERELLA EXERCISE

In the Safe Space exercise with which this book began, you moved around the studio allowing yourself to sense what place felt best to you. As you did, you may have known right away where you wanted to be, but you tried out many spaces to help you verify that "click" of certainty within you. The **Character Word Jam** approach (7.8) to character is similar, in suggesting that you can begin to "zero in" on a character choice by testing many options against each other. This exercise is utter experimentation.

The Word Jam is like the slipper scene in Cinderella. The text is the slipper, and you are trying to find—that is to *become*—the foot that fits it.

Character Word Jam (7.8)

1. Begin by selecting some phrases from your character's text that are the strangest for you to say, the words that, when you read them, seem most uncomfortable in your mouth—not like <u>you</u> at all.

2. Now take one of the chosen phrases (you can even begin with a single word of that phrase) and start to "jam" on those words: Try them out with all sorts of character choices. Change pitch, placement, intonation, and rhythm. Allow your body to change with your voice. Move as you work, play with gestures and images. Purposefully try choices you know won't feel right, and then return to ones you liked better.

3. Little by little, allow yourself to be aware of which vocal, rhythmic, and physical choices make the words you're working with <u>speakable</u>, the ones that seem to "fit" the words.

4. Once you make a choice, stick with that voice and body but move on to one of the other phrases you have chosen. If they also feel like a fit, move on to other character lines, maintaining the choices you've made.

5. If the choices you made with the first phrase do not seem to work well with other lines, try jamming on another one of your phrases. When you find something that works, try out your choices with the first line.

6. If you find a voice that somehow seems right, do not worry at this point if it feels "stereotyped" or "too obvious." You will work on refining it later. For now just keep playing with the choice you've made, allowing variations for different emotions that the character exhibits.

7. Try out your choice by working with your scene partner. Figure out what you need to hold on to and what you need to let go of so that you are free to listen and react.

"I CAN'T PLAY YOU"

It will be a good starting point for an actor, in order to grasp the initial idea about the character he is going to perform on the stage, to ask himself: "What is the differ-ence—however subtle or slight this difference may be—between myself and the character as it is described by the playwright?"

—Michael Chekhov, *To the Actor*

Kim Stanley once stated that first she listed all the char-acteristics of her character and then crossed out all the ones that she already had and worked only on the ones she didn't have.

—Alice Spivak, in Mekler,
The New Generation of Acting Teachers

As we discovered in the Not I exercise, one of the ways to think about character is to consider that what makes a charac-ter into a *character* is that it is *"not* you." But when you con-template playing someone very different from yourself, you may think, "I could never talk like that, or act like that." If the character is from a famous play, you may come to the work with an idea of what that character *should* be like—and of how unlike him or her you yourself are. "Oh, Juliet! How am I ever going to do her? She's so unbearably innocent and beautiful and rich and Renaissance and . . . !" If you have seen a previ-ous production of the play, you may have the image of another actor stuck in your mind. Or if the character is based on a his-torical personage, you may feel overwhelmed by thoughts of the historical detail you "ought" to master before attempting the role.

But if you find yourself thinking, "Oh, I could never play that part!" you must indeed have an image of what playing that part might be like. In other words, these problems and worries are, themselves, actually images, sources of energy that you can use to begin your investigation!

"I Can't Play You" (7.9)

1. Stand up and look at a space about five feet in front of you, and, as if the character you will portray were standing in that space, address him or her with some observations, such as "I can't play you, because you are . . ." Start with one specific thing: "I can't play you because you are much more athletic than I am." Or "because you are sixty years old." Or "because you have long blonde hair." Whatever.

2. Say the phrase several times, speaking toward the space where you have placed the character, as if he or she were there to hear you.

3. Then switch places. From the character's position, look back to where the actor was, and listen to what she or he was saying. You don't have to *do* anything; just listen. Perhaps the actor just seems silly to you, and you feel like smiling. Perhaps the actor seems to be complimenting you or insulting you. Just take it in.

4. If while you are standing in the character position you feel like reacting verbally or otherwise, do so. You do not have to try to *play* the character. Just trust whatever voice or gestures happen.

5. Then return to the actor's position. Look back toward the character again. If you have a reaction to the character, that's fine. If not, just go on and name another way in which the character is unlike you.

6. And then return to the character position again, and take in this new piece of information. Just let yourself be seen as the actor sees you. For instance, if the actor says that your arms are muscular, or your voice is high or your mind is clever, **let yourself just feel what it is like to be perceived that way**. Take it in. Let it work on you. She sees you as having long blond hair. What is it like to be seen that way?

7. If while you are standing in the character position you have an "actorly" thought, return to the actor's spot, and let yourself voice that thought as the actor. If while standing in the actor's position you have an impulse that seems to be the character's, cross back again.

8. Keep switching from one side to the other, letting yourself listen to what the "other" one has said and allowing thoughts and reactions to happen.

9. Little by little you will find that you can distinguish the actor's thoughts and impulses from the character's. And little by little you will find that you can spend longer and longer periods in the character's position.

10. Take the time you need to go through as many details as you want. When you have worked on one character trait for a while, move on to another. After you have worked with the voice, try out some text.

11. Don't worry if the choices you come up with in this exercise do not quite match the ones you found in the Character Word Jam. You can mix and match later.

12. Try out the choices you have made with your scene partner.

AUTOBIOGRAPHY

An actor must love dreams and know how to use them. . . .
An actor is completely free in creating his dream, as long
as he does not stray too far from the playwright's basic
thought and theme.

—Stanislavski, *Creating a Role*

Constantin Stanislavski loved to fantasize. In *An Actor Prepares* he tells the following story:

Let me tell you about an old woman I once saw trundling a baby carriage along a boulevard. In it was a cage with a canary. Probably the woman had placed all her bundles in the carriage to get them home more easily. But I wanted to see things in a different light, so I decided that the poor old woman had lost all of her children and grandchildren and the only living creature left in her life—was this canary. So she was taking him out for a ride on the boulevard, just as she had done, not long before, her grandson, now lost. All this is more interesting and suited to the theatre than the actual truth. Why should I not tuck that impression into the storehouse of my memory? I am not a census taker, who is responsible for collecting exact facts. I am an artist who must have material that will stir my emotions. [Stanislavski, 1936, pp. 87–88]

When preparing a role, Stanislavski did not restrict himself to actual memories; he would fabricate intricate imaginary details to understand a character's actions.[2] The **Character Autobiography** exercise (7.10) is just such a flight of fantasy, but since the training we have been pursuing here is corporeal, our method of creating a character biography is done not just with the mind but with the full body. What it involves is not writing but "living through" a personal history for our characters by entering a long improvisation that can supply us with images and "memories" for our scenes on stage.

Note: The Character Autobiography is a long exercise. I would suggest reserving a minimum of an hour and a half to complete it.

The Character Autobiography (7.10)

1. Begin by finding a place to lie down on the floor and just think through everything you know about the character: What the playwright says about the character. What other characters say. What images you have.

2. Then put those thoughts away. They may inspire part of the work, or they may not. This exercise depends on your trusting what comes up, whether or not it seems to "make sense."

3. Now relax using any relaxation technique you like. Let go of all other thoughts and concerns and tensions as fully as you can.

4. Let yourself become aware of your breath. There is nothing but your breath.

5. You begin with the moments just after the character was born. At first there is nothing but breath itself. Then, during the next few minutes, you begin to discover your body. Discover that you can open your eyes, that your body has parts that can move, and that you have a voice.

---

2. The elaborate history that Stanislavski created for Iago in order to justify the character's actions in the first scene of *Othello* are told in Jean Benedetti's new book, *Stanislavski and the Actor*.

6. As you discover, let yourself explore such questions as, What kind of a world is this into which you have been born? Is it bright or dark, loud or quiet? How does your mother touch you, hold you, feed you? And so forth.

7. Are there other voices around you? Who takes care of you? Do they change you when you are wet?

8. As you start to move your body, the questions about the environment spread: Are there many rooms in your house? When you are taken outside, what is it like?

9. During the next hour or so, the questions progress through the discoveries of crawling, walking, going to school, and being an adolescent. (What do you say when you start to talk? Who sings a lullaby to you?) At each age, conquer the physical tasks, and allow the questions about family, friends, environment, activities, skills, dreams, and events act as goads to your imagination, which invents details of habit and of important life moments as you improvise. (Do you have chores you must perform? Are you ever punished?)

10. If, as you work, images that belong to what you know about the character's past appear, that's fine. But if images from your own past or from other sources crop up, accept them also. It is important that you trust every image, every event, every impulse you have, discovering your history as it happens.

11. When your character has reached the age he or she is in the play, allow yourself to improvise the events that lead directly up to your entrance: How you met the other characters, what happened between you, what occurred right before your entrance.

12. Enter the scene you are playing, improvising at least the first few beats of the scene before you stop.

13. Take time after the exercise to digest, to remember what parts of the improvisation were strongest for you, and to take notes.

Over the course of three days, my class has experienced the Character Word Jam, the I Can't Play You, and the Character Autobiography exercises. After each exercise the actors have improvised or run parts of their scenes with their partners. After the final session, we gather to talk.

"Interesting, but confusing," says Sandra.

"What do you mean?"

"I mean each exercise led me to new images. And each one

felt exciting and useful while I was doing it. But now, when I compare what I found, not all of it fits together. For instance, the voice I came up with for Martha (in *Who's Afraid of Virginia Woolf*) in the I Can't Play You exercise was extremely loud and raucous, but the voice I developed for her in the Character Autobiography was more nasty and whining. How do I choose?"

"There is no right answer. Martha's husband, George, says that she brays, and even the playwright refers to her braying in a stage direction, but ultimately you must decide for yourself. What sounds like braying to Albee might sound like whining to you. Besides, you have to be very careful with such stage directions. Sometimes they have been added by directors or editors. But even if, as in this case, they seem to be the playwright's own ideas, you can never be sure that they are going to work for you. Remember, Albee doesn't have to go on stage in front of an audience and perform this part; you do. So you have to make decisions that feel right to you.

"So if you found different character adjustments in each exercise, perhaps you need to mix and match, taking images from here and gestures from there, and vocal choices from a third source. Or perhaps by playing with the various choices you will hit on a completely new choice that works even better. What is important is that you let yourself really plunge into each choice you are trying, rather than constantly second-guessing yourself. And, ultimately, you must find choices that allow you to connect with the lines and the actions of the script.

"Remember, all of these exercises are simply ways to get your own creative imagination started. Partway through your rehearsal process you may realize that some of the choices you made earlier conflict with actions you discover as you work. Then you may have to throw out those old choices and find new ones. But it is important that you let yourself have the courage of your convictions. **It is better to make a strong choice and have to change it later on than to hang out forever waiting for divine inspiration.**"

REHEARSING CHARACTER SCENES

If I have to play a character with a foreign accent or a regional dialect, I consult a specialist, and . . . I work around the clock on the sounds and rhythm of my new speech pattern. I get records of it so I can listen all day. I go to films where people talk the way I am supposed to. I make my friends and family the victims of my continuous practicing. I try to speak with my new speech pattern until it becomes second nature, until I stop hearing myself or checking myself.

—Uta Hagen, *Respect for Acting*

It is important to remember that the character work we have been studying does not replace any of the scene work we studied before; it adds to it. In order to rehearse a character scene, you must still open your body, your mind, and your voice to the words and the actions in the script, and you must still listen and react to your personal imagery and to your partner. Moreover, since character work can, as we have seen, interfere with other acting tasks (like listening), you must pay extra attention to these underlying skills as you add character choices to your acting.

There is no one "right" order in which to rehearse. Some people like to spend time making character choices on their own before working with their partners. But if you do so, be careful not to short-circuit your creative process or cut down your range of choices too quickly using the excuse "This character wouldn't do that." It often works well to spend a couple of rehearsals (using the Dropping-In exercise or some equivalent work) just listening and reacting to your partner, finding your own, personal responses to the scene before attempting character. Then you might work on the character choices, both on your own and with your partner, improvising your way through the scene to discover actions and impulses that the character inspires in you. After you have made character, emotional, and blocking choices, you might try using your character preparation as a warm-up, thinking of it as part of the preparation that leads you into the lines of the scene.

Remember, you are "sketching" the scene, making more and more decisions and becoming more and more specific as you go along. As you progress, you will have to change and correct previous decisions: Discoveries you make during a character-based rehearsal may force you to alter some of the blocking you had set while listening and reacting, or, conversely, a rehearsal devoted to listening and reacting may prompt you to cut down on character habits or gestures you had adopted in your solo character explorations but that now seem to interfere with your ability to stay present. At each stage of the work, you must dare to make tentative decisions so that you can move on to tackle the next set of tasks. As the details get more and more intricate, it can be important to keep good notes.

In my acting class, the students present their character scenes twice, just as they did the first set of scenes. Often in these scene presentations, many of the same acting problems we have already spoken about can surface again. So in order to concentrate on those questions that pertain directly to the character work, I shall describe here only one presentation of each scene.

PLAYING COMEDY

Aisha and Joan have done careful work on their characters for the first scene of *Paper Dolls*. Their characters, Margaret-Elizabeth and Lizzie, are waiting in the customs room at the Canadian border while the Canadian customs agents test some suspicious white powder they discovered in Lizzie's valise. The actresses have drawn these two aging beauty queens with impressive detail. Joan's Margaret-Elizabeth is flamboyant; her every gesture takes up space, as if she were always showing herself off for an invisible audience. And Joan has done a good job of capturing the sound of an African-American accent transplanted from a Southern childhood to a Northern city. Aisha's Lizzie is tense and emotional: she opens and closes her handbag often with a fumbling gesture that bespeaks her age.

Joan and Aisha have made judicious cuts and worked out careful blocking. After their scene presentation, the two actresses are happy with what they have accomplished, but, as Joan says during the feedback, "I just think it could be a lot funnier than it is. This is a comedy, and I know it should be funnier."

"Where, for instance? Can you think of one place that should be funnier than it is?"

"Well, the conversation about the baking soda."

"Okay, let's run that part."

Aisha and Joan set up the moment. Their actions are so detailed that they are able to pick up the scene with almost no preparation.

LIZZIE: There's no need to get nasty, Margaret. Especially since you *know* I always travel with it. Did I *ever* visit you and didn't have it with me? I never travel without baking soda—never. I don't know why you actin' like this is the first time you've ever seen me with it.

M-E: Why do you need so much of the goddamn stuff?

LIZZIE: And I don't know why you shouting at me, Margaret. Now you just stop it!

M-E: Why do you need so much of the goddamn stuff?

LIZZIE: Margaret, *soda* is *very* pure . . . *very* natural! Smell my feet!

M-E: Lizzie! Lizzie!

LIZZIE: You can't smell 'em! Every day I sprinkle that stuff between my toes . . . *you cannot smell my feet*!

M-E: Lizzie! Lizzie!

LIZZIE: TEETH! SEE! SEE! UNDER MY ARMS!

M-E: Lizzie!

LIZZIE: CLEAN THE HOUSE WITH IT!

M-E: Lizzie, for Christ's sake!

LIZZIE: I EAT IT!

M-E: Don't you dare sit there and tell these customs agents this bizarre baking soda story . . . 'cause if you do they gonna . . . YOU *EAT* IT?

Joan is right. For some reason, the scene is not terribly funny as they have done it. The moment of Lizzie removing her shoe and lifting her foot daintily to Margaret-Elizabeth's face is hilarious, but as the scene builds, the humor does not.

"What's going on in this scene for you, Joan?"

"I'm mad."

"Okay, how mad are you?"

"Well, I'm pretty mad, as mad as you can get over some baking soda. I mean it's not *King Lear*, I guess."

"Oh, but it is."

"It is?"

"Absolutely. You're a black woman in the hands of these white policemen. They could put you in jail. Maybe they could do worse than that."

"I know, but that's not funny."

"Exactly, for Margaret-Elizabeth this situation is *not* funny. The characters in comedies are often living through personal tragedies. What makes it funny to us is that *they* are taking seriously a situation that *we* can see is ludicrous."

Joan and Aisha run the scene again. It is clear how Joan was holding herself back before. This time, as she plays each moment fully, she seems ready to throttle Lizzie by the end, but the scene is much funnier for us. Then, suddenly as she begins her last line, Joan stops.

"But, if I'm taking what she is saying so seriously, I don't know how to do this line. How can I *not* react when she says 'I EAT IT!'"

"I thought you were really mad."

"Absolutely."

"Good, then you don't have to listen to her so politely. What happens if you just keep talking right through her line about eating it? Maybe as she speaks you're just taking an in-breath, preparing for your next attack."

This time, when Margaret-Elizabeth finally interrupts her own anger to hear what Lizzie has said, her "YOU *EAT* IT?" has become a hilarious double take.

"So," I conclude, "what we discover here is that even the comic timing of the long pause between Lizzie's 'I EAT IT!' and Margaret-Elizabeth's 'YOU *EAT* IT!?' is built on your taking this comic situation seriously. To make comedy work, you have to do some very serious acting."

THERE IS NO STANLEY KOWALSKI

At the end of class, after Aisha and Joan's presentation, Veronica and Brian come to me to ask for help. "We've got problems," Brian explains, "both of us."

"It's me," says Veronica. "For some reason, I just can't concentrate on the work. I feel like I'm going nuts."

"It's not just her. I know I'm not doing this part right, but I don't know why."

I meet with them privately the next day and ask them to show me what they've got, no matter what stage their rehearsal is at. When they run through the scene, Brian's problems with his character are clear. His Stanley is quite tentative, his vocal choices keep changing, and his body work seems self-conscious. But I don't see the problem with Veronica's work. She has clearly used her character work on Blanche to continue her exploration of being beautiful. Since Blanche's beauty is more ethereal than that of the "Hungarian" character Veronica had created, rather than touching her own body, Veronica plays with the costume, the makeup and the tiara Blanche wears, and the Hungarian accent has been replaced by a light Southern drawl. But, even though the rehearsal seems to be going well, in the middle of the scene, Veronica suddenly stops and turns to me, in tears.

"I feel like I don't know what I'm doing. I keep forgetting the business we planned. I can't remember when I'm supposed to pick up the fan. No matter how many times we do it, something always goes wrong. I don't know what's wrong with me."

I think I do, but I say, "Well, if you can stand living with your confusion for a few minutes longer, I'd like to deal with Brian's problems first."

Veronica is not overjoyed, but she says she can wait. I turn to Brian. "Show me some of the character choices you have for Stanley."

"Show you?"

"Yes, it seemed to me that sometimes you were doing things that were not at all Brian-like. For instance, when you picked up the beer bottle and waved it in the air. Let's begin with that."

Brian grabs the bottle and says Stanley's line: "I used to have a cousin who could open a beer bottle with his teeth." His voice is full and luxurious. He brings the bottle down to the table. "That was his only accomplishment, all he could do—he was just a human bottle-opener. And then one time, at a wedding party . . ." But now Brian's voice has lost its vibrancy and his body has contracted.

"What happened?" I ask.

"Let me show you something else," Brian says. "I worked on animal images, and I came up with this image of an orangutan for Stanley. Look." Brian runs through the same lines again. This time his arm swings up with the bottle in a large, lazy arc. And his voice is more guttural. Again he stops.

"That seemed good," I say. "What's the problem?"

"But I don't know what Stanley Kowalski is really like. How can I know if I'm making the right choices?"

"Brian," I say, "there *is* no Stanley Kowalski. There never was. There never will be. There is a film with Marlon Brando. And there have been hundreds of other actors who have played Stanley Kowalski. And there is an orangutan in the zoo. But

Stanley, himself, does not exist. All that exists are the lines that Tennessee Williams wrote. That's all there ever is of any character, even a historical character. The character in the play is what *you* make of it. If you doubt your Stanley, you kill him. If you believe in him, you bring him to life. Tennessee Williams's lines are a gift to *you*. But no one can tell you how to use that gift. You have two interesting choices there to choose from. Either one will work. Now, there is nothing more to do but to dare to choose.

"I'm going to work with Veronica now for a minute, but while I do, select one of your character choices and just practice sticking with it fully."

I turn back to Veronica.

"So, tell me, is this problem with Blanche something that has been happening all along in your rehearsal, or has it just begun recently?"

"It's been getting worse every time we rehearse. And yesterday it started happening even when we were not rehearsing. I was leaving my apartment and I kept feeling like I was forgetting things. And the worst thing was last night. I was out with a friend of mine and she told some story, some stupid joke, but afterward I kept worrying about the characters in the joke as if they were real!"

"And whenever you work on the scene . . . ?"

"It just gets worse. I keep thinking Brian is angry with me. He said he wasn't, but maybe . . ." Veronica finishes on the edge of tears, "maybe I'm going crazy."

"Veronica, I want you to just go on telling me about how you feel. And then, when I give you a signal, just pick up the lines in the scene—anywhere at all, whatever lines come to you. First go stand at Blanche's dressing table. Good. Now go on telling me what you were saying about what's happening to you."

"I don't know. I think maybe I'm becoming prematurely senile or something. I can't remember when to pick up the fan. I can't remember . . . and when I tell myself just to calm down, I feel . . . I don't know. It's like my body is falling apart. Maybe

I'm really going crazy." Veronica laughs again, but the laugh is strangely light and hollow.

"Now!" I say. "Start Blanche's text anywhere."

Veronica toys with the fan and launches into the middle of Blanche's big speech:

Physical beauty is passing. A transitory possession. But beauty of the mind and richness of the spirit and tenderness of the heart . . . *(Veronica picks up the fan, but immediately puts it down again)* . . . and I have all those things . . . *(again she picks it up, and begins to fan herself)* . . . aren't taken away, but grow! *(Veronica is almost crying now, but her voice has taken on Blanche's drawl again, this time with a bitter edge.)* Increase with the years! How strange that I should be called a destitute woman! When I have all these treasures locked in my heart. *(Her anger struggles to overcome the tears welling up.)* I think of myself as a very, very rich woman! But I have been foolish—casting my pearls before swine!

I signal Brian, who picks up his line, "Swine, huh!" As the two plunge forward in the scene, I call out: "Good, now, both of you, trust your character choices and concentrate as actors on the little things, on the actions, on the timing. Be precise. The acting will take care of itself."

This time, the scene is enormous. Stanley and Blanche are performing an exotic dance, a ritual of sex and violence.

BLANCHE: Let me—let me get by you!
STANLEY: Get by me? Sure. Go ahead.
BLANCHE: You—you stand over there!
STANLEY: You got plenty of room to walk by me now.

But we can feel the electricity that fills the space between the two characters, fills it so full that Blanche feels she cannot pass.

BLANCHE: Not with you there! But I've got to get out somehow!
STANLEY: You think I'll interfere with you? Ha-ha!

Brian's laugh reverberates. The two actors lean left and right like two boxers in a ring. Then he smiles and slowly steps toward her.

STANLEY: Come to think of it—maybe you wouldn't be bad to—
    interfere with.

When they have finished the scene, I ask them to take a long time "warming down." "Take all the time you need to remember what you did, the little choices you made, little moments you found. And take time to note your gestures, looks, and tones of voice. Then take some more time to put it away, to let it go, to physically shake it out and to return to your own body."

When they are ready, I ask, "Well, how was that?"

The two of them say nothing. They just turn to each other and hug.

"Yes," I say, "after that scene you may need to make some human contact with your scene partner. It is like a nightmare, and it takes some time to wake up.

"A couple of years ago a similar thing happened in my class to an actress who was working on the character of Laura in *The Glass Menagerie*, the scene in which Laura's mother confronts her for not attending her secretarial lessons. It seemed to all of us watching that the actress playing Laura was doing well, but she insisted that she did not feel good about her work. She complained that she didn't feel free in her acting, and that all her character choices just made her feel weak and silly. She kept saying, 'I feel like I just can't do this part.' But her problem was not that she couldn't do Laura; her problem was that she *was* doing Laura, and doing it so thoroughly that she had begun to feel Laura's symptoms as if they were her own."

"But how can you know?" Veronica asks. "How did you

know that what I was running into was not my problem but Blanche's?"

"Two things. One was that when you were acting, you did not seem crazy. You seemed to be playing the beats of the scene. Whatever was happening for you was working for Blanche. And the second thing was what you said. You kept saying that you couldn't remember things, and that you felt like you were going crazy. Those phrases sounded eerily like a character description of Blanche.

"But in the end, there is no way to be sure except to try it. Of course, it is possible that you will discover that the problem you have run into is just some old acting habit of your own, or that the character choice you've made really doesn't work. But first, *give yourself the benefit of the doubt*. Trust that maybe, after all this training, and all this scene preparation and character preparation, just maybe the track you're on, and the unpleasant territory that track is leading you through, is the right track after all.

"The fact is that when a scene starts going well, especially a scene with strong character work, the emotions you experience are always a mixture of your emotions and the character's emotions. And if the character is miserable, or crazy, a part of you is going to feel miserable or crazy too. For that reason, **when you are doing strong character work, it is very important that you take time to *warm down* after each rehearsal.** A character can get under your skin, and, for the sake of your own sanity, you must be sure that you have let it go before you try to interact with your everyday world."

TRADUTTORE, TRADITORE[3]

The scene Carlos and Maria have chosen is from the second act of Lorca's *Yerma*. Juan and Yerma have been married for

---

3. *Traduttore, traditore* is an Italian adage meaning "translator, traitor."

three years, but they still have no children, and for Yerma, this is a tragedy. Juan, however, is content without children. He is a cold man, concerned only that his wife stay at home and avoid promoting gossip. In this scene, Yerma pleads with him, "Men have their own life, the cattle, the trees, their conversations; but women don't have anything else but that: having children, and looking after them." But Juan is unmoved. "I don't want people pointing me out," he says. "That's why I want to see that door shut, and everybody home where they belong."

At the end of the scene, Yerma, with apparent equanimity, sends Juan to eat lunch with his sisters; then she explodes into a powerful monologue that begins:

> ¡Ay qué prado de pena!
> ¡Ay qué puerta cerrada a la hermosura!

> Oh what a field of torment!
> Oh what a door closed upon misery!

As Maria and Carlos begin the scene, I keep my fingers crossed. I do not expect all of the emotions to be full or all of the images to be clear. I only hope that the two actors can communicate the tenderness and the violence of this scene—that Carlos can keep his energy encased within the uptight character of Juan, and, conversely, that Maria can allow her voice to carry the fullness of Lorca's words.

I can see immediately that Carlos has created subtle but strong character choices that allow him to live fully within the character of Juan. In fact, he has created a sort of mask, a small, cynical smile that gives us the impression that Juan is satisfied with his life, and at the same time, that there are energies within him that he will let no one see.

Maria has chosen to wear a long white dress that almost touches the floor, and I worry that this costume choice may put her further out of touch with her lower body. But the opposite proves true. As she starts the scene, Maria's body seems grander, stronger, larger than before.

In English some of Yerma's lines seem almost weak or whining:

But I don't sleep. I can't sleep.

But in Spanish, the vowels in these lines are not high *ee* sounds but low *oh's,* and the consonants are not sibilants but powerful plosives and dental consonants, so the words roar and explode with bitterness:

Pero yo no duermo, yo no puedo dormir.

Most of Maria's audience cannot understand the words, but they are transfixed by the sounds and with the vehemence that fills Maria's voice. Like an animal finally freed after a long trip in a cage, Maria's body moves with an energy and freedom we have never seen before. And her voice! As she begins Yerma's final monologue, she plants her feet wide on the floor, and she strikes her chest as she cries:

> *¡Ay qué prado de pena!*
> *¡Ay qué puerta cerrada a la hermosura*
> *que pido un hijo que sufrir y el aire*
> *me ofrece dalias de dormida luna.*

> Oh what a field of torment!
> Oh what a door closed upon misery!
> I ask to suffer for a child and the air
> Offers me dahlias of the sleeping moon.

As she continues, Maria's voice swells to fill the space, and for the first time she seems comfortable in her own body, even though Lorca's words ask her to speak of the body itself:

> *Estos dos manantiales que yo tengo*
> *de leche tibia, son en la espesura*
> *de mi carne, dos pulsos de caballo,*
> *que hacen latir la rama de mi angustia.*

> These my two fountains of warm milk
> Are, in the thickness of my flesh,
> Two pulses of a horse's veins,
> That thrash the branch of my anguish.

Maria's voice and body tremble as Yerma's blood itself seems to cry out:

> *¡Ay pechos ciego bajo me vestido!*
> *¡Ay palomas sin ojos ni blancura!*
> *¡Ay qué dolor de sangre prisoniera*
> *me está clavanco avispas in la nuca!*

> Oh breasts blind under my clothes!
> Oh doves without eyes or whiteness!
> Oh what pain of imprisoned blood
> Is sticking wasps in my neck!

Suddenly Maria falls to her knees. For a moment I worry that she has lost control, but it is not Maria who has fallen, but Yerma who has come to the end of her anger. As tears fill her eyes, she reaches the last section of the monologue:

> *Pero tú has de vinir, ¡amor!, mi niño,*
> *porque el agua da sal, la tierra fruta . . .*

> But you must come, my love, my baby,
> For the water gives salt, the earth fruit . . .

By the end, the coolness and beauty of Lorca's final vowels seem to soften Maria's voice. Her arms reach upward, or rather seem to be pulled up toward the clouds, as Yerma calls to her sky-borne dream of children:

> . . . *y nuestro vietre guarda tiernos hijos*
> *como la nube lleva dulce lluvia.*

> And our womb bears tender children
> As the cloud carries soft rain.

When she finishes the speech, the class applauds. And none of us can think of anything to say. Maria just smiles and shakes her head.

"I don't know," she says. "It was as if I was not there, as if all I had to do was get out of the way and let Lorca do the work."

The language we heard as children, the vowels and consonants that provided us with our first words of love, of fear, and of admonition, holds enormous power for us. It is not that we can never learn to act in another language, but rather that there is always something special about those first sounds, something that connects directly to ancient parts of our being. For words are not just signs or meanings; they are also vibrations and tones and music. Like music, they touch us in unconscious ways, and like music they can bring us directly to emotion. If you have not tried acting in your first language, I strongly recommend that you do so.[4]

4. Grotowski was fascinated with the transformative effect that sound could have on the performer. Lisa Wolford reports, "Grotowski speaks of vibration in connection with the Hindu science of mantra, suggesting that specific sounds affect an individual's psychoenergetic state in physically objective ways" [Wolford, p. 119]. And in his late work, Grotowski often urged students to work with the songs of their ancestors, which would hold special significance for them.

FIELD OF DREAMS

I never had a single role where I did not start out with clichés.

—Vasili Toporkov, *Stanislavski in Rehearsal*

When Sandra and Peter present their scene from *Who's Afraid of Virginia Woolf*, the emotions and beat changes are clear, and Peter has created some very precise work with the props for the character of George. For instance, as he makes a drink for Martha, he throws the ice cubes into the glass to punctuate George's words. But it seems as though all this lovely detail is somehow restricting his acting freedom. For some sections of the text, his insecure George works quite well:

MARTHA: You make me puke!
GEORGE: What?
MARTHA: Uh . . . you make me puke!
GEORGE: That wasn't a very nice thing to say, Martha.
MARTHA: That wasn't *what?*
GEORGE: . . . a very nice thing to say.
MARTHA: I like your anger. Think that's what I like about you the most . . . your anger. You're such a . . . simp! You don't even have the . . . the what? . . .
GEORGE: . . . guts? . . .
MARTHA: PHRASEMAKER!

But at other points in the script, Peter's careful character voice and gestures seem to be undercutting the scene. What the audience receives is a George who is always timorous and tense, not the ragged but lively veteran of the wars with Martha.

Sandra's problem seems more extreme. She is clearly struggling with the character of Martha, especially with her voice. Although the Character Word Jam exercise has led her into raucous "braying," now, as she presents the scene to the class, her voice sounds small and tentative, and sometimes she even whispers.

"I don't know," she laments afterward, "I'm just not comfortable saying Martha's words."

"On the other hand," I respond, remembering how large and slovenly she had looked when she spread herself out on the couch, "you seem to be finding some strong, interesting choices for her body, no?"

"Yes. I like feeling big, like that. It's just the words. Every time I open my mouth, I don't believe I'm Martha. It just feels false. It feels like a stereotype or a cliché."

"I understand," I say, "but before we try to deal with that, I'd like to ask Peter something: What is George feeling on the line 'I'm six years younger than you are'?"

"Proud."

"What's the whole line?"

"'I'm six years younger than you are. . . . I always have been and I always will be.'"

"Sounds almost like a child."

"Well, they both play a lot of childish games with each other, like when Martha says she's 'firsty.' But I can't let myself really act like a child. I mean, I'm trying to play a character who is twenty-five years older than I am. If I act too childish, won't I completely lose the character?"

"Maybe, but right now you are holding on to the character work harder than you need to. You've done a lot of detailed preparation for this. You've got a voice and gestures that work well. Let's see what happens if you just ease up a little on your grip as you say the line. Can you two pick up the scene one line before the 'six years younger' line? And this time, Peter, keep doing your character voice and gestures, but let yourself go. Let yourself really play the childish pride."

MARTHA: You're not so young yourself.
GEORGE: I'm six years younger than you are. . . . I always have been and I always will be.

MARTHA: Well . . . you're going bald.
GEORGE: So are you.

Peter's George pouts and sits down on the couch. His voice is still that of a fifty-year-old man, but his intonation is definitely juvenile. The contrast between the two is so strong that the audience breaks out laughing. As they do, George and Martha both start to laugh also. The laughter stops the action for a moment, and when Peter finishes George's line, the mood of the scene seems to have completely transformed:

GEORGE: Hello, honey.
MARTHA: Hello. C'mon over here and give your Mommy a big sloppy kiss.

"How was that?" I ask.

"Strange . . . I mean good, surprising. The script actually says that they're supposed to laugh there, but we never were able to find it before. Sometimes in rehearsal we tried, but it seemed forced, so we just dropped it."

"Yes," I respond, "laughter is not something you can force; it has to just happen to you. But before, you were working so hard at staying in character that you couldn't feel such a delicate change through your armor. Now you've discovered a whole new acting beat that makes real sense of those next lines."

"My turn," says Sandra.

"Right," I say. "The primary difficulty you were having was with the voice, so why don't you just go back to working with Martha's body? Move around the space, sit, stand, throw yourself on the couch, and so on. Good. Now use your arms and your eyes to press Martha's energy out into the space around you, especially toward the downstage wall. Good. And let yourself start the lines now, start with any line at all."

"THEY'RE MY BIG TEETH!" Sandra says loudly. And Peter picks up his next line:

GEORGE: Some of them . . . some of them.
MARTHA: I've got more teeth than you've got.

   But already Sandra's voice is beginning to shrink and lose resonation. It is plain that she is embarrassed as she hears her own large voice filling the silence of the studio. So rather than urging Sandra to do battle with that void, I turn to the rest of the class and ask them to talk in gibberish, all at once, creating a sort of sound container against which Sandra can expand her character's voice. As soon as the air is thick with the group's cacophony, I ask Sandra and Peter to start the scene within this gale of gibberish. As Sandra's voice grows stronger with each line, I motion the audience to reduce and then to eliminate their noise entirely. Now we can see that it is not just the voice work that has grown. Now Sandra's Martha is clearly drunk. At one point she lets herself trip over the furniture and fall to the floor. At another she pushes George onto the couch so strongly and with such un-Sandra-like nastiness that the whole audience gasps.

   "That was *fun!*" she says at the end. "That was the most fun I have ever had on stage. Absolutely."

   "And it didn't feel false to you any more?"

   "Not at all. I mean, I knew I was Sandra, but I felt perfectly comfortable wearing Martha. I don't understand it."

   "Well, it will be important for you to do it again, soon, without the class noise, while your body remembers what you did with your voice, using your eyes and body to build that safe space for yourself. I just want you to note that the feeling of 'truth' came *after* taking the chance to be large, not before. We all have many judgments against overacting, against creating characters who are large or strong or stereotypical. But if we play it safe and try to avoid what feels false, we create a self-fulfilling prophecy: 'I can't do *that*, it isn't real. . . . See, I couldn't do it.'

   "Often, if we take the risk to push past those fears, if we dare to be larger than life, we find that **life itself will grow large enough to fill the forms we have created**. If you dare to create a larger form, your emotional truth will rise up to fill it. As they say in the film *Field of Dreams*: 'If you build it, they will come.'"

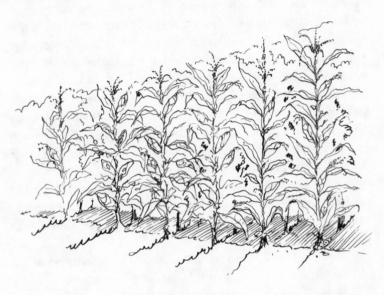

With these scene presentations, my students have reached the end of their semester, and we have reached the end of our physical acting curriculum. Before the last class is over, I gather the group together to say a few parting words:

"We have covered a lot of ground in a very short time, so during the next day or so, I suggest you take a few minutes to think back over what you have learned in this class. As you do, notice how much more aware you have become of your body and of the ways in which your body contains information for you, and recall what you have learned about how you can access that information. Perhaps certain forms, like the Cat, have become second nature to you. Perhaps certain *plastiques* act as keys to strong personal image—emotional landscapes. But more important than these particular discoveries, take note of the changes that have taken place in your attitude toward the work, toward your own inner life, and toward others. Because as you opened your bodies, you have also opened yourselves, both inwardly and outwardly. You have learned to value emotions, images, and parts of yourselves that you used to treat as off-limits. And you have learned to accept as gifts whatever images or impulses your text, your environment, and your partners send your way.

"When we did the Tiger Leaps, we noted that courage is not a matter of fearlessness, but rather a matter of accepting, and thereby transforming, fear. This new ability of yours—the ability to welcome both your own imagery and the difficulties that the outside world throws at you—depends on that kind of courage. And that courageous approach to your process is fundamental to your art. It is a work habit that will serve you in theater—and in life—forever."

Note: These students we have followed will go on to more advanced acting classes, but this book cannot follow them there. In leaving the curriculum at this point, we leave unexamined several questions raised by this physical training. We have not described how this work supports monologue preparation, or how it creates a corporeal vocabulary for the "embodiment" of Shakespeare's language, nor have we spoken about how this kind of training can serve a company or a director rehearsing a play. Yet before ending, there are a few issues of art, life, and survival that I feel we should address.

Acting, Sanity, and Survival

SELF-JUDGMENT AND STAGE FRIGHT

It is as though we insert . . . judges between ourselves and our experience, which is like making love with our clothes on.
—Eloise Ristad, *A Soprano on Her Head*[1]

I wouldn't give a nickel for an actor who isn't nervous.
—David Belasco, in Aaron, *Stage Fright, Its Role in Acting*

As a practice that requires enormous openness and vulnerability, acting is at once the most joyous and the most terrifying of the arts to practice. And of all the afflictions of acting, the torments of self-judgment are the most corrosive.

All performing artists face the fears of exposing themselves to an audience. But unlike singers and dancers whose music and choreography provide stylized containers for their inspirations, actors are asked to present real, live human beings, beings very like themselves, on stage. They are required to feel—and to proclaim in public—what most people would scarcely allow themselves to say, or even to think, in private; they must act like fools, fall in love, murder, and grieve in front of hundreds of strangers night after night. It is not strange, therefore, that self-judgment and stage fright plague actors at many points in their work.

1. *A Soprano on her Head* is a wonderful book about freedom and creativity in musical training and performance. Many of its lessons can be as useful to actors as to musicians.

No less than others, the students in my acting class often encountered fears and judgments that interfered with their acting work. The first time we studied the Cat, Maria worried that she was not doing it right; in the Bad Acting exercise, Brian "didn't dare to be loud" because he was afraid it would "sound like acting"; and during the Not I exercise, Veronica ran into very strong internal judgments against allowing herself to feel beautiful. Each time one of the actors encountered this sort of obstacle, I would ask him or her to notice it, to acknowledge it, and then to find some way to work with it. But there are times when self-judgment can become such an overwhelming or paralyzing experience, that it does not seem possible to simply "put it into the work."

Judgment appears in many guises. It may seem like a voice in your head criticizing your work, it may feel like free-floating anxiety, or it may arise as the fantasy that your coworkers or teachers are denigrating your work. (In fact judgment also appears in *positive* forms, but most of us don't find positive judgments problematic!)

Few acting teachers have discussed the problem of judgment in general, but many have spoken about that particular variety that actors experience in front of an audience: stage fright— the eerie feeling that there are people out there watching you, coupled with the notion that their opinion of you (or rather, your fantasy of their opinion of you) is more important than your action on stage.

But acting teachers express a great variety of opinions about how one should react to stage fright. Lee Strasberg cursed it, claiming stage fright was "the most vulgar preoccupation of all" [Strasberg, p. 57]. Following Stanislavsky, Strasberg taught actors to overcome stage fright by giving themselves something to concentrate on, a "circle of concentration." This solution, which many acting teachers prescribe, seems to serve many actors well, especially those who perform in plays requiring fourth-wall realism, plays in which they can concentrate so entirely on the on-stage reality that the other reality—the audi-

ence out beyond that fourth wall—simply fades into the back-
ground.

One problem with this method is that it tends to isolate the
actor from the audience, and this isolation will undermine any
kind of theater that requires contact with the audience (like
Shakespeare). Bertolt Brecht felt that this separation worked
against the pedagogical purpose of theater, and that it allowed
the audience to remain mindlessly comfortable voyeurs to events
on stage. And for Grotowski, the actor-audience relationship
was the quintessence of theater. Without the actuality of the
actor-audience relationship, he pointed out, one might as well
be making movies.

But Stanislavski's circle of concentration is only one remedy
for stage fright. Other acting teachers just *condemn* it:

> *How do you help students cope with stage fright?*
>   I yell. I say, "What the hell are you doing in this class
> if you have stage fright?" What the hell can I do? Some-
> times I get very tyrannical with certain students. They
> need it and ask for it. [Elinor Renfield, in Mekler, pp.
> 152-3]

On this technique, I have no comment.

Some teachers, like Sanford Meisner, counsel actors simply
to accept the fear: "So you're going to be nervous! *Be* nervous!"
[Meisner, p. 176]. Although I agree with the spirit of Meisner's
statement, I don't believe his advice is sufficient. "Being nervous" can interfere with your other acting tasks; it can prevent
you from using the center of the stage, or speaking loudly, or
looking out through the fourth wall.

Michael Kahn goes a step further, suggesting that actors
actually employ their nervousness:

> It's not being nervous that stops the actor from concentra-
> tion. It is the fear that the nervousness is wrong and it is
> the energy that the actor invests in covering up the ner-

vousness that results in the actor's intention no longer
being the character's. The actor's intention then becomes
to cover up his nervousness. . . . If you are feeling nervous or insecure, those are powerful feelings. Put them
into the scene. Use them as the character. [Kahn, in Mekler, p. 333]

With this method, the question becomes: *how* do you put
nervousness and stage fright into a scene?

Kahn's suggestion that you "use" the fear "in character" will
work well in some situations. I recently coached an actor who
was running into self-judgment as he worked on Macbeth's
entrance after killing Duncan. As he struggled to find the right
imagery to bring the scene alive, he kept thinking, "This is
bad. I'm faking the emotion. I can't play this scene." I suggested that as he spoke the line "Macbeth hath murdered
sleep!" he look out at the image of all the acting teachers and
directors who had ever terrorized him with criticisms like the
ones that were running through his head. As soon as he did, the
fear of the criticism immediately served the scene. Macbeth was
terrified, and no one but the actor himself knew that the "ghost"
who was terrifying Macbeth was that of an acting teacher.

But what if the emotion your character is supposed to be
feeling at the moment doesn't happen to be fear? In that case,
you must somehow *convert* the energy of fear and judgment into
a usable form. Warren Robertson puts it this way:

The first thing I do is get [acting students] to accept fear
because it is also energy. . . . energy is neither good nor
bad. It is all life. And if you interfere with one kind of
energy, you somehow interfere with all of it. . . . The
energy behind fear is the same energy we laugh with and
cry with. [Roberston, in Mekler, p. 114]

Ultimately, **self-judgment is a kind of imagery**. The difficulty
is that it is an imagery that loudly announces, "I am not

imagery. I am not part of your work. I stand outside your work and comment on it." And this is a very powerful message. The question is how to turn this message inside out and transform this critical force into usable, creative energy.

To start this process, remember how you worked in the Just Stand exercise. You kept your focus directly on the audience and simply noticed all the impulses you had in reaction to the feeling of being seen—including fear and embarrassment. Then you fed the energies of those reactions through your body, treating them as a source of physical movement. As soon as you did, you discovered that what seemed at first to be a solid wall of fear was not monolithic. It was actually built out of many diverse reactions including aggression and sexuality. And then you found that by *joining* those energies, pouring them through your body rather than fighting against them, you could begin to play with them—as an aikidoist plays with the aggression that others throw at him. In other words, once you allowed yourself to be *moved* by the energy—even the energy of fear—instead of denying it, you discovered that even this fear could serve as a doorway into anger, sensuality, or other playable reactions.

In our scene work, you built on this approach by placing your strongest personal images downstage and by filling the downstage wall with imagery that served not as a solid fourth wall, but as a kind of scrim between yourself and the audience. By accepting the audience energy into your body and by projecting your imagery downstage, you were able to convert stage fright from a negative experience to an acting source.

But what about those judgments and negative thoughts that are so omnipresent for you that they interfere with your work even when an audience is not watching? What can you do with the voices in your head that constantly compare your work to that of others, the voices that hold you back from daring to be fully committed to each moment even while you work alone with a scene partner or in class?

One technique for dealing with this pervasive kind of judgment is the **Judgment Work** exercise (8.1) developed by Linda

---

Judgment Work (8.1)

1. Find a place in the studio where you feel comfortable working. Begin by doing an exercise that involves your full body and often provokes judgment when you do it. The Cat is a good container for this work, but other ones are possible. The important thing is that the exercise you choose strongly engages your whole body.

2. Simply do the exercise you have chosen, and let yourself notice the judgments that arise. Try to be clear about exactly what the judgments are. Try to hear the particular judgmental voice in your head, its tone and its vocabulary.

3. Let yourself feel "where" this voice is speaking to you from. Is it behind your back, to one side, or in your face?

4. Then step out of the exercise, stand where the "judge" seems to be, and let yourself say the words or thoughts the judge was saying to you. You don't need to do a good acting job, but do try to get the tone of voice down. You can use the actual words or gibberish.

5. Now step back into the "actor's" position and listen to the judge talking to you. You may notice two reactions within yourself: one is just to "take" the criticism; the other is to answer back. Choose the second, and, as you respond, let your body reenter the physical exercise. **Make eye contact with the judge and direct your energy at it.**

6. If judgment returns, again step out to personify the judge.

7. You can repeat this process several times.

8. Finally return to the physical exercise itself, putting all the energy of both the "actor" and the "judge" into the work.

Putnam. It combines the Grotowski physical training with Gestalt psychology techniques.

ACTING OR THERAPY?

To me it doesn't matter whether or not people pursue acting careers. If acting class makes their lives richer and gets them to open up and lead warmer emotional lives, it's worthwhile.

—Alan Miller, in Mekler,
The New Generation of Acting Teachers

For some people, the Judgment Work exercise can be very powerful—so powerful, in fact, that we may begin to wonder, as we did after the Not I work with Veronica, if this work is acting or psychotherapy.

Since the process of acting, this *via negativa* we have been traveling, requires opening ourselves to all the emotions, images, and "characters" we carry within ourselves, it is inevitable that it should lead each of us into encounters with precisely those parts of our being that have lain hidden for years. And encountering hidden parts of ourselves can certainly be therapeutic. But suggesting that acting training *can be therapeutic* is not the same as saying that it *is therapy*. In therapy, the process of psychological discovery and personal change is the very purpose of the work. But in acting, our encounters with and transformations of the self are not ends in themselves; they are way stations and rites of passage through which we must proceed on our journey toward becoming an artist. The pilgrimage itself includes both these transformational experiences and the careful, technical training that leads us into and out of these moments.[2]

Lee Strasberg used to tell actors never to employ a personal memory that was less than seven years old. But some terrifying experiences may prove "workable" when they are only a few months old, and others may be too volatile to make into art even twenty years after they occurred. The issue is not how long it has been since an event etched itself into our body and memory, but whether we possess *acting containers* strong enough to "hold" the image in question. For, in order to make art out of our inner lives, we need to possess (artistic) forms that can safely contain and transform our raw emotions into art. Part of our job as artists is to search out and to create such containers. But if, during our search, we encounter experiences

2. From 1986 until his death in 1999, Grotowski's "Theatre as Vehicle" experiments at the Pontederra Workcenter dealt directly with the actor's ability to transform his own being. As Lisa Wolford writes, "Grotowski's work continues to presuppose that the human being is, to a large extent, capable of reconstructing himself" [Wolford, p. 132].

that are too powerful to be contained, we must move our discovery process out of the studio and into a therapeutic space. It serves no artistic or therapeutic end to let the work drive us crazy.

So if you encounter emotions, images, or memories in your acting work whose energy you cannot corral into your creative work, be careful. You may be crossing the line from art into therapy. The safe thing to do at such a point is to stop the exercise, take note of what happened, and use this experience as a good excuse to enter therapy. Most acting classes simply cannot supply the personal attention and support that therapy demands.

On the other hand, the very awareness that acting is *not* therapy, that it is *only* an art form and not life, can sometimes make strong images and personal memories easier to handle than they would be in a therapy session. For many people, therapy carries with it a pejorative, "medical" overtone or a sense of shame that is totally absent in an acting class. So sometimes acting can actually provide a safe space in which to discover (and perhaps even enjoy) parts of your being that are difficult to acknowledge in a standard therapeutic environment.

A couple of years ago, a young woman with a childhood history of abuse came to study acting with me. The visceral memories of whatever had happened to her in the past had created patterns of fear that affected her voice and made her uncomfortable with her body whenever she was filled with emotion. Over the years, in order to live with the powerful images she carried inside her, she had developed ways of insulating herself from these energies. For instance, as part of her warm-up, she would dance with soft, flowing movements that allowed her to feel good about herself, but that created a sort of distance between her body and her own deepest feelings.

When her class undertook the Judgment Work, she quickly found herself encountering impulses of great violence, especially in her arms. When I saw her hitting the wall of the studio, I suggested that she move a few feet back and allow the image of what she was hitting to exist in front of the wall. As soon as she did, her body was seized by waves of anger; she screamed and cried and tore at her images. Watching her I worried that she might be entering material that was too volatile for her to handle inside the acting work, and I thought of interrupting, but as I watched, I saw that for all the violence of her movements, she was not out of control. Her eyes remained open, and her gestures were precise and varied. When I suggested that she try using her fingers and fingernails to battle her imagery, she was able to take the suggestion and put it into the work. . . . So I decided to let her continue and refrained from interrupting her work.

After the exercise was over, as she sat in a corner making notes in her journal, I asked her how the work had been for her. "Wonderful!" she said. "For the first time, I realized that my judges are all in my mind."

In the end, no one but you can know whether the feelings you encounter in your work can serve your acting or whether they should be saved for the therapist's office. When in doubt: safety first.

A STRADIVARIUS IN THE RAIN

If your friend, the concert violinist, were to leave his precious instrument out on the porch during a rainstorm, what would you think? And what would you think if every time clouds gathered, he went out to the porch and *put* the violin there?

And a violin can be replaced.

But many actors treat their instruments no better. They feed them poorly, they get them overtired, and every day they fill them with smoke. (Of course, your lungs don't rot as quickly as the wood of a violin; it takes several years before the damage is irreversible. On the other hand, cigarettes are not a freak rainstorm. Each time you light up, you are actually making a *choice* to abuse the one and only instrument you will ever own.)

Because you must live with, love with, and party with the very same instrument you play upon in your work, **your personal habits and the care you take of your body** *will* **affect your art.** So, if you want to depend on this instrument of yours to make a living for years to come, you will be as diligent about eating a healthy diet, getting enough rest, and visiting your dentist as you are about studying voice or movement or emotional technique.

And that is not all. Since acting is a mental activity as much as it is a physical one, your work depends as much on your mental state as on your physical condition. When you are depressed or burned out or overworked, your mental and emotional processes are impaired, and that interferes with your art. Be careful. To ignore a depression, to endure an abusive love relationship, or to work at a day job that you hate can be inimical to your acting. There may be times when, for the sake of your sanity and your art, you must stop going to auditions, or start a new acting class, or take a vacation. There may even be moments when, for the sake of your soul—and your acting— you must stop acting, at least for a while: to go make money, or leave the city, or fall in love, or have a baby. These kinds of life decisions are essential to the care of your "instrument," so they are an integral part of your art.

So take your vitamins. Get enough sleep. Floss your teeth. Stop smoking. And get out of unhealthy relationships. If not for yourself, then for your art.

IS ACTING A SPIRITUAL DISCIPLINE?

The performing artist must be capable of risking all of himself. He must be willing and able to dissolve himself into the process of acting, to surrender: to "die" each moment and to be born fully each moment.

—David Feldshuh, "Zen and the Actor"

When people leave the theatre, they should be different to when they arrived. In the old days, people went to church once a week in order to be spiritually cleansed. Nowadays this seldom occurs. But good theatre should fulfill a part of this function. Like a shower, it should cleanse people.
                                        —Yoshi Oida, *An Actor Adrift*

Have you ever felt that you were "falling in love" with your character, with your scene partner, or with the words of your text? Have you ever felt that acting was an incredible "high," or have you experienced the sensation that a performance was happening *through* you? Many actors have experienced such moments on stage, but in this pragmatic world, centered on fame and money, we rarely permit ourselves to consider that these "altered states of consciousness" are, in fact, the very essence and purpose of our art.

Yet over the years, many actors have suggested that the best acting is actually an act of love and a process of transcendence. Michael Chekhov once declared:

Compassion may be called the fundamental of all good art because it alone can tell you what other beings feel and experience. Only compassion severs the bonds of your personal limitations and gives you deep access into the inner life of the character you study. [Chekhov, p. 100]

And David Warrilow of the Mabou Mines experimental theater company said:

I'm responsible for certain aspects of a performance, but there's a whole other level which is coming from outside of me. What I'm supposed to do is channel that, whatever it is. My image of it is that energy—light—is coming to the top of my head which is where the "soul" is supposed to enter the body; and that I am to channel it. It is channeled this way . . . goes through the vocal, physical, breathing mechanism which is David Warrilow and then it is given to whomever is waiting to receive it. [Quoted in Lassiter, "David Warrilow: Creating Symbol and Cypher," *TDR* 1985]

But how dare we believe that our work is actually a compassionate, spiritual activity? Aren't actors the most vain, self-centered exhibitionists in the world?

The answer to this final paradox of acting lies in the realization that there is, in fact, no separation between our "compassion" and our "exhibitionism." **We are most generous when we dare to be most powerful.** We are most human when we allow ourselves to be larger than life. In my acting class, it was when Maria allowed herself to fully inhabit her body and to take over the stage that she felt, "It was as if I was not there, as if all I had to do was get out of the way and let Lorca do the work."

Grotowski put it this way:

The actor's act—discarding half-measures, revealing, opening up, emerging from himself as opposed to closing up—is an invitation to the spectator. This act could be compared to an act of the most deeply rooted, genuine love between two human beings. . . . Why do we sacrifice so much energy to our art? Not in order to teach others but to learn with them what our existence, our organism, our personal and unrepeatable experience have to give us . . . in short, to fill the emptiness in our soul. [*Towards a Poor Theatre*, p. 212]

In other words, as in making love, we give most in the act of receiving. Our very selfishness becomes the source of our generosity.

Throughout this book we have noticed the paradoxes that are inherent in acting:

• The paradox that acting depends on the simultaneous experience of utter freedom and complete control.

• The paradox that acting requires us to be able to listen inwardly and outwardly at the same time.

• The paradox that we must experience ourselves as being both the actor and the character at the same time.

• The paradox that acting is both serious work and pure fun at the same time.

To act, we must overcome these paradoxes. But to overcome a paradox is to perform a miracle. And, as all the saints avow, you can perform a miracle only when you realize that the power of that "performance" is not *yours*, when you acknowledge that **as you perform the miracle, it is not really *you* who is performing.**

IS ACTING A POLITICAL ACTIVITY? OR, WHAT IS SELLING OUT?

I feel that the actor has a basic responsibility to the world as an artist. You don't do certain things. You don't do trash!
—Alan Miller, in Mekler,
The New Generation of Acting Teachers

I forgot that every little action of the common day makes or unmakes character, and that therefore what one does in the secret chamber one has some day to cry aloud from the housetops.

—Oscar Wilde, *De Profundis*

For thousands of years, actors have been accused of being whores. But these days, it is not in bed that we are asked to sell our bodies and our souls. We train to be artists, but we commonly get paid to display our bodies, or to enact scenes of senseless violence, or to sell consumer goods. And is there anything wrong with that? Is an actor responsible for *what* his art is saying, or only for how well he says it?

There are two questions here. The first is, What are the consequences of our actions on our audiences? The second is, What are the consequences of our actions on ourselves? Both questions are thorny.

What do you think? If you act in a commercial that helps GM sell SUVs, are you responsible for the effects of the pollution? If you do a voice-over for an Air Force commercial, are you implicated when our government bombs civilians?

And if you take a job you despise, what will the effect of that job be on your self-respect? If you are female and you act in a film that demeans women, how will you feel about your own body afterward? If you work for a director who insults you, how will you face your next audition?

There are no easy answers to these questions. But it may seem to you that even asking them is absurd. The economics of acting being what it is, the question "What job will I accept?" may seem to be a luxury. The only real question is, "What job can I find?" Besides, if you don't take the job, won't some other actor do it anyway?

Or perhaps you believe you must accept demeaning work now, in your youth, in the hopes of being able to do what you believe in later on. The problem is, **What you do now affects who you become, and who you become affects what you will believe and do in the future.** During the 1967 N.Y.U. workshop, Grotowski put it like this:

> The actor who does terrible things against his will to gain position, to gain money and success, and who plans to be creative later, will already have transformed himself, will already be castrated.
>
> *To illustrate this notion that to go against yourself is to go against your art, Mr. Grotowski told the story of a young revolutionary who decided to undermine the political system from within.*

This man joined the police force. He worked his way up, performing whatever ruthless acts were necessary—including the suppression of his own (secret) political beliefs.

When he reached his goal and had become the chief of police, he was completely that. He became what he did. He was no longer a revolutionary. [Crawley XVI, 5]

So what about you?

Is there *any* kind of acting job you would turn down . . . no matter what the pay? Is there any script so stupid (or sexist or violent) you would refuse the part? Is there any product so offensive you'd definitely continue waiting tables rather than accept the $10,000 the commercial might offer?

Where do you draw the line? Where do you draw the "political" line about what your acts might be saying to the audience? And where do you draw the "personal" line about what your acts might be doing to you?

The important thing is to remember that **whether or not you do it consciously, you *are* drawing a line.** If you work on a script that you hate, if you take criticism from a director who disrespects you, if you share your creativity with people who misuse it, if you promote a product you wouldn't buy yourself, or if you perform in a film that debases women's bodies, you may be selling yourself too cheaply and corrupting your own sensibilities.

The fact is that acting is both a personal and a "political" activity. It affects both the actor and his audience. Of course, in these cynical times, *politics* is a dirty word, and *political theater* has gained a reputation for being a theater of rhetoric and of protest. But political theater can also be a positive act. During the past twenty years, gay actors, playwrights, and directors have invented a genre of theater that never existed before. The theater they have built has been a driving force in gay liberation and in the fight against AIDS, and it has created acting roles and paying jobs that never existed before!

Jerzy Grotowski, who had told our workshop in 1967 that art and politics should have nothing to do with each other, later amended his opinion and suggested that theater artists indeed have a large political responsibility:

> My job is not to make political declarations but to make holes in the wall. Things that have been forbidden to me must be permitted after me; doors which have been locked must be opened; I must solve the problem of liberty and tyranny in practical ways—that means that my activity must leave traces, *examples* of liberty. It's not the same as leaving complaints about the subject of freedom. . . . All that deserves to be chucked away with the garbage. You must actually get things done. . . . This is the problem of social activity through culture. [Grotowski, 1987]

ACTING IN THE REAL WORLD

When we read about Stanislavski and the Moscow Art Theater rehearsing their productions for over a year, or about Peter Brook's travels with his company through Africa, or about the Polish Laboratory Theatre's endless hours of intensive training, we may feel inspired—or envious. For most of us in this workaday world, life in the theater is rarely as majestic or as transcendent as those artistic utopias have demonstrated it can be. Of course, we may be able to remember a few moments of incredible inspiration in our lives—performances when we soared, texts or acting partners we fell in love with, or acting lessons when something new broke free inside us. But these rare moments of epiphany may also leave us with an enormous yearning, a desire to make such meaningful artistic experiences more than occasional lightning flashes in our lives.

How can we reconcile this yearning for transcendent artis-

tic experiences with our knowledge of the "real world" of theater—the world of day jobs and tight schedules and pictures
and résumés, of stupid scripts and heartless agents and igno-
rant directors?

A complete answer to this question would probably require
an analysis of the psychology of modern capitalist society, the
prospects for social revolution, and the bittersweet comforts of
existentialism. But since that analysis is somewhat beyond the
scope of this book, this section is devoted instead to helping
you make the best of a bad situation, by building bridges
between the ideal and the possible. (See also the Afterthoughts
from André Gregory.) In the "real" world of American theater
there are some practical problems that many actors face. The
following paragraphs offer pragmatic approaches to these problems—pragmatic approaches that maintain your integrity.

If I Know What Kind of Warm-Up I Need, But the Work Situation Does Not Provide It, What Can I Do?

There are three possible answers to this question:

1. The revolutionary one: Teach the other people what you
know! If not now, when?
2. The evolutionary one: Ask the stage manager for time to
work in the space before rehearsal begins. (And then, when others ask you what the hell you're doing, teach the other people
what you know! If not now, when?)
3. And the personal one: Find a space and make the time to
give yourself what you know you need, even if you have to do it
somewhere else and on your own.

Whichever answer you choose, do your best to get what you
need.

In this world, people often try to do theater under all kinds
of crazy conditions, so very often you will not get what you need
unless you dare to demand it—from the director, from the pro-

ducer, or from yourself. Remember, you are the one who has to go out there in front of the audience. Moreover, you are the only one who *knows* what you need. You cannot expect anyone else to provide it for you unless you ask for it.

What Should I Do If the Other People In the Show Do Not Understand How I Work?

You are not at all alone in this. There are so many different acting training systems and so many different rehearsal techniques around today that shows are often cast with actors who work in very different ways. The bottom line is that you need a safe atmosphere in which to work. If you explain your way of working to your scene partner, you may find that she would be happy to accommodate your style or at least compromise with you. If she does not, you may have to do some of your work alone.

How Can I Work With a Director Who Undermines My Process?

Directors come in many flavors. Some will be happy to work with you your way, and others won't. Some work collaboratively, but many feel they are the boss. Here are some suggestions for working with directors who seem to see things differently than you do:

1. Try out the director's suggestions. You may be pleasantly surprised, or at least you may find that you are able to translate them into your own language. You may find, for instance, that you can fill the blocking he or she gave you with emotions and imagery that make the staging work for you.
2. Check out your own reactions. Make sure your ego isn't getting in the way of your letting go and learning something new. Is the director undermining your process or pushing it?
3. Talk to the director. Explain to him/her what you know

about your own work style. And listen well to what he/she says in response. You may or may not get exactly what you want, but at least you're talking.

4. If something isn't working for you, rather than just saying no—and thus creating a battle with the director—bring in *several alternative suggestions*. If you bring in only one choice, the director may feel that he or she must choose between his/her idea and yours. If you bring in several, you allow him/her the satisfaction of making the final choice. To make a job into a collaboration, you need to bring positive energy to it.

5. If you do not feel that you can safely talk to the director, use the assistant director or stage manager, or (if it is a union show) the shop steward. That's one of the things they are there for.

6. If you do find yourself having trouble with the director, don't take it out on the other actors. You may just have to grit your teeth and remember: This, too, shall pass.

7. Every once in a great while you may find yourself being seriously mistreated by a director. In that case you have to make a conscious decision about whether the indignity you are suffering is worth the money (or whatever) you're getting in exchange. If you have tried other avenues of redress, there is no shame in leaving. As e. e. cummings wrote in the poem that begins "i sing of olaf glad and big": "there is some shit I will not eat." (Though you must understand that others may not see your action in the same light, and by leaving you could hurt your future work opportunities.)

How Can I Live In the City And Still Remain Open And Available In My Acting?

Openness, vulnerability, and the ability to feel and express all our emotions are the very essences of acting, and any condition that closes you down hurts your acting. But living in a city often requires protecting yourself from all kinds of sensory overload. Faced with this difficulty, you may find that you need to devote part of your warm-up to the task of letting go of your tensions, working out your frustrations, experiencing your fears, and, especially, divesting yourself of your ordinary defenses, your toughness, your cleverness, and your cynicism.

Without these defenses, you may feel naked, or sad or weak or stupid, or violent or needy; in other words, you may feel human, and, uncomfortable as that may seem, that is what you need to feel in order to make your art.

But just as you need to remove your armor before entering the work, you must take care to put it back on before reentering that other stage they call the "real" world. So save yourself a few minutes at the end of each rehearsal for a "warm-down." Then take the time to remember and pack away your acting experience, and to "put yourself back together" in preparation for the "part" you must play in the city streets. Resist the temptation to chat with the others until you are ready.

HOW TO CHOOSE AN ACTING TEACHER

He who claims to teach Art understands nothing whatsoever about it.
　　　　　—Eleonora Duse, in *Antologia del grande atore*

In Japan there is a saying that it is better to spend three years looking for a good teacher than to occupy the same period of time doing exercises with someone inferior.
　　　　　—Yoshi Oida, *The Invisible Actor*

In his book *Impro*, Keith Johnstone writes about teachers and teaching:

People think of good and bad teachers as engaged in the same activity, as if education was a *substance*, and that bad teachers supply a little of the substance, and good teachers supply a lot. This makes it difficult to understand that education can be a destructive process, and that bad teachers are wrecking talent, and that good and bad teachers are engaged in opposite activities. (I saw a teacher relax his students on the floor, and then test for relaxation by lifting their feet eighteen inches into the air and dropping their heels on the concrete.) [Johnstone, p. 16]

Of course, if your teacher drops your heels against a concrete floor, you can't avoid feeling the pain, and the pain is a pretty strong signal that something is not right. But not all bad teaching is so obvious. If your teacher smiles sweetly while subtly insulting your work, it may be harder for you to perceive what is happening to you. At another point in his book, Johnstone relates the story of a psychotic and extremely sensitive teenage girl who was in a garden with a "very gentle, motherly schoolteacher":

The teacher picked a flower and said: "Look at the pretty flower, Betty." Betty, filled with spiritual radiance, said, "All the flowers are beautiful." "Ah," said the teacher, blocking her, "but this flower is especially beautiful." Betty rolled on the ground screaming, and it took a while to calm her. Nobody seemed to notice that she was screaming "Can't you see? Can't you see!"

In the gentlest possible way, this teacher had been very violent. She was insisting on categorising, and on selecting. Actually it is crazy to insist that one flower is especially beautiful in a whole garden of flowers, but the teacher is allowed to do this, and is not perceived by sane people as violent. [Johnstone, pp. 15–16]

Teachers can exercise enormous power over the directions of our lives. When I entered college, I was a math major. But my freshman calculus teacher was such a terrible bore that within two months he had killed my interest in math. After that, it took me two years of trial and error, taking courses with professors in many departments, to learn the most important lesson: a good teacher can make any subject fascinating, and a bad teacher can destroy your interest, even in material you love.

But good teaching is not simply a matter of intelligence or insight. I once worked in a group led by a very perceptive actress, a woman who could tell exactly what you were feeling by just looking at you—and who didn't hesitate to tell you what she saw. Under her tutelage, actors often reached strong emotional truth, but they did so with no self-confidence because they were afraid that at any moment the teacher might yell at them, "I don't believe you! You're not angry, you're terrified!"

It was only much later, after I myself had been teaching for several years, that I realized that it is no great feat to perceive what an actor is feeling. The difficult part is helping the actor to attain that sort of perception about himself, rather than imposing it from the outside.

As a student, you put yourself into someone else's hands, and you grant that person the power to make judgments about your work. If the subject you are studying is intellectual, a good teacher can make you feel intelligent, while a poor teacher can make you feel stupid. If the subject is artistic, a good teacher can make you feel safe, creative, and self-confident, while a poor teacher can leave you heartbroken.

Of course, one of the things that will help you feel creative and self-confident is the technique itself. It must be a system that makes sense to you, one that you can use on your own when the teacher is not present. It must also offer you tools that speak to the needs you have at this particular point in your training.

But in the end, it is not the technique that will sustain you. Any technique you learn will tend to fall away as you create your own way of working by combining the lessons you have learned with your inner instincts—just as the chrysalis falls away from the wings of the emerging butterfly. Yoshi Oida puts it this way:

> It doesn't really matter which style or technique you learn. In fact, you could train in disciplines as different as aikido, judo, ballet, or mime, and gain equal benefit. This is because you are learning something beyond technique. When you study with your master, the skills are only the language of understanding, not the purpose. [Oida, 1997, p. 112]

The most important thing about choosing an acting teacher is not the technique he or she teaches but whether you feel safe and inspired working in his or her presence. There may be some exercises you do not like, and there may even be days when everyone else in the class seems to be having a good time while you feel like you're just not getting it. That's to be expected. But it is absolutely essential that even on those bad days you feel *safe* in the work, safe enough to keep working and safe enough to talk to the teacher about your experience. That's the bottom line.

Here are a few questions that may help you evaluate how a particular teacher's style is working for you.

• Does the teacher's way of working make you feel eager to participate? If you feel uncomfortable or belittled in your teacher's presence, or constantly conscious of the teacher's presence, you will not take big risks. If, on the other hand, you feel excited about what *you* are doing, the teacher is creating a safe workspace.

• How does the teacher give criticism? It is not that there is a *right* way, but that there must be a match between the teacher's style of giving criticism and your way of hearing it. If the teacher puts things in such a way that you have a hard time taking them in, that critical method will not serve you.

• When the teacher asks a question, is it a rhetorical question, a question to which you know there is a "right" answer? Or is it a question that makes you really think about your own process?

• Are you getting your money's worth? Some teachers are very helpful when giving feedback on a scene, but they leave the rest of the class with nothing to do but watch week after week. If you don't like the way the class time is structured, your resentment may interfere with your learning.

• When you are watching others work, are you learning to be more perceptive as a watcher? Are you coming to understand from the outside what is working and what is not?

• How do you feel each time you leave the class? In order to learn you must feel inspired and joyous about your art.

At its heart, acting training is a *via negativa*, a way back toward freedoms we enjoyed years ago. It is a route no one can chart for us, a course we must find for ourselves. The best pilot for this journey may not be the one with the finest maps, but the one who instills in us the courage to find our own way, the teacher who reawakens our joy in the process of discovery itself, and reminds us that theater is, as Max Reinhardt wrote:

> the happiest loophole of escape for those who have secretly put their childhood in their pockets and have gone off with it to play to the end of their days.

Afterthoughts
from André Gregory

André Gregory's connection with Jerzy Grotowski began when both of them were young interns at the Berliner Ensemble. But it was in 1968, when he saw the Polish Laboratory Theatre perform at the Edinburgh Festival, that Gregory was astounded by Grotowski's work. That fall, he founded The Manhattan Project, including in it several actors from Grotowski's N.Y.U. workshop. During the next four years, The Manhattan Project practiced the physical training exercises of the Polish Laboratory Theater while they developed their productions of Alice in Wonderland *and* Endgame. *Over the next thirty years, André Gregory and Jerzy Grotowski developed an ongoing friendship and respect for one another. It was Grotowski who made it possible for Gregory to carry out some of his experiments in Poland, and it was the stories of these experiments that became a part of the script for the film* My Dinner with Andre.*

The manuscript of this book was finished in January 1999. That same month, after many years of illness, Jerzy Grotowski died. A month later a small memorial in his honor was held at the St. Marks Church in the Bowery. One of those who spoke there was André Gregory. His remarks at that memorial so entirely captured the essence of Grotowski's spirit that before publishing this book, I asked Andre if he had anything to add to what I had written.

There is something very important you somehow leave out of your book, namely the question of time. Jerzy's actors worked on their training exercises for years and years and years. He rehearsed his theater pieces for years. A young woman from Asia who worked with him in the eighties told me a wonderful story. Jerzy spent a few hours a day over a period of three years working with her alone on a piece she wanted to develop. At the end of the three years, he suggested she invite a handful of friends including himself to witness her work. After she performed it this one time in front of this handful of witnesses, Jerzy said to her, "Your work is excellent, you finished the process. There seems no reason to do it again." Three years' work for one performance. Time. The question of time.

For the last thirty years, I have taken at least fifteen months and sometimes three years to rehearse plays. When I was a young director, I used to direct plays in four or five weeks. But in that amount of time, all you can do is decide what you want to say and then find the best, most colorful, most articulate way to say it. But if you work on a play for two or three years, you don't find what you want to say; you discover what you don't want to say, what you are afraid to say, what you want to say finds you. The process is a long and arduous descent into the unconscious, and a long, arduous ascent toward the conscious.

The same is true for actors. When you rehearse for a short period of time, a lot of possibilities come up, and then you choose the best one. But if you rehearse for a long period of time, the choice that finally appears is not just the "best" choice, it is the *inevitable* choice, the *only possible choice*—not only for yourself but also for your acting colleagues. It's equivalent to the poet finding the best word for his poem, or the composer finding the perfect note for his symphony. Once you have found the only possible choice for one moment, you must find the only possible choice for the next moment. After years of research, you finally have a score, a collective score, that can be performed every night. A beautiful harmony better than structure and chaos. It is a process that takes years.

Cieślak compared a score to the banks of a river. The banks are the result of years of research. They remain fixed. The performance each night is like a river which is fluid. It all takes time.

Similarly, to get the most from the *plastiques* also requires a great deal of time. My company, The Manhattan Project, practiced the *plastiques* every day for three or four years. During those years, our relationship to the exercises went through many stages, just as one's relationship to a play or to a person goes through changes over time.

At first, when you begin to work with the *plastiques,* your work is filled with the struggle and the uncertainty of meeting somebody you love. It's new, it's difficult, it's exciting, but it's also awkward and fearful. Then, as in any true love affair, you start to get the hang of it, and you find the joy of expression. You can stay up all night, talking to the person you love, and you can discover exciting new things within each *plastique* you practice. Then comes the commitment, you get "married" to the *plastiques.* You think, "This is great. I love this work." Now when you work, you find you can express everything. Even the kitchen sink comes up. That is the "honeymoon." But then, when you have been working with the *plastiques* for six to eight months, they become routine. And then you find yourself thinking, "This is nothing but boring." But *boring* is a key word.

In 1969, when the actors of The Manhattan Project had been practicing the *plastiques* for over a year, I invited Jerzy Grotowski to come see them work. Of course, since Jerzy was there, all the actors wanted to show off, so as they practiced they felt rage and ecstasy and every other possible emotion. But Jerzy said, "No. Do the exercises with nothing. Just do."

The work is not about expression. The work is a practice. The work is a prayer. In every really meaningful activity, you have to go through "boring" to get to the next stage. In psychotherapy, you have to go through boring. In relationships, you have to go through boring. In order to change from your thirties to your forties, you have to go through boring. And you can never discover the fullness of your journey unless you take that time.

In fact, I first learned about the importance of taking time not from Grotowski but from Brecht. I watched him rehearsing at the Berliner Ensemble, and he would work and rework his productions for years. One gesture in one moment could take many weeks. From Grotowski what I learned was something else. I learned that the search toward authenticity involves a stripping away, a letting go, again, a process that takes years. I learned that time alone is not sufficient for actors to discover authenticity.

The psychoanalyst W. D. Winnicott wrote that we come into the world authentically who we are, and then, because we're shrewd little creatures, and we know the world will criticize that authentic person, we camouflage ourselves and, after a certain point, we can't remember who we are anymore. The process of psychotherapy, Winnicott suggested, is to take away, and take away, and take away until you're finally left with the authentic "you."

To enact the truth on stage, the actor also needs to be authentic, and so he too must remove the layers of camouflage that hide the being he himself never knew he was. And to fully reveal himself, an actor needs to know that his authenticity is valued. What Grotowski provided was a workspace in which it was acceptable for actors to be fully themselves, a space in which they felt mirrored. In an atmosphere of safety like that, an actor can show not only who the world expects him to be but who he authentically *is*.

The process of rediscovering authenticity is like the process of a child learning to walk. It depends on time, but it also depends upon the support and delight of those around him, not just in the accomplishment—the walking—but in the learning process. If adults were to criticize little infants every time they fell down, they would never learn to walk. But in fact the falling is just as interesting as the walking. It's delightful to watch little children in the process of falling as they learn to walk. Similarly, I find there is nothing that an actor does that is not interesting to me.

So, with sufficient time and with delight in the process, real growth and transformation can take place . . . if you have the desire and the dedication to go into the unknown. Grotowski spoke so often about the importance of going into the unknown that at one lecture a young woman asked him, "You keep talking about the *unknown*. What is it that you love so such about the unknown and about going into the unknown?" And he said, "Did I say I loved it? I go there screaming and resisting." It takes a great deal of time, most especially because of the resistance and fear, to go into the unknown. If NASA could take years to get to the moon, if Proust can take years to write *Remembrance of Things Past*, why can't we in the theater take the time we need to do our work?

But let's be practical. It is essential to be practical. It's impossible to work without being realistic and practical since we live in a culture where time is money and no one is willing to subsidize a long rehearsal period. The question is how to rehearse a long, long time if that is your calling, if that is your necessity. With *Vanya on 42nd Street*, which we rehearsed over a period of four years, we would rehearse for the summer, then the actors would depart to make money (you must make money, you have to live) and then we would come back again and work some more and leave again and come back again and work some more. It takes time.

I'm not saying that you have to be a fanatic. I personally like actors, who, as Artaud said, are "like martyrs at the stake, signaling to us through the flame." But not everyone has the calling to do that. And yet I do think it is important for all of us to remember that the theater has its roots in the sacred. And I do believe that the role of the artist is an incredibly important one—particularly in this culture where nobody cares about artists anymore, where everything is business.

Perhaps that is why Grotowski's work is so little known today. Today the authentic human being and the authentic human act, with all of its complexity, ambiguity, and questioning has become politically suspect and politically dangerous. Under the totalitarianism of capitalism and a consumer culture, the act of being totally human, authentic, and questioning is too subversive for us to witness—because that act itself makes us see that we are all implicated in the evils of the world.

We no longer value art that makes us see the truth. We have become like those geese who no longer go south for the winter, who no longer even remember that there is a south to go to. We are like Monica Vitti in Antonioni's *Red Desert*. We have mutated into something that *seems* human. We have lost our ancient taste for authenticity. We have forgotten who we are. We have become another kind of goose.

In the face of this situation, Grotowski's exercises are not just an artistic method, they are also a spiritual practice. They are like sacred texts that offer us clues to help us search for artistic and personal authenticity. A spiritual practice takes time. Every morning before sunrise we practice, we say our prayers over and over and over again. It takes a lifetime.

Bibliography

Aaron, Stephen. *Stage Fright, Its Role in Acting*. Chicago: University of Chicago Press, 1986.

Adler, Stella. *The Technique of Acting*. New York: Bantam Books, 1988.

Artaud, Antonin. *The Theater and Its Double*. Trans. Mary Caroline Richards. New York: Grove Press, 1958.

Benedetti, Jean. *Stanislavski: An Introduction*. New York: Theatre Arts Books, 1982.

————. *Stanislavski and the Actor*. London: Methuen; London: Random House UK, 1998.

Benedetti, Robert. *The Actor at Work*. Englewood Cliffs, N.J.: Prentice-Hall, 1976.

Brandon, James. "Training at the Wasela Little Theatre: The Suzuki Method." *TDR/The Drama Review* 22, no. 4 (T80 1978).

Brecht, Bertolt. *Bertolt Brecht Poems 1913–1956*. Ed. John Willett and Ralph Manheim with the co-operation of Erich Fried. London: Eyre Methuen Ltd., 1976.

Brestoff, Richard. *The Great Acting Teachers and Their Methods*. Lyme, N.H.: Smith and Kraus, 1955.

Burzynski, Tadeusz, and Zbigniew Oshiński. *Grotowski's Laboratory*. Warsaw: Interpress Publishers, 1979.

Chekhov, Michael. *To the Actor, on the Technique of Acting*. New York: Harper and Brothers, 1953.

Cole, Toby, and Helen Krich Chinoy, eds. *Actors on Acting*. New York: Crown, 1949.

Crawley, Tom: "The Stone in the Soup, a Journal of Jerzy Grotowski's First American Workshop." Unpublished manuscript, © 1978 Thomas Crawley.

Croyden, Margaret. "Notes from the Temple: A Grotowski Seminar." *TDR/The Drama Review* 14, no. 1 (T45 Fall 1969).

Delsarte, François. *Delsarte System of Oratory: Containing All the Literary*

Remains of François Delsarte (Given in His Own Words). Trans. Abby L. Alger. New York: Edgar S. Werner, 1883.

Dixon, Michael Bigelow, and Joel A. Smith ed. *Anne Bogart, Viewpoints*. Lyme, N.H.: Smith and Kraus, 1995.

Feldshuh, David. "Zen and the Actor." *TDR/The Drama Review*, 20, no. 1 (T69 March 1976).

Flaszen, Ludwik. "Conversations with Ludwik Flaszen" (reported by Eric Forsythe). *Educational Theatre Journal*, 30, no. 3 (1978).

Foley, Kathy. "My Bodies: The Performer in West Java." *TDR/The Drama Review*, 34, no. 2 (T126 Summer 1990).

Grotowski, Jerzy. "Il n'ést pas entièrement lui même." *Les Temps modernes*, April 1967.

———. "Les techniques de l'acteur: Rencontre avec Jerzy Grotowski" (par Denis Bablet). *Les Lettres français*. 16/22 June 1967.

———. "Le théâtre est une rencontre." Interview by Naim Kattan. *Arts et lettres* (Supplement to *Le Devoir*). July 1967.

———. "An Interview with Grotowski." Interview by R. Schechner and T. Hoffman. *TDR/The Drama Review* (T41 Fall 1968).

———. *Towards a Poor Theatre*. Ed. Eugenio Barba. London: Methuen, 1976.

———. "Odpowiedź Stanisławskiemu" (statement at a meeting with actors and directors at the Brooklyn Academy of Music in New York January 22, 1969) *Dialog* 5, 1980.

———. *"Tu es le fils de quelqu'un."* *TDR/The Drama Review* 31, no. 3 (T115 Fall 1987). © JG 1987. Trans. Jacques Chwat; translation reviewed and edited by Ronald Packham.

Hagen, Uta, with Haskel Frankel. *Respect for Acting*. New York: Macmillan, 1973.

Hornby, Richard. *The End of Acting: A Radical View*. New York: Applause Theatre Books, 1992.

James, William. *The Principles of Psychology*. Vol. 2. 1890. Reprint, New York: Dover, 1950.

Johnstone, Keith. *Impro: Improvisation and the Theatre*. New York: Theatre Arts Books; New York: Routledge, Chapman and Hall, 1981.

Kumiega, Jennifer. *The Theatre of Grotowski*. London: Methuen, 1985.

Lassiter, Laurie. "David Warrilow: Creating Symbol and Cypher." *TDR/The Drama Review* 29, no. 4 (T108 Winter 1985).

Linklater, Kristin. *Freeing the Natural Voice*. New York: Drama Book Specialists, 1976.

————. *Freeing Shakespeare's Voice*. New York: Theatre Communications Group, 1992.

Mamet, David. *True and False: Heresy and Common Sense for the Actor*. New York: Vintage, 1999.

Meisner, Sanford, and Dennis Longwell. *Sanford Meisner on Acting*. New York: Vintage, 1987.

Mekler, Eva. *The New Generation of Acting Teachers*. New York: Penguin Books, 1988.

Moore, Sonia. *Stanislavski Revealed: The Actor's Guide to Spontaneity on Stage*. New York: Applause Theatre Books, 1991.

Oida, Yoshi, with Lorna Marshall. *An Actor Adrift*. London: Methuen, 1992.

Oida, Yoshi, and Lorna Marshall. *The Invisible Actor*. London: Methuen, 1997.

Reich, Wilhelm. *The Function of the Orgasm*. Trans. Vincent R. Carfagno. New York: Farrar, Straus and Giroux, 1973.

Richards, Thomas. *At Work with Grotowski on Physical Actions*. London: Routledge, 1995.

Ristad, Eloise. *A Soprano on Her Head*. Moab, Utah: Real People Press, 1982.

Sabatine, Jean. *The Actor's Image*. Englewood Cliffs, N.J.: Prentice-Hall, 1983.

Spolin, Viola. *Improvisation for the Theater*. Evanston, Ill.: Northwestern University Press, 1963.

Stanislavski, Constantin. *My Life in Art*. Trans. J. J. Robbins. Routledge/ Theatre Arts Books, copyright 1924 by Little, Brown, and Co., 1943 by Elizabeth Reynolds Hapgood, renewed 1952, published since 1948: Theatre Arts Books. Reprinted in 1996 by Routledge/Theatre Arts Books, NY.

————. *An Actor Prepares*. Trans. Elizabeth Reynolds Hapgood. New York: Theatre Arts Books, 1936.

————. *Building a Character*. Trans. Elizabeth Reynolds Hapgood. New York: Theatre Arts Book, 1949.

————. *Creating a Role*. Trans. Elizabeth Reynolds Hapgood. New York: Theatre Arts Books, 1961.

Stebbins, Genevieve. *Delsarte System of Expression*. New York: Edgar S. Werner, 1886.

Strasberg, Lee. *A Dream of Passion*. Boston: Little, Brown, 1987.

Suzuki, Tadashi. *The Way of Acting*. New York: Theatre Communications Group, 1986.

Tairov, Alexander. *Notes of a Director.* Trans. William Kuhlke. Coral Gables, Fla.: University of Miami Press, 1969.

Temkine, Raymonde. *Grotowski.* New York: Avon Books, 1972.

Toporkov, Vasily Osipovich. *Stanislavski in Rehearsal: The Final Years.* New York: Theatre Arts Books, 1979.

Wolford, Lisa. *Grotowski's Objective Drama Research.* Jackson: University Press of Mississippi, 1996.

Yakim, Moni, and Muriel Broadman. *Creating a Character: A Physical Approach to Acting.* New York: Applause Theatre Books, 1993.

Zarrilli, Phillip B., ed. *Acting (re)Considered: Theories and Practices.* London: Routledge, 1995.

Permissions Acknowledgments

Grateful acknowledgment is made to the following for permission to reprint previously published and unpublished material:

Linda Segal Crawley: Excerpts from *The Stone in the Soup, A Journal of Jerzy Grotowski's First American Workshop*, unpublished manuscript by Tom Crawley, copyright © 1978 by Thomas F. Crawley. Reprinted by permission of Linda Segal Crawley.

Luc Delahaye and **Magnum Photos Inc.**: Photograph of Moslem refugees from Srebenica arriving at Tuzla, Bosnia, airport camp. Copyright © 1995 by Luc Delahaye and Magnum Photos Inc.

Hill and Wang and **International Creative Management, Inc.**: Excerpt from *The Rimers of Eldritch and Other Plays* by Lanford Wilson, copyright © 1967, copyright renewed 1995 by Lanford Wilson. Reprinted by permission of Hill and Wang, a division of Farrar, Straus and Giroux, LLC, and International Creative Management, Inc.

Elaine Jackson: Excerpt from *Paper Dolls* by Elaine Jackson. Reprinted by permission of Elaine Jackson.

Methuen: Excerpt from *Top Girls* by Caryl Churchill, excerpts from *An Actor Adrift* by Yoshi Oida and Lorna Marshall, excerpts from *The Invisible Actor* by Yoshi Oida and Lorna Marshall. Reprinted by permission of Methuen, London.

New Directions Publishing Corporation and **The University of the South**: Excerpts from *A Streetcar Named Desire* by Tennessee Williams, copyright © 1947, 1953 by Tennessee Williams, copyright renewed 1975, 1981 by The University of the South. Published by New Directions. Rights in the United Kingdom administered by Casarotto Ramsay Associates Limited, London, on behalf of The University of the South. Reprinted by permission of New Directions Publishing Corporation and The University of the South, Sewanee, Tennessee.

Routledge, Inc.: Excerpts from *An Actor Prepares* by Constantin Stanislavsky, Norman Hapgood, and Elizabeth Hapgood, copyright © 1989. Reprinted by permission of Routledge, Inc.

Barton Silverman/NYT Pictures. Photograph of Mariano Rivera, courtesy The New York Times Company. 229 West 43rd Street, 9th floor, NYC 10036.

Taylor & Francis/Routledge, Inc., and **Methuen**: Poem "Weigel's Props" from *Bertolt Brecht Poems, 1913-1956*, edited by John Willett and Ralph Manheim, copyright © 1976, 1979. Rights outside the United States administered by Methuen, London. Reprinted by permission of Taylor & Francis/Routledge, Inc., and Methuen.

Theatre Communications Group: Excerpts from *Yerma* by Federico Garcia Lorca, translated by W. S. Merwin, translation copyright © 1965, 1994 by W. S. Merwin. Reprinted by permission of Theatre Communications Group.

Viking Penguin and **IMG Literary**: Excerpts from *The New Generation of Acting Teachers* by Eva Mekler, copyright © 1987 by Eva Mekler. Reprinted by permission of Viking Penguin, a division of Penguin Putnam Inc., and IMG Literary.